Innovation
Judo

Innovation Judo

Disarming Roadblocks and Blockheads on the Path to Creativity

Neal Thornberry, Ph.D.

Innovation Judo: Disarming Roadblocks and Blockheads on the Path to Creativity

Published by Evolve Publishing, Inc.

www.evolvepublishing.com

Cover and interior design by Ramsdell Design

Page 34: Shopping cart photos used by permission of IDEO.

978-0-9893222-4-9 hardcover
978-0-9893222-9-4 paperback
978-0-9893222-5-6 ePUB
978-0-9893222-6-3 ePDF

Printed in the United States of America

10 9 8 7 6 5 4 3 2 1

Contents

Foreword

This book has been in the works for four years and was motivated by the incredible innovators I have met in my work, travel, keynote speeches, and business seminars. These were special innovators as they were able to innovate and create value for their organizations regardless of the obstacles put in front of them.

I also embarked on this book because of the skepticism I often run into in my talks and classes from students and participants who say that they can't innovate within their own organizations because of the ponderous rules, processes, procedures, and risk-averse orientation that their companies have compiled over the years. So when I said that I thought they could indeed innovate in these environments, I was forced to find real-life examples as a counterpoint to this skepticism. This challenge sent me on the quest for Innovation Judo masters, innovators who succeeded against the odds by utilizing a little-known and unique set of skills called Innovation Judo Skills that you will learn about in this book. I especially want to thank those who have allowed me to profile them in this book as exemplars of these skills: Walt Pullar, Jim Repp, Russ Sabo, Steven Paljieg, and Chris Kluckhuhn. They each sat through several long hours of interviewing, then reviewing, and finally correcting what I got wrong. You will find their stories to be as lively, compelling, and inspiring as they are in person.

I was also motivated by my dear wife, Meg, who after suffering through my last book, *Lead Like an Entrepreneur*, was still willing to go through the arduous book-writing project yet another time. She prodded me when I needed it, critiqued when she could, and never wavered in her belief that I had something uniquely different and practical to say to innovators and the leaders of innovation.

I also want to thank my wonderful friends and colleagues in the Navy with whom I have worked these last 5 years. Although a civilian and someone who has never served in the military, I was welcomed aboard the Naval Postgraduate School with open arms. Our military are incredible people who sacrifice more than most of us will ever know; certainly more than I knew. I am proud to have been a part of their education and hope that I have enriched their lives in some small way.

I also want to thank my colleagues at Babson College for allowing me the opportunity to take a joint appointment with them and NPS (Naval Postgraduate School) for my one-year sabbatical in Monterey, California, which turned into five.

Also, I want to recognize my great publisher Karen Krieger at Evolve Publishing who believed in my work and encouraged me to get it into print. While some others passed on the concept of "Judo" as a good metaphor for the unique set of skills that I talk about, she got it right away and signed on. She gave me the right contacts and advice at the right time, and was a true partner, always checking with me to make sure that I was happy with the process. Karen, along with Jennifer Welsch and the good folks at Book-masters, finally made my ideas come to life on the printed page.

The chapters in this section will make it clear why innovation often fails in established organizations and why some counterbalancing mechanisms like Innovation Judo are critical. Logic works in a logical world, but, unfortunately, most organizations are not logical despite their attempts to be so. Instead, they are often encumbered with politics, difficult personalities, competition for scarce resources, and hangovers from previous regimes and structures. Add to this the fear that often follows the innovator when he or she suggests doing something radically different or new and it is no wonder that so many organizations are innovation-challenged.

But some innovators are neither discouraged nor dissuaded in their quest for doing things better, faster, cheaper, or differently because they possess a particularly effective, secret leadership skill set you will learn about in this book. In Part I, you will learn about this skill set and why it is so important for disarming roadblocks and blockheads that stand in the way of creativity. You will also be able to assess your own organization in terms of innovation friendliness by looking at four different types of innovation landscapes you might encounter within your organization that have different varieties of roadblocks and blockheads. Just as in the martial arts form of Judo, you will need to assess your organization's opponents to innovation to deploy the right moves to neutralize or defeat them. At the end of Part I, you will learn that Innovation Judo can only work if you have the right mindset. Without this mindset, you will be perceived as a manipulator, not an innovator.

CHAPTER 1

....

The Innovator's Secret Weapon

SAVING LIVES OR PLAYING IT SAFE?

The Ninja Library: Quietest Place on Earth

When Walt Pullar was an active Navy SEAL, there was a great immediacy in the decision-making process. With bullets flying, long debates were not an option, and the danger of the situation forged strong teamwork and support. But now that Walt was no longer an active operator but working in Navy acquisitions to support his colleagues in Special Ops, he faced a very different enemy, the bureaucracy. Add to that the politics involved in any large and complex organization, especially one that reports to an even bigger government bureaucracy, and decision making can become laborious and exhausting.

"What do I do now?" Walt thought to himself as he pondered a critical decision he had to make where lives were at risk. "Do I push the envelope now and make the decision by myself, or do I wait until everyone agrees?" Breaking, bending, or challenging rules in a bureaucracy can be both career limiting and career ending, something that bureaucrats know very well. "But sometimes," Walt thought to himself, "you have to act for the greater good." But how do you stick your neck out without losing it? That is the critical challenge that many innovators face within their organizations and is the main subject of this book.

Here was Walt's dilemma. He was working on equipment innovation for special operators and was passionately involved in improving helmets for Navy SEALS and other special forces. He knew from his research and his personal experience that the current helmets were inferior especially when measured against the increasingly perilous missions special operators were being asked to perform. The helmets were not up to scratch with the technology that needed to be embedded in them like wireless communications capabilities, night vision capabilities, and most importantly, ballistic strength. A high-powered bullet could easily penetrate the current helmets with fatal results. Walt and his team had developed a truly innovative prototype that was about 80 percent up to specs and demonstrated that the ballistic protection of these helmets was now truly life-saving. But the quality control lead, who did not work for Walt, would not okay the manufacture of these helmets until they were 99.9 percent perfect. For Walt, 80 percent was good enough to start saving lives, but the bureaucracy and a process standard stood in the way.

What should Walt do? What could Walt do? Later in this book, you will see how Walt cleverly handled this conundrum and saved lives and kept his job in the process by practicing a unique set of leadership skills that innovators use to succeed against the odds. Walt could have played it safe, but he didn't. As you will see from his story, he had to call on these skills several other times in his career.

For you and me, Walt's decision might seem obvious. Sometimes, especially with lives at stake, 80 percent is good enough. But that is a logical conclusion, and many organizations don't run on logic. This is why innovators need Innovation Judo. It is also the reason I wrote this book—to help others innovate for the greater good even when they are overwhelmed by their own organization's roadblocks and blockheads.

AGAINST THE ODDS

For the last fifteen years of my business career in the private sector, as the head of IMSTRAT LLC, I helped organizations utilize innovation as a tool for remaining competitive and viable. In my current part time role as Director of Innovation Initiatives in the Center for Executive Education at the Naval Postgraduate School in Monterey, California, I am doing the same kind of work with the Navy. While the Navy is different in many fundamental ways from for-profit businesses, the challenges of developing, nurturing, and sustaining innovation are the same.

The military, like most hierarchical organizations, has a tough time engendering and sustaining innovation, and in the past military leaders in particular had difficulty seeing the connection between being an officer and being a business leader. But then again they never had to. They are by trade "warfighters," and that is why most of us admire and honor them. But they are business leaders as well who manage huge businesses worth billions of dollars while facing increasing pressure from Congress and America's citizens to be better stewards of our limited dollars.

It has been a great privilege and honor to work with the U.S. Navy over the last five years. I have never worked with such uniformly dedicated and honorable people. Their sacrifices are significant and they all willingly put themselves in harm's way on our behalf. I had the chance to fly out and live on a carrier for a couple of days, and just practicing for warfare is dangerous. Every day eighteen-year-olds stand on the deck and help plane after plane land and take off in a highly dangerous environment. Just standing in the wrong place on the carrier deck can be deadly if one of the arresting cables that catch the plane's tailhook comes your way.

Today the Navy, like most large organizations, is under tremendous pressure to do more with less in order to create "readiness at cost." In the old days if there was a budget shortfall, the Navy asked congress for more money, therefore the mantra was "readiness at any cost." Those days are over. Now all our forces must learn to live within their means, which requires cost cutting, increased efficiencies, better asset management, a better trained and more effective workforce, continuous innovation, and entrepreneurial thinking. Cutting costs without cutting capabilities is the tricky part! And no one in this country wants to be less protected.

Yet getting permission to try something new in the military or any large company for that matter can require a great deal of persistence, patience, and perhaps a little masochism. One innovator whom I interviewed at ADP, a large data processing organization, told me his secret to succeeding as an innovator was to make sure that, when the door was slammed in his face, he let it hit him in a different part of his face each time. Not bad advice if you like a door hitting you in the face, but innovating within an organization should not be this painful. It often is because so many organizations are built for consistency and predictability, not for innovation and change. These are paradoxical challenges, which few organizations have been able to manage simultaneously without descending into schizophrenia. I will show you how some organizations have cracked this code in the last section of the book, called "Counterbalancing."

A BOOK THAT SHOULDN'T NEED WRITING

As a business school professor and management consultant, I am supposed to write books. It's not only expected in academia, it is generally rewarded. Although I enjoy the intellectual challenge of writing and the real people I meet through my research, *Innovation Judo* is a book that shouldn't need to be written because it would mean that most organizations are good at innovating and they listen to and embrace their employees' suggestions for doing things smarter, faster, cheaper, better, and differently.

Unfortunately, this is not the case. Statistics tell a rather different story about most organizations' ability to innovate especially long term. For example, 84 percent of business leaders think innovation is critical to their future success, but nearly 95 percent of the new products developed by these companies fail in the marketplace. Less than 1 percent of the 2,000 new patents issued each year deliver a profit (Webb & Theun, 2011), and the average life span of a company on the original S&P 500 between 1920 and 1998 was sixty-five years. By 1998, the average tenure of a firm on the expanded S&P was only ten years (Arie de Geus, 2002).

When I was doing the research for my last book, *Lead Like an Entrepreneur: Keeping the Entrepreneurial Spirit Alive in the Corporation* (McGraw-Hill, 2007), I noticed a number of innovative leaders who also worked in bureaucratic, risk-averse organizations, but they did not have the black-and-blue marks that my ADP friend had. Somehow, they had figured out how to

7

outsmart and outmaneuver the organizational roadblocks and blockheads that were thrown in front of them when trying to introduce something new without taking any hits. They were clearly sticking their necks out but not losing them. They seemed to enjoy the whole challenge of being told no, then doing it anyway and succeeding. Some of you might relate to this little chip on the shoulder, a key characteristic of *Innovation Judo masters*.

I was struck by the fact that these folks were doing very innovative, impactful things and making names for themselves despite the fact that many of them were working within some pretty wacky, risk-averse organizations. They were very clever about how they got stuff done and did not hurt their organizations in the process. Instead, they helped their companies by temporarily disabling organizational impediments to innovation just long enough to get their innovations adopted and implemented.

They didn't spend years trying to change the culture, to make it "innovation friendly" to their ideas. They used one or more Innovation Judo principles to temporarily disable the organization's innovation killers just long enough to give their ideas a fighting chance. People who truly want to innovate within their companies will probably need to utilize some of these Innovation Judo principles, if not all, if they are to succeed. And Judo is the apt analogy as these leaders were disarming without harming. Judo is known as the gentle art because it disables without disabling. Karate and Jiu-Jitsu on the other hand can do permanent damage, which is the last thing an innovator wants to do to his organization.

A SECRET LEADERSHIP COMPETENCY

A lot of organizations have difficulty admitting they need Innovation Judo masters because they don't realize that their organizations are "Idea Kremlins"—places where ideas go in but never leave alive. Nonetheless, my Innovation Judo masters succeed not because they are good soldiers or have other traditional attributes like loyalty or are hard working, but because they use their Innovation Judo skills. They make the organization work for them not the other way around. And they don't practice this art for self aggrandizement but for the greater good. In this book I will explore how they do it in an easily understandable and applicable framework so that you can learn how to innovate despite the odds that are often stacked against you.

Machiavelli was spot-on in 1513 when he wrote,

The innovator makes enemies of all those who prospered under the old order, and only luke-warm support is forthcoming from those who would prosper under the new.

—*Niccolo Machiavelli,* The Prince *(1513, p. 51)*

For those of you who strive to be innovative: *forget about fairness.*

In a fair, logical world, Innovation Judo would not be necessary, but this is not the world we live in. We can debate whether the world is flat (Friedman, 2005) or curved (Smick, 2008), but we can't debate whether the world is fair or not because it isn't! The righteous don't always inherit the earth, and one bullet can bring down a life of good works. The most loyal of employees can find themselves at the company's "right sizing" guillotine without warning. And innovation is not always welcome even though it could potentially improve an organization's performance. So let's be clear that this book is not intended for those who believe in the "think and grow rich" mantra.

Innovation Judo requires a proactive and planful application of principles, but first you must understand the innovation cycle and see how innovation is important to you and your career development. Be assured that innovation is the right coattail to grab if you want to step up, stand out, and stay alive within your organization. In a recent IBM survey (IBM, 2012), innovation was one of the top items Fortune 500 CEOs wanted in their employees and their companies. It is also on the top of the CNO's (Chief of Naval Operations) wish list. However, wishing for it and getting it are not the same, and large, established organizations usually have a poor track record for innovation.

It is not about being passive, philosophical, or resigned about the roadblocks and blockheads you will inevitably face when trying to innovate. Instead it is about aggressiveness (in a unique form), cleverness, and never being discouraged when you hear the word *no*. And as Judo disarms rather than harms, you will not be behaving badly by applying these skills. You will not always need to use these skills, but given today's complex and often wacky business environment, Innovation Judo skills might make the difference between being employed and being unemployed.

CEOs, LISTEN UP

Now, before any of you CEOs think about sending out the lynch mob to get me for recommending that people learn how to outsmart your organization or encourage them to bend the rules, think twice. You actually need these people. In fact you might have been one of those people who got to the top because you had superior Innovation Judo skills—you knew how to work the system better than your peers. But now you may also be a victim of your own organization's blockheads and roadblocks. You might not want to admit you need to nurture and promote Innovation Judo masters, but as you will see from the stories in this book, they can often get the apple of innovation without breaking the cart.

CEOs will often tell me that they have much less power to make things happen in their organization than others believe they have. President Gerald Ford was an excellent example of this phenomenon. When Gerald Ford was president, he discovered that the White House had a mouse infestation problem, so he ordered their extermination. You would think for the commander-in-chief of the most powerful military nation in the world that this order would be completed immediately. Not so. It took Ford over a year of internal and infernal bureaucratic haggling and bungling to get the little critters packed up and shipped out. It turned out that there were two separate groups tasked with getting rid of rodents in the White House. One group only dealt with mice who visited from the outside, and the other group only dealt with ones who had moved inside permanently. These two groups fought each other for over a year before the mice were finally exterminated.

If you think mice were difficult to eradicate due to organizational infighting, think about how difficult it can be to get a radically new idea accepted, let alone implemented in any heavily siloed company. Even though you may be the top boss, complex and wacky organizational rules often make it difficult for you to communicate a new idea and then actually have others follow through and implement it.

If CEOs spent as much time busting their own company's bureaucracy or going after organizational wackiness and complexity as they do focusing on stock price or cost cutting, they would create an unbelievably more healthy, vibrant, and innovative organization. Unfortunately, many CEOs are prone to increasing their organization's barriers to innovation rather than to decreasing them. They do this by adding even more systems of controls, processes, structures, and formalities that strangle innovation. Later in this book, I will show you many examples of organizational roadblocks and blockheads so you can see why Innovation Judo is such an important tool in the hands of the innovator.

HR FOLKS, SUPPORT INNOVATION JUDO MASTERS— YOUR COMPANY PROBABLY NEEDS THEM

In this book I will explore the seven Innovation Judo principles that you need to master to become a black-belt innovator or leader of innovation. You will also learn how to implement these principles based on the amount of wackiness and complexity in your organization. HR people need to recognize and appreciate these skills and value them in recruitment, placement, and promotion decisions. It doesn't take too many Innovation Judo masters to make a big difference in an organization as you will see from the Jeep Rubicon story mentioned later in the book.

The seven secret principles are as follows:

1. Discipline
2. Leverage
3. Circling
4. Opening
5. Speed
6. Unbalancing
7. Redirection

All of these principles must be pursued in the spirit of "right-mindedness" to be effective, or you will become a manipulator not an innovator. Because right-mindedness is so important in practicing Innovation Judo for great effect, I will devote an entire chapter to this topic.

NO ILL WILL

Please read this book with hope. Human beings were born to be innovative. We are hardwired for it, and we exhibit this quality every day. Whether opening a beer bottle when no bottle opener is handy or using chewing gum for an application other than its intended purpose, we always have this God given talent at our sides. But often, we get disillusioned by organizations that claim they desperately need innovators and risk takers that work unconsciously to inhibit rather than embrace our natural creativity. With the right amount of moxie and a clever mind you can learn to cut through the red tape without being cut. I will guide you through using the seven principles and give you explicit advice as to when and how to use each principle and when you will not have to use any principles at all.

Keep in mind that I am not proposing the use of Innovation Judo if clear logic works. In the ideal world you could present an innovative idea to the higher-ups or your peers, and they would not only listen; they would also help you pursue it. And in the very few companies that have built a culture of innovation it is not only possible to convince with logic it is probable. For those companies that are not by nature innovative or have lost that spirit somewhere along the road, Innovation Judo will remain an important skill set until, or if, a culture of innovation emerges in your respective organization. The good thing about Innovation Judo is that it does not rely on the presence of an existing innovative culture to be effective. In the last section of the book, however, I will talk about how senior leaders can embed innovation into the organization so that Innovation Judo becomes less important. But, even in the most innovative organizations like P&G, VMware, Apple, Google, Kimberly-Clark, or Zappos, employees may still need to use some Innovation Judo principles from time to time.

REAL EXAMPLES

Throughout the book I will give you examples of Innovation Judo masters and how they apply their art not only for the good of their company but for the good of their careers. Innovators are in demand even though they are often organizationally at risk if they aren't careful. These are the real corporate black belts, not the ones who know how to instill Six Sigma in their sleep. Instead they are passionate innovators, the heroes who keep their ideas alive through implementation despite the obstacles thrown in their paths. They often pass their art on to others either by mentoring or by being keenly observed by novices wishing to learn their art. The Japanese word *sensei* means "teacher" or "instructor." If you are serious about being an innovator you will need to find your sensei and then be one. In the last chapter of this book I will show you what it takes to do both of these.

Are these techniques 100 percent guaranteed to get you what you need? Nothing in life is 100 percent guaranteed save death and taxes. But in the long run applying these Innovation Judo principles will help you not only step up and stand out, they will help you stay alive within your organization. You will become the person who not only brings fresh ideas to the table but knows how to implement them in any organization.

Some of my advice may seem counterintuitive, but trust me, it is not counterproductive. For example, sticking your neck out right now is actually good advice despite some associated risk with doing so. And if you stick it out in the right way, you will increase your survival potential, more so than if you put your head in the sand or duck for cover. And this is especially sage advice in today's very turbulent business environment where innovation is needed more than ever.

CHAPTER 2

Innovation Judo Unmasked

A SECRET LEADERSHIP SKILL

I have been a fan of the martial arts since I was a teenager. At the risk of showing my age, I first got turned on to martial arts by watching Bruce Lee in the *Green Hornet* television series. When I got to college I had to take a compulsory physical education course, which met once a week. I could choose Judo, swimming, running, or push-ups, and because I have always liked learning new skills, I signed up immediately for Judo. Swimming to me has always been "staying alive in the water," so the Judo decision was easy. My instructor was an American who got his black belt in Okinawa while in the service. He was not only a Judo expert, but also an excellent teacher. I enjoyed the two-hour lessons so much that I took the Friday afternoon classes throughout college.

What particularly appealed to me was the basic principle of Judo, which is to utilize your opponent's force against him while protecting yourself and not causing bodily harm to the other person. We got to practice this art not only in class but also in competitive tournaments sanctioned by the U.S. Judo Federation. Our instructor set these up because he believed you could never really master the art without the experience of combat in the ring.

I will admit to being stunned a few times in tournaments, but I was never really injured. Judo is not only a good self-defense method but a strenuous sport as well. For those of you not familiar with the sport other than from casual observation, it takes years to be a Judo master. You must master the technical side of course, but there is a sixth sense that only comes with years of practice—Judo masters can anticipate their opponent's moves often before the opponent has actually started the move. They follow very subtle cues, like eye motion, tenseness, etc., and they watch for or create an opportunity where they can make their move and overcome their opponent. Check out this website for a speed demo of some different Judo moves: www.youtube.com/watch?v=pFM-xRKbSec.

Unlike karate, Judo rarely involves direct frontal attacks or aggressiveness. Judo masters take their time and wait for the other person to attack and then redirect the opponent's energy to defeat him or her. The other thing I liked about Judo is that often the smaller, quicker opponent wins over the larger, more muscular, and often slower opponent. Not a bad analogy to working as an innovator in a large organization. Following is a brief definition of judo.

Martial Art that emphasizes the use of quick movement and leverage to throw an opponent. Its techniques are generally intended to turn an opponent's force to one's own advantage rather than to oppose it directly (http://www.merriamwebster.com). The traditional explanation for the meaning of JUDO is: "The word judo consists of two Japanese characters, ju, which means "gentle", and do, which means "the way". Judo, therefore, literally means the way of gentleness. However, the two words JU and DO have much deeper and wider meanings. JU can also mean Giving and Flexible. Like the willow branch that is flexible and does not contend with the wind so too does a student of Judo not meet force with force unless it is to their advantage or for a further purpose. The meaning of DO is the way, the path or system or philosophy. By renaming Jujitsu to Judo, Dr. Kano gave Judo a higher meaning and distinguished it from ancient Jujitsu. (http://www.svjudo.com/judo/meaning-of-judo)

Shortly after taking my first semester of college Judo, I was visiting some friends at a local fraternity house. One of the frat brothers started to push me out of the house and sort of joked that I should leave because I had not pledged. I pushed him back, and then the horseplay got a little more serious. He decided he was going to show me who was stronger and rushed me like a football player. Instead of pushing back on his force, I let him grab me and went backward with his force. As we picked up speed, him going forward pushing my lapel and me going backward, I suddenly turned my hips in the same direction he was pushing me, put my hand on the back of his belt, and did what is known in Judo as a hip throw. Just like in practice, it worked perfectly. He went head over heels and landed flat on his back in the middle of the frat house foyer—unhurt, but very stunned. And that was the end of the pushing match.

Going head-to-head with innovation roadblocks and blockheads is not only an effort in futility; it can also be career limiting. The secret to outwitting and outmaneuvering these obstacles requires using the organization's own negative forces to defeat it. It also involves looking for and exploiting weaknesses to your advantage. Like my frat house example, I knew that my pushing him back would make him angry and that he would charge me with reckless abandon, thus allowing me to use his energy to my advantage.

Besides the hip throw, which I described earlier, there are numerous other moves in Judo that put the opponent at a disadvantage. Simply stepping out of harm's way at exactly the right time can cause an opponent to go right by you, sometimes falling embarrassingly on her face. Foot sweeps knock an opponent's foot out from under him just as he is about to put his foot down, thus compromising his balance and causing him to fall on the ground. Other Judo moves involve getting the opponent on the ground and grappling with him like a wrestler, but using key pressure points instead to make the opponent give up. Envisioning these moves will help you remember how to apply these techniques in the corporate setting.

HERO OR HEEL?

Let's take a look at two examples that highlight the importance of the innovation Judo skill set and will start to introduce you to the seven secret principles. We start with General Billy Mitchell (1879–1936), innovator and self-imposed victim.

Brilliant but Flawed: General Billy Mitchell

Billy Mitchell was an innovator and visionary of his time. By many he is considered the father of the U.S. Air Forces, and Gary Cooper played him in a 1955 Hollywood movie titled *The Court Martial of Billy Mitchell*. From the title of the movie you can guess that he didn't really get to enjoy his fame.

During his time, he was more infamous than famous, at least to his superiors who had a hard time handling his unconventional ideas about the role of air power in the military. They had an even harder time with his personality, especially his willingness to openly challenge the status quo and to publicly question not only his superiors' collective IQs but also their motives. After returning from duty in World War I, he was convinced that naval fleets were extremely vulnerable to attacks from the air and that air power had the potential to completely knock out a nation's entire Navy. So adamant was he in his beliefs that he informed the U.S. Navy that its surface fleet would soon be obsolete; not exactly a career-enhancing move on his part. He was constantly annoyed by the bureaucrats who were so keenly invested in the status quo that they refused to see the future.

He was eventually court-martialed for issuing the now famous statement accusing senior leaders in the Army and Navy of incompetence and "almost treasonable administration of the national defense." He was subsequently found guilty of insubordination and suspended from active duty for five years without pay. Mitchell elected to resign February 1, 1926, instead, and spent the next decade continuing to write and preach the gospel of air power to all who would listen. He eventually died from a confluence of physical ailments in 1936. Most of his innovative ideas later became realized, and Mitchell received many honors following his death, including a commission by the president as a major general. He is also the only individual after whom a type of American military aircraft, the B-25 Mitchell Bomber, was named.[1]

Some Important Lessons

Billy's story, while both sad and honorable, has many lessons for innovators or those trying to lead innovation.

---

[1] www.airpower.maxwell.af.mil/airchronicles/cc/mitch.html.

1. Innovators are essential to every organization because they challenge the status quo with something newer and better, and help prevent their organizations from obsolescence. And, some, like Billy Mitchell, are game changers.

2. They are not always embraced for their views, and in some cases are vilified for them especially if they are not organizationally savvy.

3. The innovator by definition takes risks. We always need some "china breakers," but they need to be careful of how they do this if they want to survive the breakage.

4. Billy Mitchell was his own worst enemy. Despite his great ideas, he irritated others, especially his superiors, with his style and approach. People rarely help you when you call them stupid or incompetent.

5. He was not an Innovation Judo master. As you will see from the profiles in this book, Judo masters don't get court-martialed or demoted. Instead, they get promoted. They use their Judo skills to temporarily disable their opponents. They don't try to overpower, kill, or belittle them. They use smarts, guile, and finesse to get their ideas into action, while understanding that innovation is not always a welcome lodger.

I was both intrigued and saddened by reading Billy's story. He was courageous, inventive, and a pot stirrer to be sure, willing to take on the conventional wisdom and the keepers of the status quo. But he was also flawed in his ability to sell his ideas and to deal constructively with the roadblocks and blockheads he faced. How disappointing to be the brightest bulb on the tree and to be right, but so inept at leading innovation and making the organization work for him that he could never realize his dream in his lifetime. It would be easy to blame the Army, the Navy, or the government for his downfall, but that would not take into account his own flaws that kept him from becoming an Innovation Judo master.

Billy Mitchell was intellectually brilliant but organizationally naive or insensitive. Clearly, many institutions need a good stick of dynamite once in a while to get things started, but it was Billy's lack of understanding or caring about how to stick his neck out without losing it that really cost him. Hopefully, this book and your newfound Innovation Judo skills will help you be an innovative leader while avoiding the chopping block. And like Billy Mitchell, the more interesting and groundbreaking your ideas are, the more likely they are to meet equal but opposite resistance.

Not a Dummy: John Kilcullen

Now let's look at another innovator, but one with Innovation Judo Skills who was able to survive and thrive in his organization despite the fact that some of his superiors, like Billy Mitchell's, were out to stop him. John Kilcullen, the founder of the "Dummies" book series, and an example of one of my Judo masters, exemplifies what I mean by "sticking your neck out" without losing it.

I met John when writing my last book *Lead Like an Entrepreneur*. I became a fan of the Dummies books when I read *DOS for Dummies*, the book that started it all. Like most reasonably intelligent people, I thought the DOS manual would be very helpful.

For those of you who remember trying to learn DOS, the manual was arcane, written by techies, and almost incomprehensible to the normal person. So, it not only took a long time to read, it made bright people feel stupid. John's breakthrough book made sense out of the nonsense, and made the complex simple. John did not write the book, but he created the business and the brand that endures to this day. That formula has worked for two decades, and we now see titles like *Golf for Dummies*, *Wine for Dummies*, and even *Sex for Dummies*.

When I talk about the Dummies success story in my classes as an example of innovation against the odds, I always ask how many people own a Dummies book. Inevitably about 20 to 30 percent own one, and the rest certainly know the brand name. Interestingly, *Sex for Dummies* is a best seller even though I have only found one person in my class who ever admitted to owning that title.

At any rate, the Dummies brand is a huge success and has a global brand following. John had been in the book business for many years as a salesman and a manager, and he remembered having a conversation over dinner one night with a friend who lamented that no one wrote books for him, a dummy. Of course John's friend wasn't a dummy, but he was made to feel dumb by complex things being written complexly. That idea stayed with John until he had a chance to actually bring it to fruition when he started working at IDG Books.

Like many innovators, his idea of books for dummies did not resonate with everyone at his company, including the chief financial officer (CFO) who was not convinced this was a good idea for IDG, and thought it would hurt their overall brand image. In addition, he didn't like the idea that it represented a very different financial model for IDG. IDG was in the media and advertising business where revenues came in before the ads were run. With books, you had to print them first, hope they sold, so revenues could not be predicted in advance. In fact, the CFO stated on record that he so disliked John's idea, that he would starve John's start-up for cash. Some other IDG executives also shared the CFO's views. John's peers were also not all on board because they feared that this atypical venture would damage the company's stock, something that many employees were vested in. Peers can often be enemies of your innovation because they did not come up with the idea and they are afraid that you might not only stand out if your idea succeeds, but that you might also make them look bad in the process.

John not only got his Dummies idea accepted in a company where powerful senior leaders were against it, he wound up creating a quarter of a billion-dollar franchise and got to run it as well. This one innovative idea made tons of money for IDG, and it also assured John's career success at IDG and his future successes at organizations like *Billboard Magazine*. And he had a blast doing it. But as with all attempts at being innovative, there were risks. This was an untried venture in an untested market, some powerful senior leaders at IDG were against it, and John was new to his job.

How did he succeed where Billy Mitchell failed to survive and thrive, and enjoy his creation? First, he had to have a great idea, and then he had to figure out how to disable the innovation killers within IDG just long enough for him to give his idea a chance to prove itself. Unlike Billy's Mitchell's "bull in the china shop" approach, John used humor and cleverness in the form of Innovation Judo. When faced with a powerful enemy to his idea, the CFO, John did not rant, rage, or complain. Instead, he sought first to get "top cover."

Top cover is an extremely important Judo principle for any innovator. I will talk more about this topic later under the *leverage* principle, which is one of the innovative leader's greatest weapons. Top cover is a military term and refers to a fighter pilot whose job it is to protect other planes in formation. They do this by flying above the squadron, thus watching out for enemy fighters that might try to attack. This position gives them the greatest chance of protecting their squadron because of its vantage point, and diving is faster than climbing. As you will see in my Innovation Judo profiles, many masters use top cover for leverage.

Like John, you may want to seek top cover as well to protect your ideas long enough to give them a chance. In this case, John was able to convince Pat McGovern, the founder and entrepreneur behind IDG, to give him a chance even though the CFO was on record as being against the idea. And of course the founder of IDG has a little more clout than the CFO. With a little top cover from Pat, the CFO begrudgingly gave John $1.5 million to try to prove his concept or fail as the CFO hoped.

The $1.5 million was just enough money to test the idea, and when John got down to his last $200,000, as he said to me, "I got brilliant and realized that Dummies was a brand not just a book." His original concept was to have titles like *DOS for Dummies* and *MAC for Morons*, but with cash running out he realized the real gem was in creating a branded franchise. John challenged the traditional publishing model that highlighted the author by selling the books using their brand, not the authors. While everyone in my class can spout the titles of the Dummies books they own, almost no one remembers the authors' names—except perhaps for Dr. Ruth Westheimer, who wrote *Sex for Dummies.*

John also used another Judo principle: *unbalancing*. John put the CFO's name and a personal dedication to him in all their first books: "We would like to thank Bill for his help in bringing this book to market." As soon as the Dummies brand made a profit, John and his team removed Bill's name and put Pat McGovern's name in the book and then dedicated their success to him because he had the foresight and vision to give John and his team enough top cover to test the concept. As the book series started to make money, the CFO called John and suggested he should do other books like *Golf for Dummies* and *Finance for Dummies,* etc. John had also been able to *redirect* the CFO's negative energy through his demonstration of positive cash flow.

And, of course, the rest is history. A little "in your face" to be sure, but this ploy gave John and his team the emotional incentive to go the next mile and prove Bill wrong. And, of course, Bill was a little surprised and unbalanced by being thanked and initially honored in a book enterprise that he tried to kill. Interestingly, the CFO later became one of John's best allies because of the success of the first *DOS for Dummies* book. In fact, it was the CFO who later asked John, "Why don't you do *Golf for Dummies* and *Wine for Dummies?*"

John Kilcullen's story is inspirational on several points. First, he had to have an innovative idea. He also had to take some calculated risks in trying something new that the company had never done before, with very little in the way of resources or emotional support. And to really succeed, he had to figure out how to utilize Innovation Judo principles to temporarily neutralize a powerful enemy in order to help his creative idea triumph over adversity.

From his story we are now able to discern some of the Judo principles that John employed: *unbalancing, surprise, leverage,* and *redirection.* John was able to couple these with humor to soften the blow. By the way, in this story when I use the word *enemy,* I don't mean that John and the CFO disliked each other. To the contrary, they both had a great sense of humor and enjoyed having a few beers together. But the CFO was an enemy of the innovation, and this is where John had to resort to Innovation Judo skills. Now that you have a good understanding of why Innovation Judo is such an important part of an innovator's skill set and mindset, I will go into greater depth about the various organizational roadblocks and blockheads that you will inevitably meet on the pathway to creativity. Identifying them before running into them is of great importance.

ROADBLOCKS AND BLOCKHEADS

In the next chapter, I will explain many of the innovation roadblocks and blockheads that you will have to anticipate and plan your Innovation Judo moves around.

THE HARD PART

One of the reasons companies have difficulty with innovation is that they do not understand how the true cycle of innovation works and that the *ideation* part is not really the major challenge for innovators or those tasked with leading innovation. The real challenges, which are rarely discussed, exists in the company's ability to work through the lesser-known phases like *intent, infrastructure, investigation, infection* and *implementation/integration.* These phases often attract innovation killers because they are the places where a good idea has the greatest chance of being derailed.

Innovation Judo and the Innovation Cycle

Figure 2.1 shows the standard innovation cycle that most researchers typically use to describe how the innovation process works. This particular model comes from a book called *The Innovator's Playbook* (Deloitte, 2009). As you can see from the model, the four stages are idea generation, idea selection, idea implementation, and idea diffusion. The logic makes sense. First, an organization has to have some mechanism for generating ideas in order to start the innovation process. Then, it has to create a decision mechanism in order to winnow many ideas down to a few. After the choice has been made, the company enters into the implementation process and the diffusion of innovation to other parts of the organization.

Standard Innovation Cycle

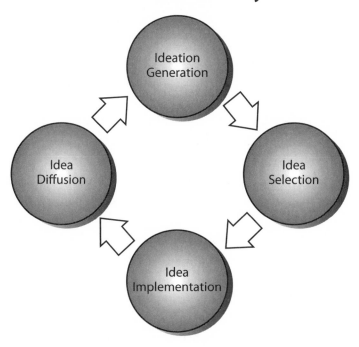

IBM, for example, runs a worldwide Innovation Jam on the web. It invites thousands of people both inside and outside the organization to send in ideas about a particular challenge, global warming for example, where innovative solutions could be very helpful. The Navy has a similar web-based idea-generating tool to seek creative solutions to the problems of international piracy. At IBM all these thousands of ideas are collected and then sorted by a committee that decides which ones they want to pursue immediately, put on the shelf for a later look, or discard immediately. Once the core ideas are selected, they are then given to appropriate groups in the company to further develop and implement. Finally, they publish the innovations so that others within IBM can leverage them if they choose to do so.

While Figure 2.1 is clear and makes sense, it is misleading for the corporate innovator. It leaves out several of phases in the innovation cycle where roadblocks and blockheads are most likely to appear and thus the need for Innovation Judo. I use the term *roadblocks* to refer to organizational impediments to innovation like bureaucratic policies, structures, processes, values, and rule sets; and *blockheads* to refer to people who stand in the innovator's way for nonlogical reasons. Like the engineering manager who tries to block an idea from marketing because it wasn't his or the CEO who tells his people to take more risks and then fires the first person who makes a mistake. When you look at the other stages that I have added to the innovation cycle (see Figure 2.2), you begin to see why Innovation Judo is more appropriate in some phases than in others because these are the places where roadblocks and blockheads are more likely to appear.

MISSED STEPS

Let's take a look at each of these steps in turn.

The 7I Model of Innovation

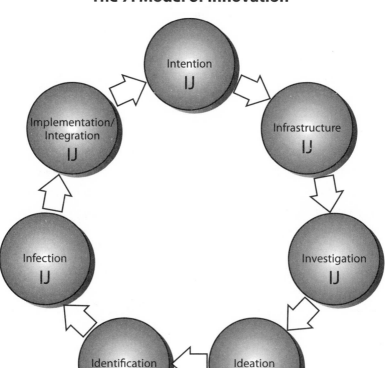

Intention

The first, and most important step is intention. Innovation is a tool—not a destination—and therefore, it requires that the organization clarify the intended purpose of this tool. Understanding the "why" of innovation is essential for generating ideas. This is no small task and requires some soul-searching so that innovation is not just a concept. For example, I once worked with an executive who called me in to help his company "innovate." I asked the executive committee what they meant by innovation. I got six different answers. One wanted new products, another focused on creative cost cutting, and the president just said he wanted a more innovative culture. As you can see from this little vignette, this group needed to agree on their intent for innovation before they did anything else.

Infrastructure

After determining intent, companies need to answer the infrastructure questions: "How do we start the innovation process and who is going to be accountable for it? How do we incent people for giving us ideas, etc.?" I have attended numerous innovation sessions where the group identifies some great ideas but everyone looks at the floor when the boss asks who is going to take ownership of the idea to see it through to completion. In Chapter 11, I will go into detail about this infrastructure challenge. Some companies create purpose-built units like skunkworks or innovation cells, others expect to create innovation cultures where innovation becomes a shared value, and in some organizations the official channel for innovation doesn't work so people like Jim Repp, who I profile later in this book, create their own stealth organizations to provide innovation a safe haven. But the infrastructure discussions are critical before diving into ideation.

Investigation

Assuming that we have clear intent and determined who will be accountable for the initiative, then we need to investigate what is known about the problem or challenge we are trying to solve using innovation as our chosen tool. Many of you have probably seen the IDEO video that is available on YouTube. IDEO is arguably the preeminent organization regarding how to innovate. In this video, ABC News challenges IDEO to test their innovation process by redesigning the typical shopping cart in just five days. The video is great fun to watch and tremendously instructive in understanding IDEO's design thinking process. It shows how IDEO utilizes this process to great effect. When people watch this video for the first time, they are often enamored by IDEO's particular brand of brainstorming and miss the importance of their investigation phase. For example, IDEO employees fan out to observe and talk firsthand with all the people who typically come in contact with shopping carts. They talked with store owners, cart manufacturers, cart repair people, store clerks, and customers. Like anthropologists, they go into the field with open minds and video equipment.

They are expert investigators, and their unique approach yields insights about shopping carts that none of the other constituencies has seen. Only then do they start the process of creating ideas. Many companies, like Procter & Gamble and others will say that most *brainstorming* is crap (my word, not theirs) because you get the same people, in the same room, with the same experiences and views that they had last week, and in the same political and physical environment. No wonder they don't come up with any really insightful new ideas.

I believe that most brainstorming is ineffective because the participants are not informed before the ideation process begins. IDEO's brainstorming is effective because it is "informed" brainstorming. For example, in their investigation IDEO project team members find out that there are over 22,000 hospitalized injuries a year that result from people's interactions with shopping carts. If you don't believe this, just go to your local grocery store and watch kids trying to ride carts down the aisles or notice that a fellow shopper could easily run into the back of your leg while looking for their favorite pasta.

 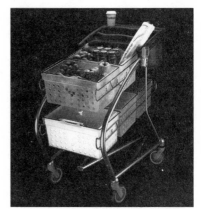

These are pictures of IDEO's redesigned shopping cart. Note that it has no permanent basket, which has been replaced by modular removable ones (thus less theft); all four wheels move in a 360-degree direction (no having to pick up the back of the cart to move it around a tight corner); it has a safety seat for children with a little play area near the handle; and on the side of the cart you will see a handheld checkout scanner so you can avoid the checkout line. The cart has no central basket. Shoppers fill modular baskets that fit inside the cart when shopping. At checkout these module baskets are emptied and removed from the cart. Their contents are placed in plastic bags, which are then hung on hooks on the cart. Since there is no central basket, this cart is unlikely to find its way onto the streets.

If the IDEO team had just sat in a room with no outside knowledge, they never would have come up with this clever design. That is why investigation before ideation is such a critical and often missed step in the process of innovation. There is no investigation step in Figure 2.1, and I believe this is an often crucial oversight on the part of people who want to get great ideas on the table. Garbage in, garbage out. Investigation allows for facts to shape the ideation process rather than the typical opinions I see in most innovation discussions. Typical discussion meetings are not innovation meetings, and the IDEO video shows you how to avoid endless opinion-oriented meetings masquerading as ideation.

Ideation

Ideation is the most fun part of the innovation process and unfortunately the one that most companies immediately jump to. Recently I was asked by a well-known government agency to talk with some of their people about their newly created innovation cell. I was one of a number of speakers who were asked to come in and share their insights with two of the people who were currently in charge of their newly appointed innovation cell. I had no notes or PowerPoint slides, but simply stood up and started to go through the common mistakes I see when companies embark on a campaign to enhance their innovation capabilities. My starting point was to show the standard innovation cycle (Figure 2.1) compared to mine and discuss how intent and investigation were often missing from these initiatives. I said if you don't know your intent, then you are doomed to follow Alice in Wonderland and struggle to find the right road. When Alice asks the Cheshire Cat to help her decide which fork in the road she should take, he asks where she is going. When she confesses that she does not know, he suggests, in that case, either road will do.

When I went through the 7I model, one of the members of this team said, "Now I know why we have been stalled. We really never figured out our intent except to be more innovative." As I said, innovation is not a destination but a tool, and if you don't know the purpose of the tool then you are bound to flounder.

When IDEO started its ideation stage, it had already determined intent and had investigated the challenge to learn new things and gain new insights that led to novel ideas regarding the redesign of the shopping cart. The ideation process involves the development of numerous divergent and often wild ideas that eventually get combined and winnowed down to a few good ones that could truly work. In the shopping cart example, the final cart has no basket, all four wheels rotate, and the cart has a scanner attached to it so you can scan your own items and make it through the checkout in record time. That is assuming you would even need a checkout.

Identification

This is the step where the real innovation work begins. Ideation is fun and most folks like being in this type of creative process. But then we face one of innovation's biggest challenges: which ideas to pursue and what resources and how much time will these ideas need. This is the idea evaluation process where we have to look at all our ideas and then winnow them down into the few that we want to follow. There is a process for this called the "opportunity process." I will go into this in detail under the IJ principles of *Discipline* and *Leverage*. Ideas have little gravitas until they start to demonstrate opportunity characteristics like durability, sustainability, defensibility, and the potential for value creation, which then makes them compelling. The opportunity process takes time, testing, and failure. "Real opportunities," as I like to tell my students, "draw people and money like bees to honey."

The ability of an innovator to present real opportunities rather than just ideas gives him or her incredible leverage for keeping their ideas afloat. Following the opportunity process also starts to move the innovator from innovator to entrepreneur where the focus is not on creativity but on turning creativity into cash.

Infection

The next step in the innovation cycle involves trying out the idea usually through some sort of pilot project to see if anyone cares. I call this the *infection* stage. The infection stage is often interwoven with the opportunity process because it is through pilot testing, experimentation, and talking with potential customers that we start to determine whether an idea is just that or an opportunity. Companies like Kimberly-Clark or McDonald's typically field test their innovations before they commit to a wholesale rollout. I use the term *infection* because it involves injecting something new into a host that may or may not catch on. If we cannot infect others with our idea, we may need to reshape or abandon it. Infections must be carefully managed because at this stage the idea starts to become known to others and thus increasingly vulnerable. You will see this later in the Steve Paljieg profile—Steve is very wary in this phase and believes you should "pick your team, one at a time." This is very counterintuitive to those who believe you should involve all stakeholders early on.

Implementation/Integration

The final phases of the innovation cycle involve *implementation* and *integration* into the business. I helped create an innovation program for Sodexho, a global food services company that felt it was losing its innovative edge. Management wanted help to innovate by creating new businesses and new business offerings. Their intent was to grow the business through differentiation and value-added services. I, and my colleagues at Babson College at the time, helped them come up with a number of innovative ideas that had real opportunity characteristics. The teams that came up with these ideas and their supporting business plans were really excited about seeing them come to fruition, but Sodexho had never really thought about how they would implement these ideas given their current business structure, and the program folded within the year.

While most authors talk about the implementation phase in the innovation cycle, they often fail to address the integration part of implementation. Implementation refers to tactics that must be employed to put an idea into practice. As you will see, this is one of the most dangerous phases for the survival of an idea. It is dangerous because the idea must not only be implemented; it must be integrated with other activities in the business and align with strategy. An innovation, even supported at the top, can still fail in the implementation phase because of department or division infighting. I have also seen great innovations supported by the middle of the organization die because they did not fit with the company's current strategy or because they might force the company to change strategy.

RIGHT TIME/RIGHT PLACE

So how are these phases related to the practice of Innovation Judo? In the 7I model (Figure 2.2), I have placed the letters *IJ* in the steps where Innovation Judo can be most useful. As you can see, it is more helpful in some phases than in others. It is helpful in the intent, infrastructure, infection, and implementation/integration phases and sometimes helpful in the investigation phase. IJ is important to intent and infrastructure because often people will try to hijack innovation for political purposes. I was asked to help set up an innovation team in the Navy a couple of years ago, and a member of the team who was in charge of Lean Six Sigma wanted innovation to fall under his purview, not for logical reasons but for political ones. We successfully fended off his attempts because oftentimes Lean Six Sigma can actually be a barrier to innovation—focusing on perfection in current products often leads to not seeking out new ones. Like Innovation, Lean Six Sigma needs to be seen as a toolkit rather than a destination. When the means become the end, then companies risk the danger of believing that process is progress.

If the investigation process is carried out like IDEO, then IJ is not necessary in this phase. I have put it here, however, as a precautionary warning. As all of you know, data can be manipulated for one's purpose as seen in today's debate over global warming. Both sides can easily put forward statistics that support their own point of view. Generally, I would not recommend Innovation Judo in this phase, but I have personally seen the need for it. I was recently on a committee to investigate our organization's "value to the world." Our intent was supposed to be unbiased research into how we made a difference due to our educational presence and offerings. In our first meeting, I was stunned to find out that there were no customers present nor were there plans to involve them. Our group consisted solely of internal faculty and administrators. As you can imagine, the final report gave us glowing comments about ourselves. What a surprise!

Innovation Judo really comes into play in the infection and implementation phases. This is where the most consequential roadblocks and blockheads appear. Innovative ideas don't really scare people all that much until people see that they might actually be implemented. Even if an idea looks very logical and attractive on the surface, implementation requires a lot of action within the organization if the innovation is significant enough. Significant innovation requires change, and people often resist change, sometimes out of unfounded fears and sometimes because the change can affect the beneficiaries of the status quo.

Implementation/integration is where the idea needs to be woven into and through the system. Most innovators will tell you this is the roughest patch for them. The ideas now start to become reality, and significant innovation changes lives both inside and outside the organization.

Innovation is never done in a vacuum. It is inextricably woven into and affected by an organization's culture. If the culture is illogical (wacky), then the innovator is in for a tough time. Innovation Judo is particularly important for innovating in wacky organizations, and most organizations have some form of wackiness that innovators must confront. Wackiness is a kind of organizational craziness that exists in many companies and creates its own set of roadblocks and blockheads.

THE WACKY FACTOR

In the next chapter I will explain how all organizations have some degree of wackiness in the way they operate. Some more than others, and this is why innovators need defense mechanisms. Wackiness expands with organizational size and complexity. As an innovator you are likely to face some wackiness that is not easily removed through logic or frontal attacks. Many would-be innovators give up when they hit a roadblock or blockhead and decide that innovating in their organization isn't worth it. The people I have profiled in this book not only saw these impediments coming, they used Innovation Judo strategies to mitigate them.

I have worked with many companies over the years, and a CEO will often opine that his or her company does not have enough good innovators who are willing to try stuff and ask permission later. This CEO, of course, is the first one with the gun to blow the failed risk taker away. One CEO, with whom I worked, actually said in the same sentence to his VP that he wanted to encourage risk taking but would not tolerate failure. This is a perfect example of wackiness. This CEO's statement is rubbish, of course (you can't innovate without mistakes), but it is one of the reasons that Innovation Judo is such a critical toolkit. Without Innovation Judo as a backup strategy, you are damned if you do or damned if you don't. If you don't step up to take a risk then you don't get noticed, and if you take a risk and fail with this kind of CEO, then you can get fired. That is, unless you have deployed Innovation Judo to mitigate these risks.

CHAPTER 3

The Wacky Factor

THE WACKY FACTOR

The culture around here is easy to explain:
We do all of the work, and they take all of the credit.

Innovators throughout history have faced both roadblocks and blockheads on their path to creativity, and so will you. Galileo, the famous Italian astronomer, was sentenced to life imprisonment for his radical view at the time that the earth was not the center of the universe as suggested in the biblical scriptures. His sentence was softened somewhat by having his imprisonment served under house arrest, but he was found guilty despite his ability to provide scientific evidence as to the truthfulness of his views. Galileo faced both roadblocks and blockheads that were irrational given the evidence. Roadblocks are typically embedded in the organization in some fashion and often kill or suffocate innovation even when the organization has the best of intentions. And blockheads are exactly what you think they are: people who intentionally want to block your ideas for equally irrational reasons.

In Galileo's time, the societal view was very much ordained by the views of the Catholic Church, and the church said that the earth was the center of the universe. It was conventional wisdom at the time, what you might call the predominant culture (shared values) of the populace. Add to that a pope who was totally invested in the scriptures' view of the earth as center of the universe, and you have two huge impediments to Galileo's innovative work. A "corporate culture" roadblock that had existed for centuries and a senior executive blockhead (no disrespect intended) who was totally invested in the status quo. Both irrational, given the evidence, but rather than rational to the organization and to the pope. I call this irrationality "the wacky factor." Wackiness does not yield easily to rationality as Galileo found out. For the innovator to succeed in the face of wackiness, roadblocks have to removed or neutralized, and blockheads need to be outsmarted. And this is where your skills as a Judo master will be the most helpful.

WACKINESS DEFINED

I have purposefully tried to avoid other terms that are used to describe organizations that actually do a lot of things not in their own self-interest. Some authors have used the terms *dysfunctional* or *toxic,* which are far too pejorative and not really fair to these companies because neither companies nor individuals are usually purposefully or totally dysfunctional.

So, I prefer to use the term *wacky* to describe organizations that torpedo themselves because they have failed to identify and/or remove innovative roadblocks and blockheads. In this book I will focus primarily on how organizations kill innovation despite their desire for it. Unfortunately, there are no psychotropic drugs for organizational wackiness so Innovation Judo will have to do until CEOs spend as much time eliminating their wackiness as they do in trying to cut costs. The best corporate innovators are the ones who know their own organization's wackiness and have prepared strategies to deal with it.

Since I am creating a new label for certain types of organizational behavior, we need to define the term. I define *wackiness* as "Systematically and often unconsciously doing things that actually prevent or inhibit achieving what you most want." We see this in human beings all the time: the woman who keeps marrying the abusive husband, the bachelor so desperate to meet someone special that his neediness actually repels potential partners, and the insecure individual wanting so much to be important that they either behave in a totally overbearing manner or wear their insecurity like a bull's-eye.

The Illogic of Wackiness

We sometimes deride these folks because their behavior is so opposite from what they want that we can't understand what is wrong with them. Why don't they know what everyone else knows about them? How can the CEO who says he wants innovation and then shoots the first mistake maker not realize the wackiness of this mixed message? But we also understand and are sometimes sympathetic with the difficulty we all face in seeing ourselves as others do and then doing something about our foibles.

Generally wacky human beings are easy to identify. Their wackiness affects others who create a pretty short feedback loop. For example, I am a "caraholic"—I love cars. Unfortunately there are no twelve-step programs for caraholics, but I do have my own feedback loop who reminds me of my caraholism and keeps me in check: my wife. While my wife is more direct with me about this personality defect, my neighbors may also chime in: "Hey, I thought you just bought a new car," or "You're gonna need a new garage," or "You must be the DMV's best friend."

Companies don't generally have these kinds of direct feedback loops unless they purposefully build them, and most don't. Who wants to tell the CEO that his company is messed up? Or that the IT system we just spent millions of dollars on is worse than the last one? Or that the company's values displayed in the main lobby and on every employee's business card is a "load of crap." This kind of candor in large hierarchical companies is incredibly rare and demonstrates that wackiness is hard to get rid of especially if no one is willing to tell you about it. Even the most open admirals with whom I work rarely get the whole truth because although they may be wearing casual clothing, everyone can still see the admiral's stars and watch what they say.

Innovation is often a victim of organizational wackiness, and that is why so many companies fail at it. The example I used earlier of the boss saying he wants innovation but then shoots the mistake maker is an example of wackiness. He is both a roadblock to innovation and a blockhead for sending mixed messages. IBM also demonstrated wackiness when it measured fledgling businesses on the same financial measures as its mature businesses. Very few of these new businesses survived beyond their first year because they could rarely meet the same ROI (return on investment) that IBM's mature companies were required to give. The effect was that IBM was killing its newborns before they had a chance to get off the ground. They have now changed their practice, and their new business start-ups are not measured on financial results at all for the first year and instead are measured on project milestones. IBM had to do a lot of work on feedback loops before they understood why their new babies weren't making it. Thankfully, IBM is a great company with lots of smart people, and it has been able to survive a number of near-death experiences by recognizing wackiness and then eliminating it.

I recently worked with an organization that was very sophisticated in market research and analysis and could probably tell you what type of shoes their targeted consumers wear. But then they created a process for going after these targeted consumers that was so regimented that it left little room for innovating outside a narrowly prescribed corridor of "acceptable" innovation. All of these acceptable ones are what we in the innovation field call "derivatives" or simple innovations regarding product features and forms like shape and size or packaging changes, etc. It was very hard for people to see this disconnect as they have put countless days and thousands of hours constructing the process not realizing that is was in fact limiting their ability to hit a really big home run. There was no re-direction of all this misplaced energy in the right direction because there was no one willing or able to tell the CEO that he was wrong.

Later in this book, I will show you how to use the Judo principle of *redirection* of an opponent's energy, to build a specific kind of feedback loop for innovation that redirects the energy of both blockheads and roadblocks. It is a simple and powerful technique that most companies are surprised by and are enthusiastic to use. This loop also takes advantage of *leverage, speed,* and *unbalancing,* which exemplify three of the seven secret principles.

AN ASTOUNDING LACK OF CANDOR

Interestingly, most of the CEOs that I know opine about the lack of transparency and candor within their companies, but they don't realize that they need to spend as much time on ridding their companies of all the wackiness as they do on cost cutting or the company's stock price. Getting rid of wackiness, however, is no small task since it can become so engrained in a company's culture. Instead of complaining, Innovation Judo masters have an innate understanding and acceptance of wackiness as a fact of organizational life, and have figured out how to neutralize it, work around it, or use it to their advantage.

GE's "Work Out" program was about as close as we have seen to a CEO, Jack Welch, going after his own company's wackiness. Welch did a lot of cost cutting and deselecting (the new politically correct word for *firing*) in his days at GE but railed at the phrase "mean and lean." Instead, he preferred "lean and agile" as he felt, and rightfully so, that if you take a bunch of folks out of the organization but leave the same amount of work behind for others to do then you will become lean, but you will also become mean. An employee now asked to do two jobs for the same compensation instead of one could turn any employee mean, and fast.

So GE put a number of teams together consisting of both outsiders and insiders. The mission of these teams was to go after nonvalue-adding activities that wasted the company's time and money and got in the way of GE's ability to do business. Welch's view was that if you take people out of the organization, you should also try to take wasteful work out as well. It was only partially successful because wackiness, like the roots of an old oak tree, can run deep and wide, thus making wackiness very difficult to literally "root out." But GE clearly had the right idea. If you can't root out the old tree, your next best option is to work around it to get where you need to go. The Innovation Judo master is your next best option. Perhaps even the best as they can get the job done quickly and efficiently without cutting down the tree.

REGRESSION TO WACKINESS

Since wackiness is so rife in today's organizations, it completely astounds me that wackiness is not only allowed to survive but actually encouraged to thrive. Many of us talk about our own company's wackiness around the water cooler and behind closed doors, but we have to be careful: admitting to wackiness opens us up to being labeled as complainers, nonteam players, or even worse. Also, we have to be careful that we are not bashing wackiness in front of a wacky purveyor. Wackiness doesn't just happen magically, someone creates it. For example, the HR manager who helped craft the company's values around trust, integrity, and teamwork has every employee's computer secretly scanned for nonbusiness use. Or take Jack Stempel, a former head of GM, who packed the executive board with his cronies who gave him an astronomical pay rise in one of GM's worst years of job losses.

Having worked as an educator with GE I can attest to its hard work in creating a culture of both risk taking and accountability. Welch promoted one of his managers two levels even though this manager's innovative business idea did not pan out. Welch did this so that he could send a message to the rest of the company that he was serious about risk taking and the importance of learning through failure. Almost no innovator becomes successful without having some failures. Eighty percent of Edison's inventions failed, but he learned enough from these failures to develop a couple of world-changing inventions. Rest assured that GE still has some wackiness despite the "Work Out" program. Wackiness is both inevitable and unavoidable in most organizations. The secret to keeping a lid on wackiness is to either monitor wackiness (short feedback loops) and eliminate it or develop enough counterbalancing mechanisms like Innovation Judo masters who can provide a counterbalance to its negative effects.

INNOVATION KILLERS

In this book, I will help you deal with the organizational wackiness that is most likely to derail innovation. Wackiness typically emanates from five sources; the first being people, who we refer to as blockheads, and the other four are organizational roadblocks that are the greater threats to the innovator because they are ingrained in the organization. Successful innovators will tell you that blockheads are easier to deal with than the roadblocks because outmaneuvering an individual is often easier than outmaneuvering the whole bureaucracy. But Innovation Judo skills will help you with both sets of obstacles.

1. People
2. Politics
3. Organizational Design
4. Company Values
5. Corporate Culture

People

Let's start with the people side. People who proactively or passively resist innovation on an illogical basis fall into the category of *blockheads* and are generally easier to deal with than roadblocks, which are more systemic to the organization. In general, blockheads are an easier target for the Judo master than the more embedded roadblocks. This, of course, is not necessarily true if your boss is the blockhead. Nonetheless, Innovation Judo is still effective with a blockhead boss as you will see in some of my Judo master profiles in Part III. Individuals can also band together as a group to illogically block innovation, which creates a more endemic and formidable opponent to ideas that

I call "Team Blockhead." This is often most prevalent in specific organizational functions. Later on when you read the Jeep Rubicon story you will see that Jeep engineers came up with the idea of the mass-produced, high-end off-road Jeep, but it was initially dismissed by the marketing organization because they thought, "What do engineers know about the market?" When gangs of people band together to block innovation, they tend to share values that become embedded in the corporate culture that may not allow them to recognize and utilize good ideas from others outside of their particular tribe or area.

In cases of Team Blockhead, you will discover that your challenges as an Innovation Judo master will be greater, and you will have to use multiple principles. I love the earlier quote from Machiavelli because his saying is as true today as it was in his time. The other saying I like is "The devil we know is better than the devil we don't know." Most people spend time trying to create somewhat of a predictable work environment over which they can develop mastery. This is not only human nature; it is also common sense. Being asked to embrace innovation, especially if it requires significant change and adaptation, threatens this mastery.

No wonder people resist change, let alone innovation. When a ship is sinking, everybody runs for the lifeboats because they know this is the best way to avoid drowning. But when there are few lifeboats, as is often the case in innovative endeavors, many people will resist going on an uncertain path even though the destination may be better. But if you remove all the lifeboats, people will become extremely inventive building other floatation devices. Removing the lifeboats illustrates the use of two more Innovation Judo principles, *unbalancing* and *surprise,* which I will discuss later in this book.

Ideally most people should at least be receptive to listening to new ideas about how things could be done better, faster, more efficiently, or new product or service ideas. Personality research indicates that some people are open because they are by nature open to experimentation and like to try out new things. But many others are not. The KAI (Kurtain Adaptive Index) is one such personality test that actually looks at one's natural predilection toward trying the new versus staying with the old. The more rigid people, as measured by the KAI, are not necessarily wacky but they reject innovation simply because they are uncomfortable with the new or don't want to spend the energy to try something different. When people resist change for illogical reasons, like their personality orientation, then you will most likely have to put on your judogi (Judo uniform).

Politics

You can usually get around one or two individuals who try to block your idea, but when the organization is rife with politics, the game of innovation gets much more challenging. You will have to use more of your Innovation Judo skills. I hate working in highly politicized organizations. They make work a lot harder and make you spend considerable time on non-value-adding activities. Politics waste people's energy, and they often subvert the organization's avowed mission. But, unfortunately, politics is part of organizational life from the two-teacher classroom in kindergarten to the hallowed halls of Harvard to IBM.

When self-serving behavior is infrequent or sporadic, wackiness is not necessarily endemic to the culture. When this behavior is widespread throughout the culture, it can make the would-be innovator's life a nightmare because the innovator will have to outsmart and outmaneuver the politically minded who are much less interested in the innovation than they are in self-promotion or self-defense. But it can be done, and some of my Judo masters whom I profile in this book will show you how they did it.

In my previous role as the Innovation Chair of the Business School at the Naval Postgraduate School, I have visited the Pentagon. My first thought was "Thank God I have a guide," as it would be easy to get lost there since every corner looks the same. I have worked with many of the Pentagon staffers and I know they work hard, but they often complain of spinning their wheels because of all the time and energy they have to put into dealing with the politics. Who can talk to whom, what is the right protocol, who can authorize what, etc. Most talk like seasoned boat owners about their two happiest days: when they first bought their boat (when the staffer was hired) and when they sold it (when the staffer was leaving). Staffers often feel the same: "A wonderful place to experience but not to stay."

Clearly a lot of time is wasted, but perhaps the more tedious element of these staffers' jobs is having to filter communications to their bosses who would then choose to filter it to their bosses. In fact, I have been in conversations where a staffer has told a would-be innovator, "I can't suggest that to the boss, he would never allow it." Filters filtering filters is certainly wacky, and it happens in the private sector as well. One of the antidotes to this form of wackiness is something I refer to in a later chapter as *openings*. One of the secrets to being a successful black belt in the martial arts form of Judo is to either look for or create an opening—an avenue where you see a chance to get your body close to the opponent's so you can exploit an advantage. In Innovation Judo, the same principle applies.

Jim Repp, the innovator behind the Jeep Rubicon, was told his Rubicon idea wouldn't fly within Daimler Chrysler. But, as you will see under his profile, his ability to create an *opening* gave him just the space he needed to keep his dream alive. Jim found his opening on the Rubicon Trail in California where Jeep tested their vehicles against other off-road vehicles. Many of Chrysler's executives attended these outings, which were held so far off the beaten path that tent camping was the only option. With executives out on the trail with no other place to go, Jim knew he could capture their attention without the filterers' interference. He planned his strategy for influencing executives to help him build the Rubicon with this event in mind. Finding an opening to convince a senior leader about the viability of his idea would give Jim the necessary support to get his idea to the next level. Jim saw an opening and exploited it. Some could argue that this is just another example of politics, but I would disagree. It certainly is cleverness and for the right reason. Jim's motivation was to help the company, not himself. Jim used right-mindedness. He wasn't there to get a promotion or to bad-mouth a colleague or another department. He was there because he was a passionate advocate of an innovative product.

In later profiles you will see several Innovation Judo masters utilizing this opening technique effectively. This technique becomes increasingly necessary as organizational politics increases and people purposefully want to block your access to the key decision makers. Unfortunately, we all have to play politics at one time or another in our business careers.

However, the motivation and mindset with which you play politics is very important. It is essential to the innovator that he or she be in the right frame of mind in order to sell innovation.

As an innovator, your ideas must always center around and be driven by *right-mindedness*. Right-mindedness is both a core principle of Innovation Judo and an essential prerequisite for the use of the other seven principles. When it comes to politics, you should practice Innovation Judo for the good of the company not for yourself. Although you, like me, may find politics distasteful, sometimes you have to play the game, but doing so for the right reasons makes the process more palatable and helps you avoid becoming a "manipulator." Remember, the politics involved with Innovation Judo are meant to disarm not harm, while other organizational politics are meant to hurt—back stabbing, rumor mongering, etc.

BRINGING OUT THE WORST

Political wackiness for personal reasons is also more likely to be evident and problematic for the innovator in organizations with limited or decreasing resources. Not all innovative ideas require new resourcing, but many do and you will be competing in an environment of increasing scarcity. Winning resources for your idea will mean that someone else loses. In these situations, good salesmanship is not enough. You will also have to utilize one or more of the secret principles.

My wife has been a speech therapist in the public school system for many years, and the stories she tells me about teacher rivalries, pettiness, and fights over rooms, furniture, etc., would put the executives at the old Ford Motor Company to shame even though Ford has had more than its share of politics, particularly in the past. Many years ago, a story appeared in the press about the politics and rivalry within the Ford Motor Company where there were twenty-one different levels of management. One newly promoted executive found out that his office was a couple of square feet smaller that the executive next door so that night he had the maintenance crew come in and move the wall between the two offices so that the square footage was the same. This executive was truly motivated, but for the wrong reasons. In my last few years consulting with another of the Big Three automakers, I remember witnessing an argument over who should be in my executive education class based on their level in the organization.

Jealousy and the competition for limited resources can lead to some major wackiness. Add to this an indulgent senior leadership group and you have a recipe for all kinds of wackiness. For the innovator, wackiness derived from these factors often presents itself as NIH (not invented here). For example, if your department came up with a great new idea or problem solution, members of a NIH management team will often find plenty of major faults in order to make sure the idea was killed because it wasn't theirs. In this type of politically wacky environment, you can easily predict a quid pro quo, when the other group tries to bring forth their innovative initiative.

Organizational Design

Disabling or disarming roadblocks presents a different set of challenges than dealing with blockheads since organizational processes, structures, systems, and culture are harder to remove or temporarily disable than people. For example, many companies that say they want greater innovation have incentive plans that are counter to innovation. Why not give the innovators, if their ideas are implemented and create economic value, a percentage of the action especially if the innovation is outside of their normal duties? I have heard one HR manager say this is impossible because it would screw up their expensive and exhaustively designed job evaluation and pay system. So, "Let's give them theater tickets as an incentive for their idea," he countered. It better be a great movie if the HR manager really wants to inspire innovation through theater tickets. So here you see the problem with organizational design. In this case, the HR system makes all kind of sense for a steady stable plodding company but no sense for a company wishing to be more innovative. Now it's not always about money, but clearly this HR manager needed a more innovative approach to her pay system if she wanted to scale innovation.

INCOMPETENT AT COMPETENCIES

A few years back I was asked to help develop a set of leadership competencies for a newly created spin-off of a large, bureaucratic telecommunications company. They created the spin-off because they knew that their current corporate culture would absolutely kill the new company. Then the parent company insisted on imposing their corporate bureaucracy's leadership competency model on the managers who were running this new start-up. What were they thinking? These competencies were developed for a business that had emerged from the government-regulated telephony industry, and the business was overrun with bureaucratic rules, regulations, and financial control systems that would make even the most evil bureaucrat proud.

The list of competencies included things like

- Demonstrates executive presence
- Strategic thinker

- Empathetic listener and coach
- Good people developer
- Team player

Now if you know anything about start-ups, you would have to question the validity of mindlessly applying these competencies from the parent company to the spin-off. The entrepreneurial leader (Thornberry, 2007) of this start-up should not be focusing on any of these competencies in the beginning phases. To get this new company off the ground, the leader needs already developed people, he won't have any time to play coach, and you hope he will be much more concerned about cash flow than executive presence. And tactical thinking will be much more important than strategic thinking in the start-up organization. I was instantly struck by what was not on the list like

- Thinks and acts like an entrepreneur
- Sees and seizes new business opportunities
- Can work effectively with all kinds of people both inside and outside the organization
- Ability to network
- Can change direction quickly when needed
- Use limited resources creatively

Where were all of these competencies that we know are much more germane to the leaders involved in this innovative start-up? When I was asked to help implement this competency model through an executive development program that my former college, Babson, had agreed to work on, I immediately questioned the rationale and validity of applying these large organizational leadership competencies to the new company. The HR people with whom we were working were initially stunned by my questions since these competencies were deemed sacrosanct in the parent company. By *sacrosanct* they must have confused its meaning with "Spent too much money in developing them to ever admit that they were of no value." But, they were intrigued by my argument and wanted me to meet with their boss, the VP of HR in the parent company.

After our conversation, I was no longer working on the project. The VP, who obviously had a lot invested in the model, was absolutely resistant to changing his mind. To be more specific, he went to my dean and said, "Hey, get rid of this Thornberry guy!" They subsequently applied these competencies with the help of my replacement. Not surprisingly, the new company failed in less than two years. Surprised? I suspect not. This is just one more example of design wackiness—selecting and measuring leaders with competencies that are antithetical to those needed for innovation. Similar examples of design wackiness abound.

WACKY DNA—INEVITABLE AND INCREDIBLE

As human beings, we can certainly blame our parents for some of own personal wackiness. Research on identical twins separated at birth and then reunited twenty years later shows that identical twins share about 50 percent of their personality characteristics and personal preferences like colors with each other. So it is quite okay if you want to blame your parents for half of your foibles and the environment for the other half. But why do organizational structures, processes, and systems get wacky over time? Even re-organizations are not enough to wipe out traces of wackiness.

There are several reasons. Organizational design wackiness is not usually generated on purpose or with malice, instead it usually develops over time and starts out with the best of intentions. And if these unintended consequences are not monitored and modified, then the wackiness factor grows. For example, all organizations need financial control systems, but when the finance people produce so many forms and reporting requirements that it takes away from selling the product, then this is wackiness. More and more refined financial reporting sounds like a good idea on its surface. Day-to-day understanding of how the business is performing should allow for greater accuracy and faster course corrections.

When this reporting gets onerous and keeps the sales guy off the road and not selling or causes people to fudge numbers just to fulfill the reporting requirements, then wackiness happens. And finance departments often have the mindset that if a little control is good then a lot of control must be better. They then hire more controllers who then have to justify their jobs by producing even better and more sophisticated reporting systems . . . and so it goes.

CORPORATE CONSTIPATION

I have to credit my brother Jeff for this term. In his rep business he works with a lot of name brand companies that use the electrical components and supplies that his principals make. One of his customers was lamenting the inability of his company to get things done in a timely and efficient manner. It seems that my brother's friend and his engineer crew had both a more innovative solution to a customer problem than the one the company had initially embarked on. But they could not get anyone to listen or take action on this much better and less costly solution. The original problem solvers were disinterested, and the layers of decision making needed to sign off on this new direction was sure to delay its implementation. The engineers eventually gave up trying.

This common phenomenon in large, established organizations is truly captured in the phrase "corporate constipation."

Unfortunately, there are few laxatives available for this kind of problem, but I will make a strong case that Innovation Judo is one of them. Innovation Judo masters don't wait for the unclogging and eventual explosion, they circumvent the obstruction. In the preceding example, the engineers may have given up too early. Since *leverage* is one of the core principles of Innovation Judo, it might have been a smart move to have the customer for whom the solution was intended present the innovation. Paying customers have huge leverage, and you will learn how to use the customer to your advantage should you encounter similar innovation killers.

Corporate constipation can be caused by many things: risk aversion, micromanaging executives, too stringent organizational structure and processes, silo mentality, and legal constraints. But the two biggest problems are the unbridled proliferation of controls and constipating organizational structures and processes. And corporate constipation tends to increase with organizational size and age.

THE EVOLUTION OF ANTI-INNOVATION

As organizations grow they go through very predictable stages of evolution and revolution (Greiner, 1998). Greiner followed a number of companies through their different stages of growth and noticed a trend. As companies grow, they go through fairly predictable phases of evolution followed by a crisis, which brings about some sort of revolution that leads to a new phase of growth with different challenges and different requirements. He also posits that doing more of the same in the previous period of evolution won't get you to the next phase of growth without the organization having to change many things including structures, processes, systems, controls, incentives, and even leadership. This view is very similar to Marshall Goldsmith's core premise in his best-selling book, *What Got You Here, Won't Get You There*

(Goldsmith and Reiter, 2007). Doing more of the same harder doesn't make you smarter and is less likely to lead to success.

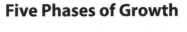

Five Phases of Growth

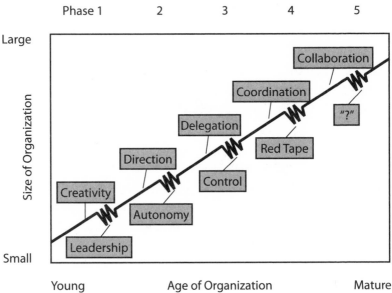

The straight lines on the figure represent periods of organizational evolution and growth. Things remain relatively calm and we focus on honing and refining our business so that it can deliver products and services to our customers in incrementally more efficient and effective ways. The squiggly lines represent periods of revolution, where things that helped us grow now get in the way. And if we keep doing what we are doing now, it will cause our business to get worse not better. These revolutionary phases can be unsettling because they often force organizations into major transformations that are potentially predictable but unavoidable. The ability of organizations to manage these periods of revolution are really the litmus tests for leadership. One of my business colleagues likes to tell people that management is easy in good times, but the real test of your leadership skills is the ability to manage in bad times. And I think there is some truth in that.

In an ideal world, the organization would be able to predict these revolutionary phases before they come and then plan for them. And we have seen some organizations do this. But often the *Titanic* has to take on a lot of water before the rabble-rousers on the party deck actually realize the danger.

Note that creativity and innovation are always essential elements when a business first starts. The founder or founders must have something new to offer or they won't get into a market unless they create it. Creating a market is clearly the pinnacle of innovation. Digital pioneers like Apple come to mind when we speak of this type of innovation. Simply delivering a service in more innovative ways than the typical supplier in an industry can give the founders a good start. EBay would be a perfect example of simply enabling a better marketplace.

In the start-up phase rules are few and the structure is informal, cash is king and the founders drive the business. Just being able to pay suppliers and employees on time is a challenge. And employees wear many hats. But as the start-up grows from 5 people to 55 to 355, these informal ways of doing business start to get in the way. You can no longer have you meetings by simply yelling down the hall, and wearing too many hats starts causing confusion both internally and externally. "Did you take care of that?" "No I thought you did!" starts becoming an all too frequent conversation. If the founders try to keep running the business in the way they did with five people the wheels start to come off. So eventually the start-up has to get more organized and more formal.

With each revolution there comes a management crisis. The first crisis is that of leadership. Can the original entrepreneur or founders continue to grow the business if they stay with their founding management behaviors? Some do survive and they start to be organizational builders not just entrepreneurs. To survive they must start to formalize the business, and they start to bring in more expertise like finance, marketing, human resources, and IT. And some of the chaos we experienced due to informality has to be reined in. Someone has to be in charge, and our once flat organization starts to look like a rectangle with a hierarchy of authority and decision making. At this stage in the company's evolution this revolutionary move is not only necessary, it is helpful.

We also start to get more formalized about how we do our accounting, our human resources, and even our meetings. This change in organization helps us grow through the next phase of evolution. If we are able to manage our way through periods of revolution then we can expect a calmer period of evolution to follow. There are several elements in this model that are particularly relevant to organizational innovation and to corporate constipation. First, Greiner tells us that the management practices, structures, processes, and cultures that helped us grow in a prior evolutionary stage may prevent us from moving to the next evolutionary stage and can actually put us in a very unstable and untenable position where a revolution will be necessary if we are to continue to be successful. And instead of disappearing altogether in the following phase of evolution, a number of these things continue and become detrimental to organizational performance in general and innovation specifically. Greiner predicts that our ability to innovate or initiate any real change will actually start to be hamstrung by our eventual movement into a very complex and unhelpful phase of micromanagement.

Of course micromanagement can happen at any stage based on the personalities of the organization's leaders who insist on knowing everything and making every decision. But they can't be everywhere all the time so some freedom to operate still remains. You will notice the words *red tape* in Greiner's model. As I said, red tape can occur at any time, but it really starts to develop with the growth of centralized functions. Eventually every organization gets too big for any group of top leaders to control personally so they must develop some key centralized functions.

These functions are usually finance, IT, and HR. As these functions take on a greater role in the organization, they create so much red tape that constipation sets in: a million reporting forms, computer systems that don't work, personnel policies that actually get in the way of performance, etc. Innovative organizations know that they have to dismantle and replace organizational design elements to move successfully into the next phase. But what ends up happening is that instead of dismantling the old structure, more structure is added, thus increasing both complexity and wackiness. As of this writing, the senate is debating how to control the "too big to fail" financial industry. The FTC (Federal Trade Commission) has failed to do due diligence for the industry, but instead of dismantling this government organization, the government has decided to add a new bureaucracy instead. No wonder our government has such a low approval rating.

All of you who work in these types of organizations understand the meaning of a legacy system. Red tape is a lot easier to build up than tear down, and very few established companies have ever listed *deconstipation* as one of their core values. The failure to limit overcontrol and overmanagement really makes it hard for motivated, well-meaning employees to get their work done. As for innovation, micromanaging makes it impossible to innovate because it discourages passion, perseverance, and cleverness. With technology as an enabler, I see an increasing move toward more control rather than less control. With the absence of any substantive deconstipation focus, employees are left to giving in, giving up, or practicing the art of Innovation Judo. While large, established organizations tend to be the most susceptible to corporate constipation, we can also find the constipated boss or coworker who is also a blockhead. Innovation Judo will be helpful under both scenarios.

AN EXAMPLE

Honeywell Corporation wanted to develop a new HVAC product to fend off its faster and more innovative rivals. So they did the right thing by putting together a cross-functional team made up of representatives from manufacturing, engineering, marketing/ sales, and finance. It is a common practice in many organizations to put this type of team together in order to create a new product using real-time cross-functional input. This team met weekly to orchestrate the design, development, and introduction of this state-of-the-art product to the market. Despite good intentions, the product rollout failed miserably. Despite those good intentions, and that the product was positioned to account for more than 30 percent of the company's future revenues, it failed. The problem was that everyone on the team knew it was going to fail, but no one intervened or pulled the plug.

Here was a strategic project that was critical to the company's success and longevity, so what went wrong? For starters, each team member still reported to and was evaluated by their own managers, who were not involved in supporting this project because they were only responsible for working on their own functional projects. Team members were allowed little time to meet, and there were no consequences for failed teamwork as long as your manager rated you well. In addition, the marketing manager, who was the head of the project team, had mixed feelings about the project's success. The new product would cannibalize a number of her existing products, and since it was unproved she was afraid her bonus would go down if these other revenue-generating products were taken out of the mix. Just look at all the wackiness going on in this story.

I often ask participants in my executive courses to give me examples of their company's wackiness. Trust me, there is no shortage of examples, and participants instantly name many. A Navy captain in one of my executive courses at NPS (Naval Postgraduate School) told me the following story. He was just being billeted (placed in a job) to Hawaii so he and his family arrived in Honolulu to take up residence in base housing. But the inside of the house had not been repainted and was on a list of houses to be redone. Since there was only one painting contractor approved by the Navy for painting houses on the base, he would have to wait his turn. The captain even offered to paint the interior himself so he could move in earlier and save the Navy thousands of dollars but was told that this would not be allowed. So the Navy put this captain and his family up in a hotel for six months, which cost the Navy $8,000. Wackiness? Definitely but it followed protocol.

Company Values

Company values provide both a challenge and an opportunity for innovators. The real wackiness regarding company values happens when the espoused values are not the real values or where the values are contradictory. It always amazes me how much time and money organizations spend on trying to articulate their values and then immediately disregard them. For example, in one company I know they have a value of "mutual respect" for each other, yet they let their highest sales performer trample over others with his arrogant and condescending treatment of those whom he is supposed to respect. It is certainly not lost on employees that the values don't apply to him. He is forgiven because he makes the company so much money. That's the real value?

The upside for innovators is that values can be used as *leverage* for innovation even if they aren't true. For example, if the company declares, "The customer is number one," then positioning any innovation aimed at the customer will be hard to ignore because the company has not only said this value is important; it also has actually put it in writing. Or if another division tries to shoot down your idea, you can bring up the "respect for each other" company value as your *off-balancing* maneuver, and that division will have to at least entertain your idea. Thus, the would-be innovator can use these written values as another Innovation Judo tool for success.

Corporate Culture

Corporate culture is the interaction among people, politics, organizational design, and company values. While most writers describe corporate culture as simply "shared values," this terminology does not do justice to the concept of culture. First, different organizations within the organization often have different cultures. I didn't realize that different geographies within the same vicinity could have such different climates until I moved to Monterey, California. Where I grew up in Ohio, the climate was consistently cloudy with occasional breaks of sunshine, but you could never predict where the sun would shine. In Monterey, NPS, where I help support innovation initiatives in a sunny microclimate, yet four blocks away in either direction you will often find fog. So even the city of Monterey has a number of different fairly predictable microclimates.

For you as innovators, I am less interested in the organization's overall climate or culture, and more interested in the microclimate(s) within which you are trying to innovate. And since innovation can often span internal and external organizational boundaries, you may find yourself quickly moving those four blocks into the fog, then rain, and back out to sunshine again, which necessitates the use of different Judo principles customized to the various microcultures you will find yourself in. In the next chapter, I will introduce you to different innovation climates (the Land of Oz, the Maze, the Asylum, and the Jungle) that could describe either your organization's entire climate or the particular microclimate within which you work. These climates are extremely important to diagnose as different climates may require different application of the seven IJ principles.

Another reason I don't particularly like the phrase "shared values" as a definition of culture is that it does not give any insight into the etiology of those values. I know they are probably listed on the company's wall somewhere, but how is the company making them real for its employees? Values emanate from the interactions I described earlier. Whenever we bring people into an organization, subject them to or inject them with the organization's politics, and try to structure their interactions and mindset, what results is the organization's culture.

The greatest challenge to any innovator and to embedding and sustaining innovation over the long term is culture. The U.S. Coast Guard has built a pretty successful innovation structure within its broader organization despite the many forces that are in play against it. For example, in the Coast Guard, and the military in general, there is huge pressure to behave tactically. This doesn't allow a lot of time for focused thinking and innovating in their day-to-day operations. There is also a very clear differentiated hierarchy that often creates a culture of subordination. Fortunately the Coast Guard has a proud history of innovation, but even it had to create a structure that allowed innovators to spend 70 percent of their time on innovation as opposed to the typical zero. You will hear more about how the Coast Guard did this in a later chapter, especially in the profile of Chris Kluckhuhn, a Judo master who was told by his boss to forget about all that innovation stuff he was involved in and get back to work.

NOT ALL WACKINESS IS EQUAL

I am sure that all of you reading this book can also come up with your own examples of wackiness, be it people, politics, design factors, or values. Wackiness is indeed pervasive. But not all organizational wackiness is equal. Some wackiness is simply irritating while other wackiness is detrimental even to the point of running a company out of business.

I can live with my computer being scanned (although not secretly) because I shouldn't be surfing the web for nonbusiness activities while I am at work. And I suppose I can handle executives flying first class while they put the rest of us in coach, but I can't accept wackiness that gets in the way of a company's success or survival and where innovation is no longer an option but a necessity for surviving and thriving.

Since organizational wackiness is not easy to deconstruct without a great deal of effort from the top, innovators in the organization only have a few choices. Give up, try to overcome the blockheads and roadblocks through sheer force, wait for Godot, or deploy one or more Innovation Judo principles. Giving up reduces frustration and risk, but it also lessens your chances of standing out. Sheer force only works when you have a lot of clout, and unless you are at the top, your clout may be limited.

Waiting for Godot is a greater problem for both the innovator and the organization. When I was growing up, my mother worked as a part-time actress and even started a playhouse that is in existence today in my hometown. It's not a good thing to have an actress for a mother. I was about seven years old when I first saw her on stage. She played a murderess who killed three other characters with a knife. I told my father I didn't want to ride home with her because she wasn't my mother. That's how good an actress she was. I did survive the event and as I got older went on to enjoy her plays and was even in one or two of them.

When I went to college as an undergraduate, I took an elective course in theater arts where we had to read a play a week and then write a paper on that play for the professor. I liked all the plays except one called *Waiting for Godot*. This play was written by Samuel Beckett, an Irishman living in Paris. It is a short play and the story of two men in a small town eagerly awaiting the arrival of a person named Godot who is coming to save the town. The men get increasingly excited as his arrival grows nearer. But Godot never shows up and the play ends. I thought to myself, "What a stupid play! It wasn't worth reading." So I wrote a very short paper to my professor suggesting the same and advising him not to assign it to his class next semester as it was meaningless. He gave me back an equally short note with an F for a grade. It wasn't until I started teaching innovation in large organizations that I finally understood the play's meaning. Many people in the organization look to the top-level leadership to fix things; to make things right. In the case of innovation, they expect the top executives who say they want innovation to create an environment that is right for innovation so that it can happen easily and effortlessly.

Sometimes, Godot does get off the train and innovation can be inspired at any level of the organization, but sometimes someone has to step up and take initiative. If you are a true innovator, you will not wait for Godot.

NIH

Previously I said that one of the biggest cultural barriers to innovation within the company is what I call an NIH (not invented here) mindset or attitude. This cultural mindset exists both internally and externally. For years, P&G was proud and quite secretive about its product innovations and inventions. In many ways, it was as secretive as the CIA. In fact, there were even restrictions against sharing innovation between divisions. It took them ten years, for example, to share the technology from Bounce with the people who made Cottonelle so that they could enhance the brand with a "super soft" product. In those years, P&G's mantra was "Proudly invented here!" and they were very protective of their patents and intellectual capital. Very little of their R&D was farmed out to others. They relied solely on their own people for innovation.

Unfortunately, this reliance on internal brains started to erode its ability to invent the $100 million new product at the rate of one blockbuster every ten years. Today, P&G requires that 50 percent of their new product ideas come from people outside the organization, and it would like to increase this percentage to 80. Its mantra is now "Proudly not invented here!" P&G went from a "We know best" R&D approach to "A lot of people know best and they don't all live within P&G" approach. P&G was one of the first large companies to embrace "open innovation" and is now proud to open its doors to all great ideas, many of which come from outside the organization.

Much of P&G's rebirth as a world-class innovator has come about under the leadership of former CEO A.G. Lafley who not only changed the company's values like NIH, he also re-organized structures and processes to encourage innovation and innovators At least within P&G there are clear structures and mechanisms in place that can enable innovative products to see the light of day and become really big winners. While P&G still has some wackiness as most organizations do, it has worked hard to create more of a "Land of Oz" innovation landscape and has been quite successful in churning out those $100 million winners.

NIH is also prevalent within companies that have a silo organization—where functions or groups often compete with each other and where cross-organizational collaboration is less than optimal. R&D, for example, might think that it is the only department that can invent things, that it knows the customer better than marketing does, and that marketing should only be supporting R&D's initiatives. When in reality, marketing may know the customer very well and knows what the customer wants, but it cannot innovate because that is only R&D's job. Research has shown that the more silos within an organization, the less innovative it is.

Makes sense! Great ideas come from diverse minds, but only if they are open minds. NIH is a closed-minded attribute. Innovation Judo masters will often find themselves trying to innovate in silos that are by definition wacky since people who work for the same company should all be on the same team. As you know from experience, this is often not the case. When internal NIH is rampant, it is one of the hallmarks of an asylum organization that you will learn about in the next chapter.

Unfortunately, there aren't many Lafleys around and waiting for one to arrive can take a long time—like waiting for Godot. But passionate innovators with a modicum of Innovation Judo skills don't have to wait for Godot. They can still innovate as you will see from the masters I profile in this book.

CHAPTER 4

···

Innovation Badlands

As I mentioned earlier in the 7I discussion, one of the better books on innovation is *The Innovator's Playbook* (2009), which emanated from research done by Deloitte. There are two versions: one that looks at innovation in the private sector and the other at innovation within the public sector. I took issue with Deloitte's "missed steps" in its innovation model, but I also found it interesting that the book doesn't mention that much about culture other than to say it's important. This doesn't offer much hope or advice to the innovator facing a hostile culture.

For companies trying to build an innovation model it is an excellent read, but it fails to give clear instructions on creating an innovative culture, especially in a wacky environment. And as all of us in the innovation field know, company culture is the hardest nut to crack. You can build the best model in the world and try to structure the organization accordingly, but if the cultural roadblocks and blockheads work to kill innovation, it is impossible to build let alone sustain innovation.

Fortunately, Innovation Judo does not presuppose an existing culture of innovation. As I mentioned earlier, Innovation Judo exists specifically for the purpose of getting around the roadblocks and blockheads that stand in your way. If you wait for an organization's culture to become innovative, you can have a long wait and wind up looking like Rip van Winkle. Oftentimes resources for innovation are put on hold when the cost cutters get out their shears. The innovator needs to know how to operate in these less than friendly cultures without waiting for some miraculous transformation in corporate policy. The good news about cost cutting is that the smart innovator can actually become a hero by showing the organization that if it did things differently it would not only cut costs but grow the business as well. This is really the area of creative asset management that is ripe territory for Innovation Judo masters, especially in today's cost-conscious environment.

WACKINESS AND COMPLEXITY

When I was growing up, my mother always worried that we might wander into the street and get hit by a car. I am sure that mothers of today share this concern and know that some intersections are more dangerous than others. I live near a town in California where crossing the street requires not only speed but a fair amount of courage. Both streets that intersect have three lanes on each side of an island, and both left and right turns are allowed from two adjacent lanes. This street corner is also at the exit and entrance to Highway 101, one of California's main freeways. And people fly.

Fortunately, they have a pedestrian control button that gives the illusion of control—because it works some of the time. This is one hairy place to cross the street as it is both complex and crazy because pedestrians take chances as they do not trust the button. Organizations also have intersections, and some are more dangerous or at least challenging for the innovator than others. Innovators need to focus on the intersection where *complexity* crosses *wackiness.*

To be an effective innovator or leader of innovation, you will need to understand the "lay of the land" in terms of these two important dimensions. Some organizations are very complex but not particularly wacky, while others are very wacky but not very complex. You also have organizations that don't have many characteristics of either, and some that have both in great supply. Your choice of Innovation Judo principles will depend on your analysis of your company on these two dimensions as some of the Innovation Judo principles you will learn may be more effective in one scenario and less so in another. In Appendix A, you will find the ILS (Innovation Landscape Survey), which you can take to help you pinpoint where you are on the intersection between these two roads.

I have already defined *wackiness* as typically arising from five different sources or a combination of these sources. And wackiness of course means "nonsensical." Figure 4.1 summarizes some of the elements I talked about in Chapter 3 that define *wackiness.* Now let's turn to complexity.

COMPLEXITY

Complexity is something different and often emerges from a quite rational thought process. When we say a person is complex we usually mean multilayered and not so easy to decipher. There is generally more than meets the eye. It may take longer to get to know someone who is described as complex. Organizational complexity is much the same. Organizational complexity can arise from an organization's size and geographical dispersion, but for the employee inside the organization the measure

Sane	Wacky
Low in politics	Watch your back, cover your ass
People promoted on merit	Corporate constipation
Say what we mean, mean what we say	Hidden agendas
	Mixed messages
Values are real	
	Promotion on favoritism
Healthy, open debate	
	Sucking up
Collegial	
	Killing what you most covet
Transparency	
	Internal combat
The customer is king	
	The boss is king

FIGURE 4.1 Elements of Wackiness

of complexity is how long it takes the average new hire to figure out how things work.

Obviously the more products, the more job specializations, the more departments, the more levels, the more locations, the more services and the more people in an organization the more complex the organization is. Getting your bearings in a complex organization can take some serious time. A small start-up with one product and ten people is not complex. There may be some complex personalities in that organization, but it is easy to observe and understand the business. The U.S. Navy, on the other hand, has 330,000 employees and that includes the active duty and reserve Navy personnel, their civilian counterparts, the Marines, and a host of defense contractors. Add to that extremely sophisticated weaponry, technology, and geographical dispersion, and you get a very complex organization that reports to the federal government, which is even a larger organization with a plethora of levels.

One measure of an organization's complexity is its use of acronyms. As the complexity goes up, so do the number of acronyms. When I first started working with the Navy, I thought they were speaking a foreign language. It takes years of immersion to understand all these acronyms, and they even have acronyms for acronyms. It makes sense for them to use acronyms of course as it makes the communication of complexity simpler.

Siemens has 360,000 people worldwide and five divisions that make everything from post office sorting machines to power plants. No one in any one part of Siemens actually knows how all the parts of the company work or what the company is working on. When I was a faculty director for an innovation-oriented executive education program for Siemens a couple of years ago, it was not uncommon for two people to meet for the first time in my class only to find out that they were working on almost identical things. This is a rather common occurrence in large, geographically disperse organizations like Siemens.

Complexity in and of itself is not the same as wackiness, but for innovators it may pose the challenge of understanding who to talk with and what doors to knock on when it comes to introducing and implementing a new idea. If the new idea is just for your own department or unit, then the pathways and doors are often pretty clear. But when the innovation crosses over organizational silos or boundaries and is a company-wide big idea then some of the Innovation Judo principles will be helpful here as well because organizational confusion can be just as impeding at wackiness. When complexity and wackiness interact, the pathway to creativity can get pretty muddled, thus creating different landscapes or cultures that you as an innovator must navigate if you are to succeed. Let's take a look at these interactions and the different innovation landscapes, or in some cases "badlands," that they can create for you. Figure 4.2 describes some elements of organizational complexity.

Simple	Complex
Runs on logic	Runs on logic
Clear reporting relationships	Unclear reporting relationships
You know where to go and whom to talk to	Three months to find anything
Organization chart is reality	Multiple decision makers, some of whom are invisible
Clear objectives and goals	Multiple and potentially conflicting goals
Decision makers easily identifiable	Multiple, sometimes hidden decision makers
Fast learning curve	Hard to explain to others
Hypo-acronymic	Hyper-acronymic

FIGURE 4.2 Elements of Organizational Complexity

A DANGEROUS INTERSECTION

Figure 4.3 represents four different types of organizational environments, some might say cultures, you could find yourself in as a potential innovator. While these four organizational typologies are not mutually exclusive, a little observation and analysis will help you decipher where your organization (or your part of the organization) sits on this two-by-two grid. The grid shows the potential interactions between the two key organizational variables: Organizational complexity and organizational wackiness. Knowing where you reside on this grid will help you decide when and where to deploy one or more of the seven Innovation Judo principles. This type of analysis can also help senior management understand why they have trouble engendering greater innovation even when they are passionate about pursuing it. In the last chapter, I will talk about what senior leaders can do to try to change the badlands to goodlands or at least ameliorate some of their negative effects.

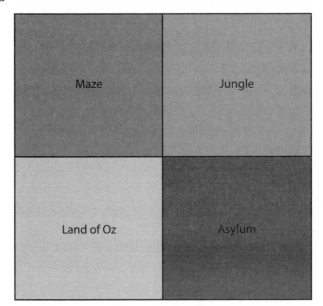

FIGURE 4.3 A Dangerous Intersection

THE LAND OF OZ

The Land of Oz is a truly magical place and not very easy to find as Dorothy can tell you. But, once you get there, it's a great place to be. For the innovator living in the Land of Oz, wackiness is low as is complexity. In this kind of environment logic, persuasion, and presenting a well-documented business case often carry the day when it comes to getting your idea heard and implemented. Bringing a paying customer who is interested in your idea is even better. Keep in mind, however, that every company has some degree of wackiness and some degree of complexity. I have never seen a zero score on either of these dimensions even in the best Land of Oz landscapes. But, relatively speaking, Land of Oz landscapes are generally easier places to innovate.

Like the Land of Oz from the movie *The Wizard of Oz,* this landscape has a clear yellow brick road that leads to a place where wishes are granted, and that is usually senior management. In the Land of Oz, facts are relatively easy to come by, there are relatively few layers of management, and while these types of organizations can be large, they are often pretty simple to understand in terms of business model, organizational structure, and performance metrics. They are the easiest landscapes in which to construct a well-lit road for the innovator and his or her ideas. And standard innovation cycle (Figure 2.1) is easier to replicate in Oz environments. It doesn't mean that you don't meet blockheads in the Land of Oz, but you won't face nearly as many roadblocks as in the other landscapes.

John Beaver invented the first disposable surgical steel knife. What a great business: His company had one product line, and a very clear hierarchy of authority and decision making. And since John was the owner and the boss you knew exactly where to go with a new idea. For the most part, organizations that exhibit Land of Oz traits are logical and function logically. There may be a few witches or flying monkeys running around, but logic rules, especially with the financials. If you can show "yellow bricks" associated with your innovation then you are on the right road. Your most important Judo principle will be *leverage* gained from presenting an opportunity rather than an idea. I will differentiate the difference between these two concepts in a later chapter, but for now, just know that a great idea has almost no leverage whereas an opportunity provides a great deal of leverage.

Sodexho, the food service company I mentioned earlier, is an example of a Land of Oz company. It is large and global, but what it does is not very complex. It provides food to universities, hospitals, prisons, oil platforms at sea, and the military. It knows how to deliver and provide food at a profit and good value to its clients. The business is not hard to understand, and if you are successful in one industry, you can do the same thing in another industry segment without missing a beat. What Sodexho wanted was an innovation program based on logic. It wanted to experiment around the edges of its core business with value-enhancing add-ons like dry cleaning services and kiosks.

I helped educate a number of their managers in the art of innovative thinking, entrepreneurial action taking, and the development of a business plan. A well-written, logical, fact-based business plan was what groups in Sodexho needed to get senior management to hear the idea and support it. During this process, I encountered very little game playing or backstabbing. Instead I saw the "good" kind of competition you want when groups strive to present the company's best opportunity.

Sodexho was also low on wackiness. Most of its employees work in small, close-knit operations and report to a very simple management structure. They are measured on their unit's performance against a contracted budget, and they get frequent feedback from upper management and their customers. They also don't compete for resources with each other because the clients pay the bills. Thus, internal competition is low, and there is no benefit for backstabbing.

Even in the Land of Oz Innovation Judo can still be a useful tool especially when it comes to moving faster. Innovative opportunities don't last long so the spoils often go to the quickest. In Land of Oz organizations, logic and plans sometimes work against the speed needed to capture an emerging opportunity. Innovation Judo, although used less often, can still be a friend to those of you operating in this innovation landscape. Eaton Corporation's Russ Sabo, whom you will meet later on in this book, had to utilize three Judo principles—*speed, surprise, and unbalancing*—in order to help his company take advantage of a great new business opportunity. The company was moving in the right direction but moving too slow. So Russ's skills gave it the shock and then the impetus to move quickly to capture this opportunity before its competitors did. While Innovation Judo is still handy for certain Land of Oz situations, it will probably not be needed as often in this landscape as it will be in some of the other, more challenging landscapes.

THE MAZE

Organizations that have developed a maze are high in complexity but low in wackiness. Global organizations that have a matrix-type structure and multiple reporting relationships exemplify maze companies. ABB is such an example. It is one of the largest engineering companies as well as one of the largest conglomerates in the world. ABB has operations in around 100 countries, with approximately 145,000 employees as of June 2012, and reported global revenue of $40 billion. It is managed through a complex global structure but with a very small headquarters staff located in Zurich. There are only five members of the Global Executive Committee (Pinto, 2006). ABB has downsized its Executive Committee from ten to five since my last visit (2003) to the company in Zurich, and I was surprised then to see such a small corporate staff. It keeps the headquarters staff at a minimum on purpose to prevent the wackiness that often emanates from large IT, HR, and finance departments. Its motto is "Think Global, Act Local."

ABB's management style is collegial, and it moves managers across the globe as part of their development. Since complex organizations are often hard to manage structurally, ABB relies on personal relationships built up over the years. These relationships make its matrix run and run well. In addition, folks at ABB know that they are accountable for working with each other, and there is very little headquarters can do to intervene due its small amount of personnel.

Innovation Judo in the Maze often has a different purpose. Innovation Judo principles are used less for speed on the highway to creativity as they are for building the highway. The Maze requires the use of more principles for longer periods of time.

For example, *speed* and *unbalancing* are not very useful, but *right-mindedness, redirection,* and *leverage* are. The barrier to innovation at ABB is not so much a matter of outsmarting bureaucrats but rather fostering employees' goodwill to make decisions collaboratively with the best of intentions and with clear logic and analytics. And because complexity is high, innovators may not be very clear about how best to pursue their ideas. In the Land of Oz the pathway to creativity is relatively clear, but in Maze organizations, there may be a number of potential roads that are not well marked. Mazes also often suffer from disintegrated innovation, which is a number of folks working on their own initiatives with little or no collaboration or integration.

Steve Paljieg, innovator of Mominspired at Kimberly-Clark, has worked in several Maze-type organizations including his current organization, Kimberly-Clark. Kimberly-Clark is a great company with a history of innovation, but it is also complex with many products, functions, departments, distribution channels, and a global organizational structure. Like many Innovation Judo masters, Steve has sometimes had to create his own network of roads to the right people to get his ideas accepted. The challenge for Maze innovators is simplifying complexity. Like Steve, they either have to discover or create the pathway to creativity since it is often not obvious. You will meet Steve later on in the book. He is comfortable with ambiguity and always, always utilizes his Judo skills with right-mindedness. This is extremely important in general, but also critical when dealing with a very ethical and customer-focused organization like Kimberly-Clark.

THE ASYLUM

In the lower right-hand quadrant of Figure 4.3 are companies that fall in the Asylum category. These are companies that are pretty simple to understand from a business model and metrics perspective but they have a very wacky culture that doesn't run on the currency of logic. Being successful often depends on politics, who you know, knocking down the other guy, bare-knuckle internal competition, and most likely a dysfunctional leader or executive team. Family-run businesses often fall into this category. I once worked for a large media company that was family run, and while they did well financially due to the father's talent, the rest of the company was a mess. Sister Zelda was on the payroll as was cousin Mike and nephew Sam. Having them on the payroll was okay, but the father had also given them really important jobs that none of them was qualified to do or even wanted to do. And, of course, all the nonfamily employees were constantly jerked around as a result of the constant internecine family fighting. It didn't help that the father was a tyrant, who once fired his secretary for buying the wrong coffee cups. The only good news is that his short-term memory was not good, so my friend in HR would just tell the employee to go home for the week and then come back as though nothing had happened. And so she did, slipping quietly back into work without repercussions.

Since Asylum organizations often run on a command and control model, internal competition for promotion can be downright nasty. In addition, what the organizational chart says in terms of power may not be who actually wields the power, thus making politicking even more necessary.

I once consulted for a high-tech services company that was in the outbound marketing business. These are the folks who make it possible for people to call you at dinnertime to try to sell you something. The company's hardware and software solutions allow them to segment the market for any particular product and start calling you because of your profile. Often, these calls are automated. This company was started by an entrepreneur who grew it to over $250 million, but when I was asked to come on board and help the management team, the company's board was just about ready to wrest control of the company from its founder. The stock had fallen from over 150 to 30 in just two years, and most of this loss was due to the incredible wackiness the founder had introduced and cultivated throughout the organization.

This company was pretty simple to understand: organizational complexity was quite low but the wackiness was high. When I came for my first meeting at this company, the founder and president had hired and fired two CEOs and had gone through two executive teams in a span of two years. He was a maniac, a brilliant one to be sure, but a terrible leader. He pitted people against one another, he managed by fear, and he only trusted a few people in the technical area who had helped him start the business. He often bypassed his subordinates in the chain of command to countermand orders, and his moods were unpredictable. As you can imagine, his erratic and irrational behavior set a pretty wacky tone throughout the rest of the organization.

But he was extremely talented and passionate about his company since it was his baby. He particularly loved the technological aspects and often had his hands in every detail. In Asylum companies, especially this one, *discipline* and the ability to exploit *opening*s become two of the most effective weapons for the innovator. *Discipline* in this case means the ability to be patient and wait for an opening as well as discipline to understand in some detail the company's technology. The president spoke techno, and if you could speak it also, he was more willing to engage. In addition, he was keen on any innovation that might improve the company's outbound marketing capabilities. The innovators in this company would have to position ideas from a technical perspective (this would surprise him), be disciplined in learning this technology, and be patient enough to wait for one of the founder's more rational moments to approach him. Unfortunately, most of the executive team members tried to only use logic with him and were not disciplined enough to wait for the right opening.

Not all companies are as wacky as the one I just described, but you can see that logic or thorough analysis and well-planned PowerPoint presentations are not enough to give innovation a fighting chance. So the application of Innovation Judo principles is absolutely essential for innovators who want to ply their trade in Asylum companies, and usually a combination of multiple principles will be required. By the way, in this company, the founder was excited by invention so if a creative idea could be presented at the right time in the right way and it worked, you were then in his trusted inner circle making your next idea even easier to present and pursue.

Jim Repp, the innovator behind the Jeep Rubicon at Chrysler, had to deal with a lot of Asylum behaviors in the old Daimler Chrysler Corporation in order to see his idea come to fruition. He was called on to utilize a myriad of Innovation Judo skills including *leverage, surprise, redirection, openings,* and *unbalancing* or the very successful Rubicon would never have seen the light of day. And because Jim was an engineer, marketing dismissed his experiential knowledge that there was a market for a mass-produced specialty off-road Jeep. And were they wrong.

THE JUNGLE

Jungles are dangerous. You can get lost and you can get eaten. Jungle organizations are probably the most difficult environments for both innovation and innovators. Jungle environments are high in both complexity and wackiness. Innovators can face both deep rivers and snakes and will need a full complement of Judo skills to ply their trade in this type of environment. It's not that these types of organizations don't want or need innovation, in fact most of the companies that fall into this category are the ones most in need of it. But, they often kill innovation by running out or wearing out would-be innovators despite the company's often adamant and sincere claims that they want more innovation.

Jungles can also be places of beauty if the explorer is confident, well-armed, has a good map, and likes the challenge of surviving and thriving in this kind of environment. Some of my Innovation Judo masters were quite successful in Jungle landscapes because they managed all three of these factors to their advantage and had fun doing it. They knew where the roadblocks and blockheads were, they were armed with Innovation Judo skills, and they were confident in their ideas. In fact, many of these people actually enjoyed working in these Jungle environments because they liked the challenge of innovating against the odds, and they did not get discouraged by the word *no*. As I mentioned earlier, for some reason, many innovators get even more inspired when someone tells them they can't do something. They smile to themselves, rub their hands together, and think, "Just watch me." Jungle companies desperately need a cadre of Innovation Judo masters because clearing the jungle can take years, and the company will eventually sink under its own weight in the quicksand.

One such innovator was a manager who worked for a large and somewhat wacky multinational corporation that embarked on an innovation training program despite its wackiness and complexity. The company wanted to create a group of managers who could lead innovation, despite the difficulties, because it knew that creating a critical mass of innovators would be easier than reducing complexity and wackiness. This company was over 100 years old and had built so many legacy systems that it would be impossible to dismantle all of them without major upheaval and turmoil. I was involved in creating this program for them, and I saw how one individual with a great idea immediately ran into a number of major roadblocks and blockheads. His idea was technical and needed some help and resources from one of the company's sister divisions, but there was not enough money or resources to actually create a working prototype. His immediate boss, who was not part of the executive team sponsoring the program, told him, "Forget all this innovation nonsense and get back to work."

Well, he was one of those innovators who loved the word *no*. He heard it from his immediate boss who told him to get back to work and he heard it from the head of the sister division who remarked that he must have too much time on his hands if he could work on pursuing a new business opportunity instead of just sticking to his real job. Now he was really revved up by the multiple nos. Many would-be innovators give up in such situations, but not this Innovation Judo master. Instead he pitched his idea to a competitor of the sister division. This division was extremely interested and immediately put together a draft "letter of intent" to partner on the technical development of the prototype.

My Innovation Judo master then took this letter back to his own company's arrogant division and suggested that he would sign the letter of intent in two weeks if his own division was not interested. Within a week, the leader of this sister division was on board and developed a business plan to pursue this opportunity. Just look at the Innovation Judo principles utilized by this innovator: *speed, surprise, leverage, redirection, right-mindedness, unbalancing,* and *opening*. He moved quickly. Instead of whining about the no, he used it as motivation to move quickly and devise an alternate strategy. He used competition as the lever, redirected the no energy into a yes, pursued this opportunity for the right reasons, surprised and unbalanced his opponent, and then utilized the opening created by time pressure to strike a deal. Because his organization was highly complex and moderately wacky, he needed to deploy more than one principle.

THE INNOVATOR'S LANDSCAPE SURVEY (ILS)

In Appendix A, you will find a survey that can help you identify which landscape you are most likely working in: the Land of Oz, the Maze, the Asylum, or the Jungle. This knowledge will help you decide which Innovation Judo principles you will want to employ when meeting a roadblock or blockhead. For senior managers reading this book, it will also give you an idea of where you need to focus your energies as well. For example, you can try to clear the jungle, or build forts that protect and buffer innovation so that it can survive. Or you might decide that a few of your rebels who are Innovation Judo masters are worth much more than you are paying them. In the last chapter, I will talk about how you might counterbalance the negative effects of complexity and wackiness so that your organization can be more inventive.

CHAPTER 5

Right-Mindedness

DON'T CONFUSE CLEVERNESS WITH MANIPULATION

Over the years I have studied both Judo and karate and have trained with a number of black belts. What impressed about all of my black-belt trainers, was their "right-mindedness." In the movie *The Karate Kid* the movie worked because of its good versus evil theme. There was the evil karate instructor who taught his students that winning matches was everything and if that meant purposefully hurting the opponent then so be it. And, of course, Mr. Miyagi represented the good side of the equation. He counseled his young protégé to be right-minded. By this he meant

- Only use your skills for self-defense.
- Try to walk away from a fight if you can.

- Be humble.
- Respect your sensei (teacher) and your fellow pupils.
- Practice self-control and discipline.

All of my instructors were like Mr. Miyagi, and they adhered to the code of ethics associated with most forms of the martial arts. In fact, all of my instructors were good at weeding out students who did not adhere to these principles.

Every once in a while I would see a new student in class who was taking martial arts for the wrong reasons. Some actually liked hurting others, and one student wanted to learn karate so he could beat up on his wife's lover. He admitted this to a few of us and he was soon ousted from the class. I remember vividly having one student who was clearly in it for the fun of hurting others. I suspect he was a bully and was there to help refine his bullying skills. He did not pull his punches in practice as we were required to do so as to demonstrate absolute control of our moves. It's not that he did not know how to control his punches and kicks; it was that he didn't want to.

My instructors were keen observers and pretty good judges of character. So my instructor at the time, Mr. Kim, observed this guy being a little too forceful and warned him several times not to make contact with his opponent other than to make the uniform move. But this bully did not heed his words. So the instructor said, "Since you are not able or willing to control yourself, I will show you what it feels like." The instructor proceeded to show him what it was like. Even though the student was bigger than my instructor, he, of course, could not defend himself very well against a third-degree karate master. The instructor made his point, and the student never came back to class again.

NOT FOR BULLIES

Right-mindedness does not affect the Judo skill set, only its application. I could use my martial arts skills to purposefully hurt others or to show off. I would still have the skills. But how you are perceived, either as a bully or an honorable person, does count because people can get even and people have long memories. Even the best black belt can't block a bullet. So it is important that those of you who need to practice Innovation Judo in your pursuit of innovation need to do it with right-mindedness or you can be perceived as highly political at best or at worst a manipulator. You should only practice Innovation Judo when you need to accomplish something really important and the deck is stacked against you or when simple logic is not enough. Unfortunately, as you saw from my examples in the "wacky factor" chapter, and the various "badlands" you might find yourself in, logic does not always win out, especially in complex, complicated, and political business environments.

MANIPULATION OR INFLUENCE?

When I am out on the teaching circuit talking to executives about leadership and wackiness in organizations, I will often bring up Innovation Judo as a skill set that can be effective in such environments when innovation is the goal. And then I give some examples like John Kilcullen and Jim Repp and the others that you will read about later on. Some participants smile and I can tell they are thinking, "Yes, I have had to use some of these principles on more than one occasion," and some participants interpret my remarks as recommending manipulation. This often happens when I describe Innovation Judo as a skill set to help you outsmart and outmaneuver your own organization.

So I give them the following example and ask if this is manipulation or just good leadership. Say one of their direct reports is an avid Red Sox fan and you don't want to put in some extra hours to do a project over the weekend. Since you know that the person is a Red Sox fan, you offer them two tickets to a game if they come through and help you on this project. After the story I ask whether this is manipulation, or just good leadership. And of course I hear both answers. Some say it is good leadership because I am connecting the organization's needs with the employee's, and some say it is manipulation since I know something about that person that I use to get them to do something. Of course this debate can go on for hours.

For me, manipulation is when I get what I want at your expense and I do so without transparency. Influence or good leadership is when I help you get what you need while the organization gets what it needs. Innovation Judo should never be used for personal gain or just getting what you need as it then becomes self-serving manipulation. It should be used when you are trying to get your job done for the betterment of the organization and you are helping yourself in the process because you are getting results despite the impediments.

This is Mr. Miyagi's mindset. He finally lets his protégé hurt the other opponent in return, but this is for the greater good—to teach the other instructor and the student a lesson in the values of karate. When Jim Repp got the Jeep Wrangler Rubicon built at Daimler Chrysler, he helped the company despite the fact that the company was not interested in building it. Jim represents an excellent example of using Innovation Judo with right-mindedness with the greater good (Chrysler's success) in mind. And if you met Jim, you would know right away that he is a selfless, stand-up guy.

STAYING RIGHT-MINDED

1. *Always tie your innovative ideas to some desired business effect.* I never really thought about the difference between goals or results and effects until I started working with the Navy. It does a good job of teaching officers to follow effects-based thinking. The difference is important as achieving results may not always get the desired effects. For example, a salesman might be given a goal to increase sales by 15 percent over the next year. And let's say that he gains that result at the end of the year by selling to too many small customers who may never order again. Compare that to attaining the 15 percent by selling to only a couple of branded multinational corporations who might be able to buy over multiple years. In addition, these big companies have a brand that could be leveraged for more sales with others, which the smaller, no-name companies could not provide. Same results but very different effects. When you are seen as keeping the greater good in mind, then some of your more risky moves are more likely to be accepted.

2. *Know your company's values and use them as justification.* As I said in the earlier chapter on wackiness, I have always been fascinated by the time and effort that companies put into creating and shaping their company values. Some organizations actually try to live by them and use them to guide employees' daily behavior. If employees live the values, then theoretically they should not need a lot of supervision in doing the right thing. The wonderful story of a Nordstrom salesman giving a refund to a customer for returned tire chains is legendary. He did so even though Nordstrom never sold tire chains. Nordstrom's value of the customer is always right was given credence by this salesman's behavior, and upper management supported his decision.

It is also easy to be cynical about a company's values. I once accused a client of mine of buying their value statements at a values warehouse. It seemed that they went to some values menu and just downloaded from the typical laundry list you find in many organizations' value statements, such as

- We respect our employees.
- We strive to be number one.
- Customers come first.
- We love teamwork.
- Our people are our most important asset.

3. *Show them the money.* Companies run on numbers. Be it profit, ROI (return in investment), ROA (return on assets), cash flow, IRR (internal rate of return), stock price, or EPS (earnings per share), the numbers count. You are always right-minded when you help your organization make money unless you do so either illegally or unethically. Companies are in business to make money, and when you can show them how much they can make with your idea, they will listen to you. Your innovation is not for you, it's for them. But to do this you must have a modicum of financial literacy. I can't tell you the number of managers and employees I encounter in an organization who do not really understand even the rudiments of finance and don't know how to communicate an innovative idea as an opportunity. Opportunities are different than ideas because opportunities have financial value (or some other value metric) associated with them.

Do yourself a favor. If you don't understand the basics, learn. Finance is the language of business, and you can't make it to the top of any organization without having a fair amount of literacy in finance. And if you are not at the top, demonstrating your financial chops can be a real differentiator in helping you step up, stand out, and stay alive. If you can demonstrate that your idea has money-making potential, then you are on the right track and in the right mind. Fortunately, becoming literate in finance is not as hard or daunting as it used to be. There are now user-friendly software packages that can help as well as simply written books like *Finance for Dummies*. In Appendix A, I have given you several references to financial self-learning resources. You can also find short courses, usually described as "finance for the nonfinancial" at local colleges and business schools.

Here is what you must know about finance if you are going to be an Innovation Judo master. Knowledge is power, and financial knowledge is essential to the innovator, even if you are an engineer who just likes to think of yourself as an inventor and not really all that concerned about the money side of innovation. Trust me, your bosses are interested in the money side. Innovation has to result in value creation for the company or you won't have many supporters unless you are just in basic research for its own sake. But even basic research isn't funded unless someone thinks this research is eventually going to pay off. So learn the basics:

- How to read a balance sheet and income statement especially your own company's annual report.
- Quick ratios—these are simple equations that can let you understand simple ratios like
  - ROI—return on investment.
  - IRR—internal rate of return. Sometimes called the "hurdle rate," this is what your company pays to borrow money, so any venture or project you might propose as an innovation has to be able to pass the hurdle rate down the road.

- ROE—return on equity.
- ROA—return on assets.
- EVA—economic value added. Is your company creating value or diluting it?
- Pay back.
- NPV—net present value.

If you would like a quick guide to some of these terms, check out the following website for MindTools (www.mind tools.com/pages/article/newCDV_45.htm). Make sure you really understand these terms. Also look at Appendix A where I have listed some of the better readings on finance for nonfinancial people.

Now, I am not a whiz in finance, but I know enough to get by. As an example of the importance of this type of knowledge, I can tell you a little story about buying my first RV. My wife and I had never owned an RV but when I took a sabbatical to work in Monterey for the Naval Postgraduate School, we decided to look into buying one. Since California is one of the most beautiful states, we figured is might be fun to take some time here to see it, and what better way than in an RV. At the time of this writing, our economy is not great, and we have record deficits, so it was a good time to buy, not sell, an RV. We reconnoitered several RV dealers in and around the Monterey area. Our final stop was Alpine RV in Morgan Hill, California. And boy did they have RVs. They were everywhere and there were deals galore. Our favorite happened to be a new 2007 leftover 32-foot Dutchman motor home with a diesel front cab and a living room slider. It was loaded and the original price was $120,000 now on sale for $89,000. Not a bad discount.

On our way home from the dealer we talked over the merits of having a motor home. Should we or shouldn't we? We decided we shouldn't unless the deal was so phenomenal that we couldn't say no. About ten minutes into our drive home, we decided we would make an offer so ridiculous that the dealer would say no, and if he took it we couldn't say no. We called our salesman at Alpine and told him we would give him $50,000. There was stunned silence. Finally he said, "Are you crazy? We are losing money at eighty-nine thousand." I then used my modicum of financial acumen. I said, "Ask your boss if he is more interested in profit or cash flow." The salesman said he didn't know what we were talking about, but he would tell his boss. And I gave them thirty minutes to decide.

After fifteen minutes the boss called us on my cell phone and said he would take $62,000. I countered with $60,000 and again reminded him that profit on a unit that doesn't sell is not nearly as good as $60,000 cash flow that would allow him to buy something that would sell. He took my offer. I can't buy a BMW for $60,000. We now are proud owners of a new motor home and are thoroughly enjoying seeing the many and spectacularly beautiful state parks and campgrounds in California.

In these economic tough times, I knew that the dealer had to be strapped for cash, especially given the huge inventory he was holding. Instead of arguing with him over price, I spoke to him in the financial terms that upper-level managers or entrepreneurs know so well. When you are struggling, cash is king. It is no longer about profit, it is just about keeping enough cash flowing through the business so that employees get paid, mortgage or rent gets paid, and suppliers get paid. Losing $20,000 on a vehicle that was paid for three years ago was not as important to the owner as keeping the doors open and the lights on. This may sound like we were treating the dealer cruelly, but in the end he needed quick cash so it was a win-win for both of us.

Note how my modest knowledge of finance helped in this situation. You are always right-minded when you understand the financial necessities of your company and can position your moves or arguments in financial terms. Money talks. Fortunately for you, financial acumen, although initially daunting, can be learned. And your ability to do "finance speak" will put you head and shoulders above most others in the organization.

4. *Show them respect.* It can be very hard to act respectful in the face of stupidity (Billy Mitchell) yet respect is a virtue and an important part of being an Innovation Judo master. Everyone sees the world through their own lenses, and even the most hardened of bureaucrats or micromanagers believes that they are doing the right things. I do not suffer fools or foolishness easily, yet I have learned to be both respectful and patient especially when I am trying to get things done that require the cooperation of others. John Kilcullen was miffed that the CFO was on record as trying to kill his idea, but he had the *discipline* to stay the course in the midst of doubt and remain *right-minded* and thus respectful.

The Massachusetts Registry of Motor Vehicles is one of those places that tested both my discipline and my right-mindedness. It represents the epitome of bureaucracy. If you are accidently in the wrong line, forget about it. Start at the end of the right line! (Assuming that they actually conveyed to you which one is the right line.) The counter personnel give you that evil eye that says, "I wish you weren't here, and if I have to be here then I must make you unhappy as well."

Perhaps I am going too far, but we are all familiar with organizations like this.

Since I am a keen observer of human behavior, I learn a lot watching human interactions. I was at one of the Massachusetts Registry of Motor Vehicles offices waiting in line when I noticed a slight altercation between the registry clerk and the person in front of me. The person in front of me was obviously in the wrong line, and when the employee told him to start over, he lost his cool. They had a little tête-à-tête, and he went to the other line in a huff. When my turn came, I started the conversation by saying, "It must be tough working with the public day in and day out. And a lot of your customers have special problems and issues that must make your job even more complex having to know the answers about so many things." She actually looked up at me (an unusual behavior for Massachusetts Registry of Motor Vehicles folks) and smiled. She said, "You don't know the half of it," and we struck up a brief but cordial conversation. I also had a problem that should have sent me to another line, but she offered to fix it for me so I would not have to wait. Manipulation you might say? I just call it Innovation Judo. I knew that while she often berates others, she is often berated. I just showed her a little respect and empathy, and I was treated differently.

It is very hard to step up, stand out, and stay alive in any organization by treating people disrespectfully or by becoming known as a self-promoting manipulator. And, of course, there are times when respect should not be accorded. Bowing in Judo is a sign of respect, even if you don't like your opponent. When you bow you always look the opponent in the eye.

When you are right-minded in your attempts to overcome roadblocks and blockheads on the pathway to creativity, you are much more likely to have a successful journey. Keeping your eyes on the prize, in this case, the desired effect of your innovative idea, helps you make the right moves in the right ways. Some of the Innovation Judo moves you practice can be seen as manipulation, but you are much more likely to be forgiven if you are seen using them for the right reasons and because you are absolutely passionate about helping your organization succeed even though it may not be naturally innovation friendly.

I put right-minded first so that you will know how to correctly put the other Innovation Judo principles into play in the right way.

Part II *The Seven Secret Principles*

This section takes you into the heart of the Innovation Judo master's playbook. It will introduce you to the seven secret principles you can master to ensure that you keep ideas alive within your organization. They are only secret because no organization wants to publicly admit that they actually need Innovation Judo masters to cut through corporate constipation and other forms of "wackiness" and who are good at making the complex simple. Armed with the right mindset, each move is helpful, but in combination, they are deadly against the opponents we identified in Part I. These principles are:

1. **Discipline**
2. **Leverage**
3. **Circling**
4. **Opening**
5. **Speed**
6. **Unbalancing**
7. **Redirection**

Not only are these principles applied differently in different innovation landscapes, but as I mentioned earlier, they are also more helpful in some phases of the innovation process than in others. For example, Innovation Judo is particularly effective in initiation, investigation, implementation, and infection and much less appropriate in intention and ideation. Other experts on innovation typically postulate only four phases in the innovation cycle and, as a result, miss the other elements where roadblocks and blockheads are most likely to appear, thus necessitating the art of Innovation Judo.

CHAPTER 6

Outwitting, Outmaneuvering

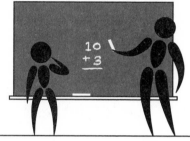

Do I get partial credit for simply having the courage to get out of bed and face the world again today?

1. Discipline
2. Leverage
3. Circling
4. Opening
5. Speed
6. Unbalancing
7. Redirection

A DYNAMIC SPORT

In the martial arts world, Judo is a dynamic sport. Winning requires physical skills of course, but it is as much a game of outwitting and outmaneuvering as it is about strength or intimidation. It is almost impossible to overpower roadblocks or intimidate blockheads so you must use your mind cleverly, learn the seven principles, and apply them at the right time in the right situation. In martial arts, opponents are always moving, often *circling* each other looking for some *opening* or advantage they can either create or exploit. And Judo masters never rely on just one move or approach as this severely limits their potential to win the match.

The real experts master multiple grips, moves, throws, and leverage points, and they use them in combination. For example, to do a hip throw you need to create an *opening*, utilize *speed* to get your body next to and aligned with your opponent, and then you exercise *leverage* by lowering your body's center of gravity below his, grab his waist, turn you body, and over he goes. Without the correct sequencing and integration of multiple moves, you could not accomplish this throw. None of the moves by themselves gives enough advantage especially when trying to overcome a larger opponent.

In this chapter I will discuss each of these secret principles, but keep in mind that they are almost always used in combination by successful corporate innovators especially when the badlands get badder. For example, *leverage* can create *openings* and *openings* can lead to *leverage*. *Circling* allows you to take a different angle of attack where your opponent's defenses are less strong. *Quickness* can allow you to apply *leverage* or take advantage of *openings*. *Surprise* and *redirection* can lead to *unbalancing*. The sequencing and combination often depends on how much *discipline* you are willing to put into studying your opponent and then practicing the principles.

You still have to be adaptive since even the best-laid plans can be upset by unforeseen circumstances. Because this book is about overcoming opposition to innovation in your organization, you will need to analyze and master moves that will be appropriate and effective in the particular organizational badlands in which you find yourself, but you will still need the full complement of Innovation Judo skills to deal with the unanticipated. As no organization is without some degree of wackiness and complexity, Innovation Judo can still help even in the Land of Oz where you are more likely to encounter blockheads than roadblocks.

THE INNOVATOR'S FORMULA

Starting with Chapter 8, you will get a chance to look at several successful Innovation Judo masters who had to operate in different badland scenarios, and you will start to see how they tailored their approaches to their particular organization's innovation landscape. As you would expect, many of these principles overlap to give you added potency in dealing with roadblocks and block-heads. I present these in no particular order except for putting *discipline* first because without *discipline* you may have more difficulty in employing the other principles. For example, if you do not counterbalance love of your idea with the discipline it takes to determine whether it is an opportunity, then you may be unprepared for those who do not share the love for your idea, and you may be too late to apply the correct Innovative Judo principles.

Remember that for the seven principles to be effective they must be focused, used in combination, and always employed in the spirit of right-mindedness. If you never need to use them, then you are lucky to be in an organization that already knows how to cultivate innovation.

PRINCIPLE 1: DISCIPLINE

Preparation

No Judo master, winning athlete, or warrior ever goes into battle without thorough preparation. Preparation is a fundamental part of the incredible discipline shown by world-class athletes. Bill Belichick, head coach for the New England Patriots, has one of the best winning records in pro football. He has talent, of course, but his team members will tell you that their real edge comes from preparation. They study their opponent's every possible move down to the last detail, they plan for possible changes in the other team's game plan, they create a customized game strategy for each opponent in excruciating detail, and they are perhaps the best team in football when it comes to exploiting the other team's weaknesses. Players who aren't prepared and disciplined in executing the game plan don't last very long with the Patriots nor do prima donnas. For the Patriots, passion often trumps skill. Tedy Bruschi, one of their star linebackers for a number of years wasn't the biggest, fastest, or most talented linebacker that the Patriots had, but he had the biggest heart and that gave him the honor of being the defensive captain for the better part of his career with the Patriots.

Preparation and passion are essential and inseparable ingredients for the Innovation Judo master. As the old Frank Sinatra song goes, "You can't have one without the other." Preparation gets you ready for game day, and passion keeps you energized throughout all four quarters.

Check Your Passion Meter

It's important to love your idea as long as you don't love it to death. Love will give you the energy and motivation to follow your idea through to implementation, but it can also blind you to its fatal flaws. Fortunately, the "opportunity process," which I will talk about under *leverage*, will highlight any flaws and give you an ample chance to reshape your idea or in some cases abandon it. And it will be essential that you follow this disciplined process. But love is important too, so you need to check your passion meter to determine how much you really like your idea. A lot of people fall out of love with an idea as soon as they realize how much work it entails to turn an idea into an opportunity. That is why so many would-be entrepreneurs at a cocktail party never pursue the idea they sketched out for you on a napkin.

First, you must see if your idea is of interest to anybody, including you. Some corporate innovators come up with their own ideas and others are told to adopt and implement someone else's. All those profiled in this book were self-generators—they came up with the big idea. But others may have to adopt someone else's idea.

When I teach, I often ask people in the class how many of them have children. Then I ask how their babies looked at birth. And they almost all say in unison, "Beautiful." I'm sorry but that's just not true. In fact, at birth, most look like little wet rubber erasers or a manatee sitting in the sun. Their eyes are squinty, their legs are crossed, and they are often wrinkly. But to their parents they are beautiful. An idea is much the same to the innovator: beautiful at birth, but on closer inspection, it may not look so beautiful to others. You cannot let love of your idea trump the discipline needed to determine if the idea is an opportunity.

You have to recognize and accept that your passion for your idea will not necessarily be widely shared, and others may call your "baby" ugly. You will need to prepare for this in a couple of ways. First, understand and accept that you will have more passion and love for your baby, and you may have to help others develop the same love that you have. You can help them by being the first to point out its flaws and by not being defensive if other people point them out. Radical ideas need to grow on people, and if the innovator is too much in love with the idea, then he or she is more likely to miss the flaws. Second, you must take the time to identify the opportunity more assiduously than you did in its ideation.

LOVED TO DEATH

I was asked by the *New York Times* to comment on a start-up entrepreneur who was trying to start an innovative Internet business for clothing like T-shirts specially made for pregnant women. The reporter asked me to predict how well her business would do in a year, and then they planned to come back at the end of her first year to see what actually happened and would then interview me again to see if my predications panned out. After looking at her and her business, I predicted it would fail, and it did in less than a year. Her enthusiasm for her idea overrode her ability to take a disciplined approach to determining if her idea was an opportunity or just an idea. Her financial predictions were much too rosy, she had not identified the hidden risks nor developed any risk mitigation strategies, and like many first-time entrepreneurs, she fell blindly in love with her idea and did not step back to see where the real opportunity lay. She had passion galore, but not discipline. The innovator must have both.

You have to love your idea, but not to death. When the reporter asked what I thought about my prediction coming true, I told him that I was sorry to hear this but not surprised. What she had really done was spend $80,000 as her "tuition" to learn that her idea did not have opportunity characteristics and her enthusiasm blinded her to its flaws.

If you are handed an innovation by someone else to implement or just told to "go innovate," you will have to check your own passion meter again. In the previous case, the entrepreneur loved her idea too much, but if it was someone else's idea, would she still love it? You can learn to love an adopted idea, but this is a more difficult challenge and you will need to make sure that you can shape the idea into an opportunity. It is in the shaping that you make the connection, and the adopted idea then becomes your own.

I am currently a part of a newly formed innovation team. In our very first meeting, one of the team members mentioned a problem defined for them by a senior executive. This senior executive also told him what solution to pursue in an innovative manner.

Wrong, wrong, wrong!

As you would expect, our first meeting started out with how we were going to implement this solution. I stopped the group very early in the meeting to decide if we were an innovation team or a tactical team. When you are given the problem and the solution, the only latitude you have to be creative is in the implementation, and then you are acting as a tactical team not an innovation team. I said that if we were a tactical team then I would have to bow out, but if we were an innovation team then we would have to approach this challenge much differently. First, we would have to validate that the problem given to us was actually the problem.

One senior leader's opinion may not be the opinion of others, thus we would have to research whether he was on target; investigation in other words. If we could not use our brains then it would be very hard for us to get into this issue emotionally. In the first scenario, "problem found/solution given," there is very little likelihood that our team would love the idea because we had very little experience creating or even investigating it. In the second scenario, "problem possibly found/solution unknown," we could develop love for the idea over time because we would have more experience researching the problem and finding a solution. If someone gives you a problem and the solution, fight back or you will really be a tactician rather than an innovator no matter what the company calls you. In my case, I knew that our team would have to fight back or be given a new charter because we certainly would not be innovators.

Innovation without passion is called work. You must have passion if you are to sustain the energy and willpower to see an idea through to its implementation. There are always failures and missteps on the pathway to innovation. It is inevitable and predictable. And, of course, there will be the ever present roadblocks and blockheads. Without personal passion you will find it very difficult to stay the course.

I often tell presenters in my innovation seminars that I have a passion meter at the back of the room and that this meter measures how excited they are about their own idea or the idea that they are trying to push. This is a joke, of course, but I make the point that if they are not excited about the idea, why should anyone else be? So part of preparation is to assess your own passion. If it is low, you need to get yourself either more excited or give it up because without this passion, you will not have the discipline to see it through.

My Judo instructor used to tell students that if we were not passionate about the sport then we should probably pick a different one. In the martial arts you are not considered to be even minimally proficient until you achieve the rank of black belt, and it takes a lot of passion to practice three times a week for three years. Passion is one of the few things that we can't teach. It has to come from inside, and if you can't get excited about your idea, then no one else will either. I have watched some great ideas presented to venture capitalists or to company executives with little or no emotion. That is one of the first things they pick up on and are immediately suspect of both the idea and the presenter. However, love can grow, and the only way it can is for you to actually roll up your sleeves and get heavily involved in the "opportunity process." Sometimes going through this process can fire up the embers, but it can also cool them if you find out your idea is only an idea, not an opportunity.

Discipline in innovation is also essential and has some characteristics that are similar to the martial arts form of Judo. Innovation Judo requires many aspects of discipline. Many innovators fail to get their ideas implemented due to a lack of discipline especially in the formative stages. If you follow the few suggestions I provide next, you will be better prepared and ten times more effective as an innovator. These suggestions will also give your idea critical breathing room for further development.

Bring Opportunities, Not Ideas

One of the biggest reasons innovation fails is that the innovator lacks the discipline to adhere to a known methodology of separating a good idea from a good opportunity. But it takes time and effort to work this process. So one of the first things you must do to counter roadblocks and blockheads on the path to creativity is make sure that you bring opportunities, not ideas, to the table. Ideas are easy to kill because they have no substance. An idea is just that. It is a concept with no proof, and thus no gravitas. There are far too many ideas in organizations and far too few opportunities. Now there is nothing wrong with ideas. They are the starting point for all innovation, and good ideas for doing things better, faster, cheaper, with less costs are essential for organizations in today's volatile and competitive environment. But I would trade a thousand good ideas for one good opportunity. You need to understand the subtle yet critical differences between these two concepts if you are to have any chance of overcoming roadblocks and blockheads. Perhaps the biggest difference between a "wannabe innovator" and a successful one is the willingness to follow a disciplined and sometime arduous process for discovering if your great idea has opportunity characteristics.

Blockheads have an easy time killing an idea. I am sure you have all heard such phrases as "That would never work here," "We tried that before and it failed," "Great idea but we just don't have the resources to do it." Ideas are defenseless but opportunities are not.

All the successful Innovation Judo masters profiled in this book loved their ideas but did the necessary work to demonstrate to others that they were not just presenting an interesting idea, they were presenting a real opportunity with high potential. Figure 6.1 shows the flow from idea to opportunity.

In Figure 6.1, note that there are three phases that an innovation must go through if it is to survive and create value for the organization. First, we have to identify it as an opportunity not

The Entrepreneurial Process

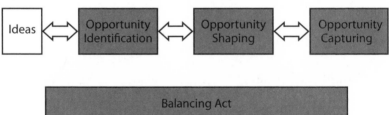

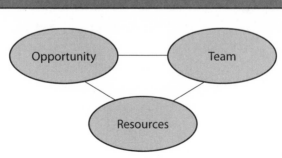

just an idea. A colleague and I had a great idea for developing an executive education program for our university around teaching HR executives to be business leaders first and HR people second. We often heard HR people complain about not having a seat at the table like the other executives who ran functions like manufacturing, finance, and marketing did. HR has often been seen as a necessary evil by CEOs and as a cost center not a profit center. Add the reluctance of many HR people to study finance so that they can speak the language of business and you have a good chance of being marginalized.

We were convinced that HR executives could benefit from a course specifically tailored to help them speak with greater authority from an overall business perspective not just an HR perspective. But, of course, we only had an idea. We now had to follow a disciplined process of identifying whether this idea was just an idea or had opportunity characteristics. Was there really a market for this kind of course? How big is it, and will companies send these people to our course for enough money, for a long enough period of time to make this innovative program value creating and thus compelling? If we were able to identify this idea as an opportunity then we had to take the next step, which is to shape it. As we talked to potential customers would our original idea of course content and marketing focus remain the same or would we need to reshape our original content? And finally, if we were convinced that our idea was a real opportunity, would we have the willpower, manpower, and resources to pull it off? Note that we have to get some good answers to these questions or we remain forever in the world of ideas.

You won't know if your great idea has opportunity characteristics until you roll up your sleeves and do the work necessary to find out. And before we would even present this idea to the president of the college, we would want to make sure that our idea has some characteristics of an opportunity.

One of our first moves was to contact HR executives to see if they would be willing to sit on an advisory board to help us build this course. We figured that if we could not get at least four to five senior HR people interested in coming in at our expense to talk about this and be on the board then the market didn't care and our idea was probably not worth pursuing. Not only were we able to constitute an advisory board, but several of the members guaranteed that if we built the course with their recommendations, they would send a certain number of their HR people to the program with a discount for sending more than one person. As you can imagine this process did not happen overnight. We had to spend our time, energy, and some money to bring these people in for a day to discuss our potential idea. But when they left, we knew we had identified an opportunity, they helped us shape it, and then we proceeded to pull faculty, staff, and resources together to build this program. The program was a great success for a number of years, and the HR participants also became our advocates for other educational courses that we offered.

This is the process of idea to opportunity. We did have some detractors at the beginning of the process, but when we brought in the advisory board, it gave us incredible leverage over the naysayers because we now had interest from those with wallets who were interested enough to put us on their busy schedules and spend a day with us. We also surprised our detractors with how quick we were able to get this idea off the ground. If we had stayed at the idea level, we would have gotten very little traction in convincing the school that we should pursue this investment over something else.

This is the process that all innovators must go through if they want to wring value out of their ideas. It is true that some innovators are only interested in the invention side of the equation and that they typically work with basic research. Most of us, however, expect our innovation to deliver value.

Opportunities then need to be balanced with the resources and the people who can make them happen (Figure 6.1). I tell my corporate clients, "Always start with ideas and opportunity identification, then worry about who can pull it off, and then look at resources last." Unfortunately, too many organizations start with the budget and then look at who's around. If you start with the budget you are by definition limiting your idea set. You will see that Lieutenant Commander Chris Kluckhuhn developed a major innovation for not only the Coast Guard but also the Air Force and private industry by not starting with the budget even though it was too small for his opportunity. If he had started with the restrictions of the budget he would never have pursued his game-changing and life-saving innovation that you will read about in Part IV.

OPPORTUNITY CHARACTERISTICS

Let's take a closer look at the differences between fluffy ideas and weightier opportunities. Opportunities have specific characteristics that can be analyzed and presented in concrete terms while ideas remain at the conceptual level. The innovator must learn the discipline of differentiating a good idea from a good opportunity or their idea will likely get very little real traction in the organization. Ideating is the fun part of innovation, but opportunity identification, shaping, and capturing is where some of the fun stops and the real work of innovation begins.

Differentiating ideas from opportunities is not done in brain-storming sessions or in meetings. It is done in the field by rolling up your sleeves to answer the following questions:

1. Who will actually care about this idea? This is the "customer" question and should be asked about customers internally and externally.
2. How many are there?
3. How much will they pay/invest?
4. For how long?
5. What are the financial implications for value creation and investment?

People in management at Kimberly-Clark like to say that a real opportunity allows them to sell more stuff to more people, for more money, for greater profit, for a longer time. Ideas won't help them do this, but opportunities can. Be clear that opportunities are not defined by market characteristics like size and structure or growth potential.

Remember, even in nonprofit or government organizations, there are always customers for whom an innovation must have some value for it to go beyond just the idea state. In the Navy it could be an admiral who is the customer, someone from the Department of Defense, etc. I am currently on a team discussing the value proposition of NPS to its constituents. We are still debating the customer question as we say we are innovative, but it's not what we say that counts. It is the recipients of our innovation who must see the value or we will get little or no traction in pursuing this innovation. Ideas do not have customers; only opportunities do!

In short we have to have some degree of confidence that our idea is

a. durable,

b. sustainable,

c. defensible,

d. value creating, and

e. compelling

before we can start calling it an opportunity.

Durable An idea is durable if it creates value over time and can withstand assaults from competitors. There is nothing wrong with one-hit wonders that can make short bursts of money, but to a company, the reliance on one-hit wonders is not a sustainable strategy for long-term viability. Some products or services are so easily copied that they have no staying power, technology often changes, which could make an innovation obsolete quickly, or the market may not be robust enough to handle new entrants. As an investor in your idea, I would need some confidence that your idea, once implemented, would have some staying power.

Sustainable An idea is sustainable if we have the willpower and resources to see it through its various stages of maturity to adulthood and value creation. Some great ideas won't show a profit for two to three years because of the start-up and development costs. Not all ideas cost money or take that long to implement, but the bigger the idea, the more likely it is to take time and money to really see it through. Do we, as an organization, have the ability to sustain the idea through fruition? If you were trying to get me to back your idea, I would need some confidence that we have the personnel and the willpower to make it happen.

Defensible Defensibility refers to how well we can defend our idea against other uses of time and resources within our company. Innovative ideas often compete with other investment opportunities vying for limited resources. Why should I put my money (time, dollars, or people) into your idea versus putting it somewhere else? Can we defend it internally? If not, then the resources should go to something else.

Value Creating Will your idea create economic value for your company and why should we believe your numbers? Now we won't really know for sure until it is implemented, but do you have some confidence in your projected numbers? Innovation without value creation may be easy, but it's not going to create any true value for the company. Innovation always has risk, so I need to be convinced that the risk is worth taking in terms of potential investment and return on investment. Value is defined simply as $V = B/C$ (Value equals benefits divided by costs). I don't talk about value creation in economic terms to the Navy, but its innovative ideas can always be presented in a value equation. For example, there is a group called JIEDDO (Joint Improvised Explosive Device Defeat Organization) whose job it is to develop innovative ways of countering the improvised explosive devices (IEDs) that kill soldiers and numerous civilians on almost a daily basis in Iraq and Afghanistan. These innovations can also create value. Saying "I save 5 percent more soldiers per month," shows the measureable value of an innovation. There is value in less deaths and injuries, lower expenses associated with treatment and hospitalization, and better mental health for families—being able to quantify these things will turn an idea into an opportunity.

If an idea is to be an opportunity, it must demonstrate a strong potential for value creation. It always makes me cringe to watch someone present a great idea to senior management or outside investors and get to the point about value creation twenty slides later. Always, always start with the formula and the following words or something close: "My, our idea, has a potential to create the following value (best to give an upside and a downside range) and here is how we can make this work."

Compelling If an idea has some evidence of durability, sustainability, defensibility, and has a high potential for value creation, then your idea starts to look, feel, and smell more like an opportunity. This, of course, assumes that you are a credible and passionate advocate of the opportunity. I have seen a lot of potentially great opportunities fall by the wayside because the innovator shows either little passion for the idea and/or has not done the work necessary to determine if the idea has opportunity characteristics. Your opportunity is also much more compelling if you point out what can go wrong and demonstrate that you have a backup plan or risk mitigation strategy already in mind.

In Appendix B, I have provided you with an opportunity template. This two-page document asks you to assess your idea against a series of questions. The more you can answer these questions, the more your idea moves into opportunity territory. The template represents an express version of a business plan, and you probably cannot answer all these questions immediately. Differentiating an idea from an opportunity is a process that all innovation must go through to determine its value creating potential and probability of success. No innovation has certainty until it is implemented, but this document will help you better understand your own idea, and it is an extremely useful document for communicating with others about your idea.

I often hear employees say that their company doesn't listen to their ideas. And I am sure this is true in many cases, but it is also true that ideas are not listened to because they are just ideas and not opportunities. The next time an employee comes up to you and offers you an innovative idea, hand them this two-page template and ask them to fill in as much as they can and you will go over it next week. If they never come back to you with that template, they probably weren't really that interested in their own idea.

Opportunities have great leverage for convincing others that you have come up with something of great potential. And unlike ideas, opportunities are hard to kill. This Judo principle of *leverage* is very helpful in the Land of Oz and Maze companies, but is less helpful in Jungle and Asylum companies where other Innovation Judo principles are more applicable. While it takes a great deal of discipline to work through the opportunity process, it also creates leverage because opportunities can open doors and move roadblocks that ideas cannot. So in following the opportunity process, you are putting yourself in a very good position to create leverage as well.

Patience

Another aspect of *discipline* is patience, and it is truly a virtue when it comes to innovation. Unlike other forms of preparation that require action, patience requires inaction or better yet inaction combined with reflection. Ideas are never born mature, and like new wine they take time to age. As they age they change. The opportunity that is identified in the first stage of the opportunity process is rarely the same one that you see at the end of the process. Patience is equally important when it comes to roadblocks and blockheads. It takes time for people to change their minds and their biases and to accept untried and untested things. But if it takes too long then you will also have to have the patience to look for openings in their defenses that you can then exploit. Jim Repp, for example, found out that no one was interested in his idea of the Jeep Rubicon. So he secretly built his own Jeep outside of Chrysler and patiently waited for an opportunity to get a Chrysler executive out to "Camp Jeep" to surprise him with what his secretly built high-end Jeep could do under near impossible conditions.

Patience is also very important for exploiting openings. In my Judo matches, we hold the lapels of our opponent's judogis (uniforms) in order to try to control the opponent or influence his movements. And we circle each other while holding on to these lapels, waiting for an opening to either get our hips into his, knock his foot out from under him, or initiate other moves just at the right moment when we see a possible point of attack. Muscling doesn't work very well unless you are exceedingly strong, but in Judo, patience is a virtue because it allows you to take advantage or create an opening, and then you have to move very quickly before this window of opportunity closes. So it is with blockheads and roadblocks.

Russ Sabo also waited patiently for an opening in which he could surprise and shock his executives into making an acquisition on which they were dragging their feet. My mother used to tell me that when she was a child her mother would tell her the exact time to approach her father with a touchy subject and when not to. So as they say, timing is everything, and you will need to be patient with not only your own idea but with roadblocks and blockheads until the moment is right to utilize your Innovation Judo skills. Also, you can be proactive in making the timing right as well, and as you will see later in the profiles.

Perhaps one of the best examples of a patient and disciplined innovator was Thomas Edison. He believed that a lot of experimentation and consequent failures were necessary in the shaping process. His famous statement that he had not failed in getting the lightbulb to work, but rather discovered a thousand ways that did not work is a great example of patience combined with the discipline of testing ideas for their opportunity characteristics.

Self-Control

As you remember from Chapter 3, Billy Mitchell did not suffer fools easily. They irritated him and he was not afraid to show his irritation by heaping insults upon his detractors. He may have felt better in the short term, but it hurt him in the long term. John Kilcullen was also irritated by his detractors, but he held his anger in check and used humor to deflect and redirect their negative energy.

Showing emotion to your innovation team is appropriate, including anger when it is appropriate, but doing so with blockheads only makes them dig in harder. Roadblocks are insulated from anger since wackiness and complexity don't respond to human emotion. Screaming at a bureaucracy has no effect, but outsmarting it does. So keep calm, even in the face of adversity, and remember the great rule of physics: "For every action there is an equal but opposite reaction." Beating up on blockheads only increases their pushback to now both you and your idea and lessens your chances of keeping your ideas alive in the corporation. And remember the supposed Mafia advice, "Revenge is best served cold."

PRINCIPLE 2: LEVERAGE

The Clever Lever

Leverage is perhaps the most powerful principle that the innovator has at his or her disposal. Since Innovation Judo masters utilize

multiple principles when faced with opposition, it is no surprise that Jim Repp was also a master of leverage. He used a number of levers to get Jeep to finally build the Wrangler Rubicon. His biggest roadblock was the marketing department who had the NIH attitude and felt that they, and their statistics, knew the Jeep customers better than Jim did. But Jim knew what he called the "Fringe Lunatic" Jeep enthusiasts in a way the marketers could not—he was one of them. Corporate marketers predicted that at best only a few hundred serious off-roaders would ever buy a Rubicon if they built it. In its first year, Jeep sold 12,000 Rubicons. As you will see, Jim also used several of the other principles that we will talk about as well.

Although there is no Latin root for the word *clever*, it is interesting that without the *c* the word becomes *lever*. In the dictionary, cleverness is defined as

Ingenious, shrewd, mental astuteness

What could be a more appropriate word for the innovator who leans on Innovation Judo principles to overcome roadblocks and blockheads? Remember our earlier story of Billy Mitchell and John Kilcullen. Where Mitchell was rude and paid the price, Kilcullen was shrewd and won the prize. Since *leverage* is such an important Innovation Judo principle, and helpful in all of the innovation landscapes, I will spend some time explaining it.

Without leverage, no rocks would have been moved, no catapults made, no pyramids built, nor any bodies thrown over your hip. Both Judo and Jiu-Jitsu use leverage. In martial arts, leverage can take a number of forms. It can involve a lower center of gravity than your opponent or using certain holds that give the Judo master an advantage. Leverage is what allows the small to beat the tall!

I recently watched a UFC (Ultimate Fighting Championship) match. The UFC allows one-on-one combat using any style—wrestling, kickboxing, Judo, Jiu-Jitsu, karate—in a mostly no-holds-barred octagon-shaped arena. The matches can be won on points, but most of the time someone is either too injured to go on or submits to his opponent through being caught in a submission hold. And while there are weight classes, the band is pretty broad. But it is truly one sport where size does not matter. Some of the biggest and strongest combatants submit to their smaller opponent due to leverage. I recently was amazed to see a smaller Japanese fighter take down a much larger Brazilian fighter by wrapping his leg around the opponent's leg and applying leveraging. Once he had their legs entwined, he fell to the ground and rolled his opponent over, coming up with his opponent's leg and foot twisted like a pretzel around his own leg. But he had the advantage because he held his opponent's foot in his hands, his leg locked the opponent's leg, and he simply twisted the opponent's foot until the pain made the Brazilian fighter tap out and submit. And all this happened in the blink of an eye. Smaller fighters often win because they get their opponent on the ground where height and weight often becomes a liability for quick movement and body leverage. Jiu-Jitsu artists often win these mixed martial arts matches more than any other style of fighter because of their cleverness in letting the bigger opponent wear himself out, make a small mistake that creates an opening, and then apply just the right amount of leverage to a limb, or in some cases a choke hold, that allows them to overcome a much larger, stronger, and more imposing-looking opponent.

Organizational Leverage

Large organizations can be imposing, slow moving, and hard to muscle, so this is where leverage can work to your advantage. Leverage is one of those laws of physics that is hard to deny. Put two unequally weighted kids on a teeter-totter and the heavier one always has the power to leave the other one up in the air, unless the fulcrum is moved to give the lighter one equal to or greater advantage. Anyone who has ever been on a teeter-totter or has to pry something open knows the importance and basic principles of leverage. The lighter kid on the teeter-totter has to move his or her weight farther back on the board in order to offset their partner's greater weight.

Judo uses a great deal of leverage especially using the body as a fulcrum. The first throw one learns in Judo class is the hip throw. You actually use your body as the fulcrum over which you unbalance and throw your partner. Much like the teeter-totter, the heavier your opponent, the lower you have to get your body beneath your opponent in order to help offset the weight advantage.

Organizations are full of leverage points if you know where to look. Innovation Judo black belts have learned that leverage can be one of their best friends when it comes to bureaucracy busting or overcoming the roadblocks and blockheads we talked about earlier. I will point out some of the obvious and not so obvious ones that you can use to your advantage in trying to clear your pathway to innovation.

Let's look at organizational levers and how you can use them. Remember that these levers are not always required nor should they necessarily be your first option if you are living in the Land of Oz. But you will need them when logic doesn't work or there is a great deal of politics involved, or your boss is mentally challenged and can't see a good idea if it ran over him.

Corporate Values

I talked briefly about corporate values earlier, but because they are so helpful as levers, they need to be explored in greater detail. One of the most exploitable organizational leverage points for the corporate innovator lies in the company's value statements. Almost all of the companies I worked with have some set of formalized value statements written down or on plaques on the wall. These are wonderful tools to leverage and exploit when the need arises.

I was recently doing a seminar for a software company. Although there were supposed to be twenty-seven people in class on any one day, there were only about sixteen to eighteen people present. They were either running out to answer emails from customers or were pulled out by their bosses to attend meetings at the nearby corporate headquarters. Many of the participants were unhappy about this because they liked the program, and the company was spending considerable money on it, but they felt they had no power to say no to their bosses. Yet the executive board had just published its list of most cherished company values, and on that list was "talent development."

None of the participants saw the opportunity to use this value to leverage their way out of often impromptu unimportant meetings. A well-placed email to the boss or one of the executives asking whether the person should attend the program, since it is part of the company's written values, is a great example of leverage. The email is not an attacking email, but a wonderful tool that utilizes the company's own value system to avoid being called continuously out of a talent development program that the participant really needed and wanted. This is why I advise my clients to never put values in writing or make a big fuss about them unless they are seriously committed to them. Values that a company truly believes and lives by can bring great strength to a company, but they can also be a tremendous soft spot that Innovation Judo masters can exploit when necessary to eliminate roadblocks and blockheads.

Generally corporate values are created at the top of the organization, and as such they have both implied and real power. Jack Welch, for example, reportedly fired an employee because he could not cite all eleven of the company's corporate values. So anyone else in GE who did not adhere to these values was fair game for exposure and thus censure. Know your company's values and make sure that you tie them to your initiatives. It is much harder to kill an initiative that is obviously in line with a core value, and even if others do not live by the values, very few in management want to admit this, so that will give you leverage.

Keep a list of the values on your office wall if they are not already there. If you get into a situation where logic isn't enough to convince people to get on board for one of your projects, or the boss says no, think how to recast your goals in terms of the company values. Try not to be too obvious. Too obvious would be putting up a wall chart of the values or listing them in an email. But you can always refer to them casually. In my talent management example, you could easily have a chat with your boss or the head of the program and say you really feel torn about going to the meeting or staying in the program as obviously senior management seems to really think talent development is critical and you want to utilize this experience to the fullest. You could also say that this particular section of the program is critical to you as you want to be able to pass this information down to your employees. Again note the leverage. Your employees and you add to the leverage. Thus, the boss insisting that you go to the meeting instead of the training class will not only let you down, but now it will affect your people as well. This is not manipulation as you are doing these things in the spirit of right-mindedness.

I do not think this use of values as leverage is manipulative. If talent development is a value then your boss has no business pulling you out of the class. Education is one of the most important investments people can make in themselves and a company can make for its employees. Education lasts a lifetime, but meetings often come and go so you have every right to use leverage to get not only what you need but what the company says it needs. The talent development example is just one of thousands of instances where people inside the business, either by design or by default, violate their organization's own values. Many people have seen a boss or person of authority dress down an employee in public even though the organization's values say "We respect our people" or "We value our employees' contributions."

Now we will turn to the customer, so you can see how using the customer as leverage puts you in an even better position, since companies need customers to create profit.

The Customer Lever

I often argue with my colleagues in finance about the fundamental purpose of a business. They like to tell their MBA students that the fundamental purpose of a business is to "create shareholder value." I counter with a view that the fundamental purpose of a business is to fill some want or need for a customer. Without doing this, there is no value to share. We don't get shareholder value unless customers are willing to reach into their wallets and pay us for our goods or services. The real value we should worry about is the value we create for the customer. If we can do that well, then shareholder value is likely to follow.

These days, customers are increasingly hard to get, keep, and please. And with our shaky economy, plenty of competitors would be happy to fill in any gaps that we are leaving open. Without customers, we don't have a business so anytime you can use the customer as leverage you are on solid ground. Customers, actual or potential, are incredible sources of leverage. Later in the book, I will give you several examples of how innovators have overcome their own organization's roadblocks and blockheads by using customers as levers to force their organizations to adopt innovation.

I worked with managers at Siemens Corporation for a number of years trying to help them inject entrepreneurial serum into the veins of several hundred of their managers through a series of executive education program. This showed me firsthand why Innovation Judo skills were a necessary skill set.

The basic thrust of the executive education program was to teach internal Siemens managers to think and act in more entrepreneurial ways. So the program involved entrepreneurial education with real opportunity identification. The team would experience eight months of entrepreneurial education interspersed with an application of entrepreneurship principles to learn how to create new businesses within the company. Participants would come in for two weeks of education where we would challenge them to come up with a new business idea. They would then go back to their jobs for six to eight weeks to see if their ideas had opportunity characteristics that could move the idea to the next stage of business potential. They would then go through another two weeks of education showing them how to turn their opportunities into viable businesses. Then six to eight weeks later they would come in with a real business plan that the faculty and internal Siemens strategic planning folks would coach them on so that they could present these plans to a Siemens board of directors for possible funding. Some of these business plans were funded, and one business succeeded in creating revenues of over $250 million two years after its inception. The actual cost of our entrepreneurial leadership program was about $2.5 million so this was not a bad return on investment.

Perhaps in all of my career initiatives this was the most valuable from a learning perspective. We were able to see what could and could not be taught about entrepreneurship and how organizational barriers often conspire to kill great new business ideas. We were also able to see how some of our entrepreneurial leaders were able to outsmart these barriers. Keep in mind that this was a top-driven initiative and despite the overwhelming support from top management, there were still many roadblocks and blockheads getting in the way of creating these new businesses. They ran the gamut from stupid HR payment policies, to petty jealousies, to outright sabotage. One of the new businesses was perceived as threatening a legacy business, so the head of the legacy business did his damnedest to derail the new business.

One of my favorite stories from this experience involved the use of a customer as an incredible lever to get Siemens to do what it thought it could not do. Siemens is large by any company standard—around 360,000 employees worldwide. One of our teams of internal entrepreneurs trying to start a new business worked for the Dematics Division of the company. One of this division's biggest customers was the U.S. Postal Service. Tasked with looking into new business opportunities, our team was not too optimistic about more work with the U.S. Postal Service. They were slashing costs and pressuring all their vendors to cut prices. So the Dematics team looked into how they might use some of their postal automation equipment in a new industry or a new application. Fortunately, one of their team members worked for the Arlington, Texas, Police Department as a volunteer officer. In one of the team's meetings, he said that if the equipment could read a letter going by one of the cameras at the speed of sound and then send it to the right location, what else could it do?

In a brainstorming session, they came up with an interesting question: If the equipment can read the addresses on letters that are literally flying by, could it read a license plate on a moving car from a safe distance? The team got excited about this idea and since one of their members was a cop, they went to the Arlington Police Department with the initial idea. They were interested but wanted answers to the typical questions you would expect from a potential customer. Will it work when both the police car and the suspect's cars are moving, going around corners, etc.? How far can the camera read, and will it log the number correctly and integrate with the police department's data entry system?

The team took the challenge and started to do some research and prototyping to come up with a camera supported by Siemens software and hardware that could read a moving license plate from a mile away. Clearly an important tool for pursuing police who want to avoid harming anyone or themselves when trying to get close enough to read the license plate of the car in front of them. Not only did the prototype work; the group patented some of its technology and wrote an extremely strong and compelling business plan.

They then took it to the Siemens board for some funding to determine the commercial viability of their new product, but they were turned down. The board liked the idea and praised the business plan, but said their investment capital was already allocated for the year and to try again next year. As newly trained entrepreneurs, the team members knew that opportunities don't wait for a year so they went back to the Arlington Police Department for funding. The Arlington Police Department did not have the money but suggested Dematics should show the product to a national police organization. They not only successfully demonstrated the product, but they also came back with half a million dollars in seed capital if Siemens would match the money. When the group went back to the board with this commitment, the board realized that they had a real opportunity because they now had a real customer and matched the half a million dollars by taking the money from another project.

This story reveals how important the customer is from a leverage perspective. I can talk until I am blue in the face about a new business idea, but my words will never match the clout of a paying customer. And customers don't always give you leverage through money; they can give you leverage by donating their employees' time, knowledge, or expertise. Very few organizations want to say no to a customer or generally piss them off (except airlines), so the more support you can get from the customer, or preferably cash, you can get for your ideas, the more likely you are to get innovative things done.

A few years ago, I was asked to help create a Strategy Formulation program for senior leaders of a well-known medical device company in the United States. The company provided a range of products and services to hospitals, long-term care facilities, and trauma units. I asked to do some interviews with a sample of this company's employees to help in the program's design, and I also asked to speak with some customers.

In a number of my interviews, it became clear that not all customers were happy, and in fact, some were downright angry. One doctor told us that he loved the company's products but hated the company. They described this medical device company as arrogant and slow to respond to customer complaints, usually blaming the customer for the not doing things the right way. Their comments reminded me a little bit about when the Audi A2000 ran over some of their owners because of a transmission problem. Audi's first response was to blame the customer for not knowing how to drive.

A lot of these customer complaints never got through to the top with the original emotions attached because it was filtered by the people down the chain of command. The salespeople who received the brunt of the customer's ire were hesitant to pass the message up the chain of command. Because the purpose of our program was to help bring about some fundamental changes to strategy to help further this company's growth, we decided to bring in one really pissed-off customer, a doctor, as a guest speaker. Although we did tell the senior executives in our class that we were bringing in an unhappy customer, we did not realize just how unhappy he was until he started to speak. The more he spoke, the angrier he got. He started out trying to be somewhat calm, but as he was describing a litany of negative experiences, his turbo charger took over and he really let go. And at the end of his talk, he said that he would dump this company in a heartbeat if he could find a reasonable substitute, and he said publically what he told us in the one on one interview: "I love your product but hate your company."

Needless to say, the participants in the course were shocked. There was stunned silence after this particular speaker left the room. Then the murmurs began, and we as the educators started to get some jaundiced looks. Eventually one of the more senior people in the group said, "How dare you bring in such a person to insult and humiliate us." Some other members started to pile on, and then one of the cooler heads suggested that we calm down and realize that the participants were now demonstrating the same arrogance that the customer had vehemently complained about. This one outside speaker probably had more effect on our client movement toward a more customer-centric organization than all of the faculty members combined. When customers speak in the right venue, they can provide you with incredible leverage to introduce your innovation.

They needed to see the face of the customer, the emotion involved in what they were creating, and how it truly affected the customer. Was there some risk on our part? Absolutely, but playing it safe and sociable would not have helped our client get the results that they wanted and needed. Bring in a customer who really likes your idea and may be willing to share in both the risks and rewards in seeing it through to completion and watch many of the roadblocks and blockheads melt away.

The Competitor Lever

Another extremely useful lever is the competition. If you hadn't noticed, Americans are very competitive. Leaders in an organization, especially those at the top, usually have more than a touch of healthy ego. They hate to lose, and thus competitor information, particularly when the competitor has some advantage, is a powerful tool for persuasion and very helpful for positioning innovative ideas. One of my clients is a multinational corporation with multiple divisions and a myriad of complex products. Large silos exist in this organization partly because of how it has grown over the years and partly because of its competitive culture.

I did not do much entrepreneurial teaching in this organization, except in one of the divisions that was deeply involved with manufacturing automation and robotics. As a result of the push for new business development, one of this division's managers had come up with a great new idea, but it would need the help from one of the company's other product manufacturing lines. When this manager and his team approached the division and asked for help in developing this new joint business idea, they were essentially told to "get lost." Actually, the manager of the other division derisively suggested that if this group had time to work on such an innovative new business venture they obviously had too much time on their hands. Not very familial, I would argue.

But the automation division manager was an experienced Innovation Judo master. Instead of getting angry, or going to the other guy's or his boss to complain, he went to a competing manufacturer and asked them if they might want to form a joint venture. This competitor was interested and wrote a letter saying so. The automation manager then sent a copy of this letter to the manager and his boss who had summarily dismissed his overtures suggesting that they should talk again to partner internally before he signed with the outside manufacturer. This time he got a much different response. Ah, the power of *leverage*. It would have been preferable if this manager had just been able to convince through logic, but as you saw, logic did not work.

Using examples of a successful competitor's innovations to push your ideas forward is like throwing out the gauntlet to potential naysayers or to senior leaders from whom you need support. None of us likes to be shown up as lesser in a contest, and this is extremely powerful ammunition for the innovator.

The Referred Power Lever

"I just ran into the CEO, and he said we should . . ."

How to Succeed in Business Without Really Trying was a very successful Broadway play that was eventually made into a movie. It is a comedic story about the triumph of the common man, a window washer named J. Pierrepont Finch, played by Robert Morse on Broadway in 1962 and in the movie version in 1967. After Finch happens upon a book titled *How to Succeed in Business Without Really Trying*, he decides to begin his rise up the corporate ladder. Following the instructions in the book, Finch lands a job in the mailroom at the World Wide Wicket Company. With the help of his handy book, Finch quickly gains promotions and outsmarts and outmaneuvers his rival, Bud Frump, who also happens to be the boss's nephew. Finch then gains the love of Rosemary, a secretary at the company. In the end, however, after Finch's ad campaign goes awry, the book can no longer help him. He is forced to rely on his own wits and performs so admirably that he is promoted to chairman of the board.

One of the tactics he uses is the referent power lever. Referent power means referring to someone who is in power and then using that implied relationship to persuade, influence, motivate, or perhaps even frighten. While working in the mail room, he runs out the door to deliver some mail and literally runs over the CEO of the company. Of course the CEO hurls epithets at Finch, dusts himself off, and goes on his way. But Finch uses this encounter to his advantage to help leverage his way to the top by saying things like "I just ran into the boss and we think . . ." And, of course, he really did run into the boss so in some ways he is not being totally dishonest.

My position is both interesting and challenging at the Naval Postgraduate School. I was brought on board to bring more innovation and entrepreneurial thinking into the Navy. Part of the reason I was offered the job initially was because I was teaching an innovation and entrepreneurial thinking class to two- and three-star admirals. Knowing all these admirals on a first-name basis gives me substantial *referent power*. Admirals are highly respected in the Navy and clearly have a lot of power. It doesn't hurt that I know them on a first-name basis and count many as my friends. I can call them on the phone and usually get a quick response while others may wait days. This referent power also gives me a fair amount of leverage in working with others in the Navy even though my formal authority at the Naval Postgraduate School is relatively weak. Getting to know others in higher authority not only makes sense, it clearly does not harm your career development potential. In addition, knowing these folks can give you tremendous top cover and leverage against roadblocks and blockheads when trying to get an idea heard. But remember, this power should only be used when logic doesn't work and with right-mindedness. I have never used my relations with admirals or other senior leaders to hurt anyone or for personal gain, but sometimes a word from an admiral or a senior executive can make the innovation ball roll just a little faster down the road.

The Strategy Lever

You might not be amazed at this but many managers in large companies cannot state their company's strategy. Try it in one sentence. What usually comes out when I ask this question in one of my executive education classes is a slogan that people think passes for strategy. For example, I have heard the following as statements of strategy:

- To be number one in the robotics industry.
- Leading the next generation of antibiotics.
- To be the provider of choice in the insurance industry.

Closer scrutiny, of course, reveals that none of these are actually strategies but goals. Most can be measured by some index but even that is not clear. Being number one in robotics could mean volume, market share, profit, etc., none of which gets us any closer to strategy. Strategy tells us how we are going to be number one, or the leader or the provider of choice. Large companies are often much better at financial engineering than strategy development and articulation. It is much easier for a CEO to say the company is going to double its market share in the next two years than it is to tell people how he thinks the company should get there. But somewhere, lurking around the organization is probably the semblance of a written strategy. If you know the strategy in depth, which most of your counterparts probably won't, you can use this knowledge to position your innovative idea as somehow linked to and supportive of the strategy even if it takes the company in a slightly different direction. How does your idea add to the company's core capabilities, competitive advantage, cost cutting, or acquisitions?

But keep in mind that many really innovative ideas can and should challenge a company's strategy. But if they appear too far from the current strategy they can be easily killed as irrelevant even though the innovation could take the company in an even more profitable direction. So striking the right balance between reinforcing a current strategy and pushing the organization in new directions that it hadn't thought about is a delicate balance. Nonetheless, it is still helpful to utilize your company's current strategy as a platform from which to launch new initiatives.

I will give you two examples. One of my former university col-leagues came to us from industry as a very successful entrepre-neur. He and several friends started Jiffy Lube, which became a huge success and was eventually bought by Pennzoil. The inno-vator at Pennzoil who said, "We should buy Jiffy Lube," probably got a few quizzical looks because Jiffy Lube is a service business and Pennzoil is a manufacturer and distributer of oil. But when you position the acquisition of Jiffy Lube as not buying a service business but simply acquiring a new distribution channel for your product then it makes sense.

When one of the internal innovators at 3M tried to get them to manufacture CDs, which were just an emerging product at the time, he used to always hold the CD in a horizontal position so that is looked very thin like sandpaper not something round, flat, shiny, and foreign to the company. 3M had a deep tradition of making paper products that were flat and thin so he wanted to make sure that the CD, which represented a very new and risky strategy for 3M, didn't appear all that different from what 3M was already manufacturing. When you propose an innovation that is congruent with both the company's values and its strategy, then your idea is likely to have greater leverage than if it looks like it came from Mars.

The Informal Network Lever

I have not always been the best networker in my career. I often as-sumed that my appeals to logic and "doing the right things" were ammunition enough to gain cooperation and dissolve obstacles. Naïveté, to be sure. In large organizations (and smaller ones too) politics, power, games, one-upmanship, and positioning are all part of life in the corporate arena. Most of these tactics are attempts to increase power and influence, much like the teeter-totter example. Sometimes they are mild distractions but at other times games and politics actually take precedence over performance. There was a good story in the *Detroit Free Press* many years ago about a newly promoted vice president at Ford Motor Company who brought in the maintenance people in the evening to knock down and rebuild the wall between his office and the VP's office next door. The newly promoted VP had found out that his rival had two more square feet of office space, so he had the wall knocked down to make it even. Clearly not a good use of corporate funds.

Obviously this guy had some clout or good relations with the maintenance folks or the wall never would have been moved. Proactively creating, maintaining, and expanding your own personal networks is perhaps one of the greatest tools that an Innovation Judo practitioner can master. The development of this network is like adding two or three other kids to your side of the teeter-totter to improve the balance of power.

THE "KCI KID"

KCI, headquartered in San Antonio, Texas, makes a life-saving product called V.A.C. This piece of equipment saves lives every day from Iraq to your hometown hospital. It is a wound healing device consisting of a special dressing encased in a vacuum system that literally pumps air out of a wound because without oxygen wounds heal faster with less chance of infection. V.A.C. also works on horrible wounds like burns or stomach injuries that might be caused by an IED. After working with the Navy over the last couple of years, it is especially meaningful for me to have had KCI as a client because I see some of those men and women who have been saved or healed faster using KCI's medical devices.

My partner and I had worked with KCI's managers over several years to help train their employees given KCI's rapid growth and move into international markets. As we like to do in our programs with middle managers, we try to involve more senior leaders as guest speakers in these programs. It not only gives participants extra motivation to be in these programs because they know higher-ups pay attention to them, it also helps the senior executives become more familiar with the program and meet some of the people who might eventually work for them or perhaps even succeed them.

So, I ask for senior leaders to come in who can speak about one or more of the topics in our general management curriculum. Most are pretty easy. We get the CEO, the head of finance, and of course the VP from sales and marketing. In one of the iterations of the program, we introduced a new module on coaching at the company's request, but since coaching is not an organizational division, it was not easy to identify a subject matter expert.

As we were asking managers at KCI who might be appropriate, the head of HR said that KCI had just hired a new young VP from Johnson & Johnson (J&J) who might be able to help since J&J is known for its coaching and talent development. So we asked Kien Nguyen,* the new VP for global research, to come speak about this topic. Frankly, I was a little worried as Kien was new. He didn't know me and I didn't know him; since he was so new, most of the class would be meeting him for the first time as well.

But, I figured with a J&J background, he would probably be okay.

---

* Kien is now the president of SomnoMed, a dental/medical supplies company.

What a surprise.

Kien was born in Vietnam and came to the United States with his mother when he was nine years old, not speaking any English. They had very little money and had to go on welfare for a while until they were able to establish a successful Vietnamese restaurant in northern Texas. Despite their initially poor economic status, Kien was encouraged to go to school, and he eventually wound up getting his PhD in physiology and later an MBA to help him understand how to go from working behind the scientist's desk to working behind the executive's.

Kien arrived in class at the appointed time and he looked much younger to me than his experience belied, but I figured coaching is coaching. I expected him to roll out the typical mantras of good coaching:

- Coaching should be learner centered.
- Practice active listening.
- Don't advise but help the person make his or her own decisions.
- Make sure the discussion sticks to a coaching one, not a performance appraisal one.

And Kien did present a brief PowerPoint presentation talking about good coaching practices. But then he told a story about his first boss at J&J who was the best coach Kien had ever had. When Kien first joined J&J as an assistant product manager, he was like a fish out of water. He was moving from an academic, behind-the-bench environment where he often worked alone to a large, complex, complicated, rapidly moving, results-focused organization where getting big things done could only be accomplished by working with others in the organization, many of whom he did not control.

His boss insisted that they meet once a week. In one of the first meetings, Kien noticed that his boss had a single piece of paper in front of him with some names on it. At a very memorable point in their conversation, the boss slowly turned the paper around so that Kien could finally read what was written. His boss then ordered Kien to remember these names and that his first important job assignment would be to systematically meet each of these people. He was to introduce himself to each person, try to get to know them, and ask for advice and help from each one. And the boss said he would follow up to make sure that Kien was completing this task.

I was totally stunned. I had never heard of a coaching story like this. Kien's boss had given him a list of the key movers and shakers who Kien would have to befriend if he was going to succeed. In fact, Kien's boss had given him the organization's informal network on a silver platter. This informal network is the one that most of us don't figure out until we are well into our jobs, and sometimes we never figure it out and this lack of understanding of who the power players really are can hurt us.

What a gift! In my career I have never had anyone do this for me. Of course we can try to figure it out for ourselves if we are adept enough and if we have enough time, but Kien's path to success was accelerated tremendously by his boss's assignment. Not exactly the kind of coaching story that I had expected, but one of the best I have heard. Kien's peers who did not have such a coach were at an obvious disadvantage.

It is now clear to me that Kien's boss, and now Kien, both practice this approach to coaching and while they refer to it as coaching, I much prefer to think of it as creating, identifying, and developing potential leverage points. The boss made this list of names from his own experience working at J&J. He knew the people who could block and those who could help, and these people were in different parts and different levels at J&J. The names weren't on any formal emailing list nor was their importance belied by their positions the formal organizational chart. But they were the people who would ultimately affect Kien's success or failure.

Kien spent a great deal of his time meeting with these people, asking them about themselves and for advice. And he was both consistent and persistent. He was then able to use these people and the leverage these relationships gave him to get things done that others could not. For a new employee this kind of leverage is incredibly powerful. It got Kien invaluable advice on how to operate in J&J, and it also gave him leverage with others outside of his realm of control because they knew he was connected. Without this kind of leverage, Kien's days at J&J would have been numbered. Like every good Innovation Judo master, Kien's boss shared his skills with his student who would never forget the lesson and choose to pass it on.

Kien's story is important because it talks about one form of *leverage* that you can use to help you step up, stand out, and stay alive in today's sometimes pretty scary corporate environment. If we are lucky we might actually have a sensei (teacher) who can teach us these things, but most of us have to build our own networks, which takes concentrated time and effort.

Have you ever had a boss who hands you the informal network lever on a silver platter? Most of us in new jobs struggle to get to know the formal structure let alone worry about the informal one. But the informal network often offsets the power in the formal network and can work to great advantage when needed. This network is the one needed to turn bureaucratic nos into yesses despite your opponent's formal power.

My work in the Navy and other branches of the military and governmental offices in general clearly demonstrates the power and necessity of this lever. The military has so many rules and regulations about how you are allowed to both acquire and dispense money that it literally has to train people for years to be able to make the systems and processes work. And with its obligatory relations with the federal government, it is also complex. It literally took me three months on the job as the innovation chair in the business school before I was able to get paid. I had to go through a paperless (supposedly less wasteful and efficient) computer program in order to send in my invoices. The program was very user-unfriendly. Changes and corrections were difficult to make, and after an hour I might have to start all over again. When finished filling in and maneuvering through an assortment of pages and codes, I finally got to the "click to submit" button. The invoice was sent instantly, and an email was generated within seconds to confirm my submission to the appropriate government contracting office.

Then I would get an email back saying "rejected." No one called to say why it was rejected, just that it was. When I finally got hold of someone who should be able to tell me what the problem was, their help was not only not helpful but also condescending. Then for each mistake I would make on the invoice, I would be directed by a faceless bureaucrat to a bulletin or pamphlet that gave me the information I needed to correct that specific issue. I always thought it would have been nice of these folks to give me this stuff up front so I could have done it right the first time.

What I desperately needed was someone like Kien's boss at J&J to point out those dots of light on the organizational chart that could have told me how to get to the right person the first time.

Identifying and getting to the right network fast is critical to the innovator. Commander Joanna Nunnan is a former leader of the Coast Guard's five-year-old Innovation Council. The Coast Guard, now under Homeland Security, has taken on a key role in the defense of our borders and in disaster relief. After Hurricane Katrina, the Coast Guard was responsible for saving over 33,000 lives. As with all U.S. military and governmental agencies, they too have bureaucratic challenges especially dealing with the government's myriad of policies, procedures, and rules, and its own hierarchy.

While Joanna's title was manager of the Innovation Council, her title should have been innovation broker. As she walked the halls of the Coast Guard headquarters in Washington, D.C., it appeared that almost everyone seemed to know her, waving and smiling as she passed by. It is no wonder that she has such an extensive network and puts it to good use in helping to bring new ideas into the organization. The Innovation Council's job is to surface, vet, and implement good ideas coming from anywhere in the organization. Joanna actively pursues people who have ideas and tries to help them implement these ideas within the organization. Chris Kluckhuhn, whom I have mentioned previously, was very much like Joanna in his ability to identify, develop, and utilize an extensive network for his innovation initiatives. And the people in this network were not only higher-ups but folks outside the Coast Guard as well. As you will see, this network helped Chris succeed even when the odds were stacked against him.

Dote on Quotes

You have all heard the term *self-incriminating evidence*. I was recently pulled aside by one of my executive students who had been given the task of innovating by his boss. He came to me for counsel because his boss said he wants innovation but doesn't really walk the talk. I gave him several Innovation Judo suggestions, and the one he found the most effective was actually quoting his boss's quotes. This kind of boss is actually a blockhead either intentionally or unintentionally. Because all people have egos, it is very difficult to deny publicly that you didn't mean what you said. Thus, if the boss uses the term *innovation* frequently even if he or she doesn't practice this value, you as an Innovation Judo expert can still get leverage by quoting them frequently in their presence.

It is a good idea to record these quotes and date them. This allows you to say, "I remember two weeks ago in our meeting on X, that you said innovation has to be one of our key priorities. And then you mentioned it again yesterday and as a consequence of your interest I wanted to bring this opportunity up to you for further actions." Notice that this is not done in an "I gotcha" manner, but smoothly integrates his words with your actions thus making it very difficult for him or her to say, "I was only kidding about innovation."

PRINCIPLE 3: CIRCLING

Circling in the martial arts form of Judo is one of the first things I learned in my college class. If both participants just stood still holding on to each other's lapels it would not only look pretty silly, nothing would happen. Circling allows you to assess the other's balance, foot movements, strength, and defenses while simultaneously trying to create an opening for the execution of different moves. They, of course, are doing the same thing to you and that is what makes the sport fun. Circling also keeps both of you moving so that you can try to redirect your opponent's energies to work against him. It isn't just about technique. For example, one of my favorite moves was to get my opponent moving in a circle and just when he was about to put his foot down on the mat, I would kick it out from under him. He would immediately lose his balance and fall to the ground. Point for me.

Circling is a *setup* principle. It does not defeat the opponent directly, but it allows you to observe them from many different angles so that you can exploit or create opportunities to neutralize their attempts to neutralize you. Circling also allows you to see small openings in the opponent's defenses, giving you just enough room to either create or walk through an *opening*. When faced with obstacles, especially if they are in the form of nonsensical or wacky rules, seams can often be found in the spaces between rules. Several of the Innovation Judo masters that you will read about were excellent at identifying seams between rules. This, or course, necessitates that you know the rules as well and often better than the rule makers or enforcers so that you can move your ideas through these seams.

Remember earlier on I mentioned an Innovation Judo master who worked at ADT who told me that one of his secrets to surviving as an innovator was to make sure that when the door was slammed in his face he offered a different part of his body for the door to slam into next time. In other words, he would come at his detractors from a different angle. Circling allows you to take a different angle of attack when either blockheads or roadblocks are in the way. Circling also gives you the opportunity to take a detour when the pathway to creativity becomes impassable. So here is how you can use circling to your advantage.

Walk Around Your Opponents

In addition to my role as Founder and CEO of IMSTRAT LLC, I am still associated with Babson College as a Professor Emeritus. Every year, Babson honors well-known entrepreneurs in what we call Founders Day to celebrate the founding of the college by Roger Babson, an innovator and entrepreneur in his own right. We invite two to three well-known entrepreneurs to come to the college, speak with our students, and share their insights on starting a business. Since entrepreneurship always involves innovation, they are by definition innovators as well as entrepreneurs.

In my experience a number of the folks who have come, such as Richard Branson from Virgin, or Barry Gordy from Motown, or Sherry Lansing from Paramount, and Magic Johnson have what I call a "strong ego sense." This means that they have a pretty high opinion of their opinions and not afraid to let other people know them. They are extremely self-assured but don't seem to ever cross the line into arrogance. And clearly their opinions have merit or they probably would not have created multimillion and even billion-dollar businesses. They typically don't suffer fools well, and they can easily run over people who don't share their vision and passion for their ideas.

They also typically possess another trait you often find in start-up entrepreneurs, which I refer to as a chip on their shoulder. As children, they probably liked their parents to say no, just so they could prove them wrong. This chip on the shoulder is an interesting and functional trait for entrepreneurs because it actually energizes them when people tell them their idea won't work or that it's stupid.

Instead of being depressed, they rub their hands together and say to themselves, "Yeah, just watch me." This trait is also highly important for corporate innovators, but it has to be leavened with the understanding that trying to bully your idea through because you love it and because you believe you are right can work pretty well for start-up entrepreneurs but can kill a corporate innovator. Don't be a "Bully Mitchell." I jokingly refer to him as "Bully Mitchell" because of the bull in the china shop attitude he took with his critics, many of whom were in government positions who could and eventually did end his employment.

When you identify a roadblock or blockhead standing in front of your idea, the worst thing you can do is try to run over it head-on. And never say aloud, "You just watch me do this anyway despite your misgivings." "I'll do it whether you like it or not." Start-up entrepreneurs can say this to venture capitalists because there is always another one they can approach. But in-company innovators have to be much more careful especially if you want to keep your job. I do know of some corporate innovators who did take their ideas to a competitor when their own company did not say yes, but this is probably a last-resort move as the new company may suspect your loyalty to them as well.

In Judo, you never rush your opponent head-on. If you do, you will be like I was with the frat boy, and allow your opponent to use your own bull rush against you. So step back when you hear an irrational no or run into a wacky factor. Walk around the barrier and see if there isn't another angle of attack you can take that is more likely to succeed. When Chris Kluckhuhn was told that there was no money to pursue one of the ideas that he presented to the Coast Guard's Innovation Council, he took another angle of attack and went after funding from folks outside the Coast Guard, both of whom were interested enough in his idea to pony up the necessary seed capital.

Chris realized that no amount of complaining, handwringing, begging, or top cover was going to get him the money. So he took a very different angle of attack that led to a positive outcome.

Walk Around Your Idea

One of the most difficult things for an innovator to do is see his or her idea as others do. It is a little bit like people who never leave their homeland. They have a very insular perspective, and it is only through traveling to other countries that you are able to see your country from a different angle. I have done a lot of traveling in my life, and I can tell you that I am a very different person for having done so. I appreciate the United States even more because I have been in many countries where freedom of speech is a rarity and quite dangerous for citizens to practice. But I have also seen more clearly why others see us quite differently than we see ourselves. I talked earlier about the danger of loving your idea to death, and one of the best ways to avoid this is to walk around your idea and see it through other people's eyes. They will spot flaws that you will never see, and they may see a different side to your idea that could make it even better. One of the things I suggest to innovators to help them keep their ideas alive is to unbalance, surprise, and redirect detractors by pointing out the risks of your idea before they do and showing that you have already developed risk mitigation strategies. Never be Pollyannaish about your idea, it only makes critics even more suspicious. I am always hypervigilant when I see an idea put forward with a hockey stick projection with no risk assessment or mitigation. It is a red flag that the innovator has not gone through the opportunity process.

Never be afraid to invite criticism, and don't be defensive when you hear it. Perhaps one of the greatest arguments for diversity involves innovation. Innovators need a team of people who share passion for their idea, but they also need a diverse team who will see the idea differently based on their unique and diverse perspectives. Edison knew the importance of having others with different lenses circling his ideas. His small innovation team had among its members a mechanical assistant from England, a German glass blower, and a Swiss clockmaker. It was no accident that Edison chose these people as it gave him the diversity that innovators need to help them turn their ideas into an opportunity.

You might not always like hearing what others have to say about your idea especially if they are negative, but it doesn't mean that you should give up. This kind of feedback is critical for opportunity shaping. And you will quickly sort out the constructive critic from the blockhead as the constructive critic usually gives you suggestions for shaping your idea versus dumping it out with the bathwater.

In many of my executive courses, I ask would-be innovators to bring an innovative idea with them to class. This is great experience because on average they get to see their idea through the lenses of about twenty other people, most of whom have no axe to grind. Remember in the IDEO video I mentioned earlier, the folks at IDEO walked around their shopping cart idea by going and visiting the maker of carts, the users, the store owners, and the repairers. This is about as close to a 360-degree circle as you can get. And some of their best suggestions came from these people.

Circle the Wagons

Lone innovators rarely make it. Venture capitalists rarely bet on an individual, but they will bet on a team. So it is extremely important that you surround yourself with at least two to three other people who have the same passion as you do for your idea. This is important for a couple of reasons. First, if you can't find two or three other people who have passion for your idea then you probably don't have a very good idea. Second, these people will help you shape and reshape the idea and are unlikely to give up on it. Third, they can watch your back. In the pioneer days, circling your wagons was great advice. It gave the settlers some protection from bullets and arrows and helped keep the enemy from outflanking you and getting to your vulnerable backside.

There are times when the innovator needs to circle the wagons. According to research on group dynamics, a truly passionate team of two can steer a group of five in their direction.[2] There is safety in numbers, and the more people you can get to support your idea in the organization, the more likely you are to have defenders from blockheads and sage advice for dealing with

---

[2] ABWE, *Teamwork: Group Dynamics*, accessed June 13, 2013, http://docs.abwe.org/CEIM/fps/Teamwork-Group-Dynamics.pdf.

roadblocks. And if your team consists of higher level bosses or customers, then you have even more protection.

John, one of my Innovation Judo masters in a large technology firm, was having trouble getting his idea accepted by upper management even though he had some stalwart supporters at his level. But the tide turned tremendously when he brought his boss out to a customer who asked, "How's that idea that John was working on in your company going? We're very interested to see if it is an application that we can use." John made the customer his ally, and the customer not only provided leverage, he also become part of John's extended innovation team and provided John with a pretty good circle of wagons. Most of us do not think of customers as part of the innovation team, but they can really add value when it comes to circling the wagons and giving you greater credibility for your idea within the organization.

There are also internal customers, although often not as powerful as the external customer, who can help as well. Most large organizations, even in the Land of Oz, have some degree of silo formation. Tony Palmer, CMO (chief marketing officer at the time) at Kimberly-Clark, worked very closely with Pete Dulcamara, head of R&E (Research and Engineering) at Kimberly-Clark, so that they could share perspectives. Kimberly-Clark's marketers visit the marketplace, working with customers to identify unsatisfied needs, while Pete and his team are trying to create products that customers may not even know they want. But because the two men are leaders and want innovation to succeed, they now train these two departments together, teaching joint courses about innovation through their Global Marketing University around the world. So now these two groups no longer complain about NIH and can proudly say, "Invented together."

PRINCIPLE 4: OPENING

In Judo, combatants continually look for or try to create openings. Openings are those little windows of weakness or spaces of opportunity that the Judo master can use to move in on his or her opponent. For example, I mentioned earlier that we hold on to each other's lapels when we are in a match and we pull on each other trying to develop an advantage. To do a hip throw properly you have to get your back lined up to touch your opponent's chest. If I cross my arms in front of my body, the opponent can't get in. But when we hold on to each other's lapels, we are both vulnerable to being moved in on but are also in a position to move in on the other person. You have to wait for the right moment to make a move: when the opponent's front side is unprotected and arms are wide apart. Once your body is past your opponent's forearms, that person can't stop you from at least getting in close enough to make the throw.

To exploit openings, you need to observe, move your opponent around, and then strike fast when you spot that opening. One of the test items on the WAIS (Wechsler Adult Intelligence Scale) asks people what the phrase "Strike while the iron is hot" means. Hopefully, most people know that this means to take advantage of an opportunity that won't be there when the iron gets cold. This little bit of wisdom is extremely sage advice for the corporate innovator especially when facing an uphill battle. So how to do you create and exploit openings long enough for you do get your idea to the next stage if you are faced with opposition?

Working with Blockheads
HOT BUTTONS: OPPORTUNITIES FOR DISARMING

I am a pretty savvy reader of people. Some of this skill is inherent in me and some of it I learned from years of being a psychologist. My wife sometimes accuses me, and rightfully so, of occasionally liking to push people's hot buttons just for sport. She is partly right, but I usually do this to make a point and sometimes create some insight in a person who is irritating me. For example, a few years ago, we moved to a new town and joined a newcomers club, which is a great way to start meeting people and developing new friendships. We would go to dinner parties once a month at different couples' homes and then eventually we would host the group at our house. For the most part we met terrific people, but every once in a while we would meet someone who had some irritating traits.

It was customary to bring some kind of dish to the host couple's house, to round out the dinner menu. One night when we were receiving our guests, a woman rushed by demanding to know where our kitchen was. We showed her and she proceeded to hand her dish to my wife and told her that she had to put it in the oven at 450 degrees and keep there for exactly twenty minutes, no more, no less. Well, she immediately irritated me by her brusque attitude so I said, "I'm sorry, but we have a problem." She looked agitated and said, "What's the problem?" I told her that we were renting the house and that there was a problem with the stove. It would only cook at 440 and 460 but not at 450, and I said it with a serious face. I pushed her control freak hot button and stood back for the predictable reaction. She became red-faced and flustered, and exclaimed that now her dish would be ruined. That, of course, took the arrogant wind out of her sails and she was pretty silent for the rest of the evening.

Now I know that in telling this story I risk being seen as toying with someone's emotions, and I admit I'm guilty, but in this particular case, she also deserved it. I knew that within a very few moments of meeting this woman that she was a control freak. I could have played to her need to control, but in this social situation it was my house not hers, and I felt some justification in using this knowledge of her character trait to deflate her.

Every person has hot buttons that you can utilize to create openings. In my story I pushed the hot button to close her off because I was annoyed with her ordering me and my wife around in our kitchen, but I could just have easily appeased her up by saying I understand how important it is to get the temperature just right, and asked her how long it should be preheated, and what shelf it should be on, and even offer to put in the thermometer to make sure that the dish was cooked evenly. In this case, I would be not only recognizing her hot button, I would have used it to try to make her a "friend." But it was my house and my party and I was more interested in trying to teach her a lesson. Not all hot buttons could or should be pushed unless you need them, and only in the spirit of right-mindedness.

I like listening to experts in the area of negotiations because expert negotiators are trained in identifying hot buttons. I often listen to an individual who not only does hostage negotiations, he also does negotiations for governments and warring factions. He admonishes his audiences to go beyond what a person says they want to understanding what they need. You will often find people who are against your idea for seemingly irrational reasons. When Billy Mitchell railed against his bosses for not understanding and accepting the inevitable superiority the airplanes would have over Naval ships, he was shot down, because the Navy was afraid that it would become irrelevant. The Navy needed reassurance not abrasive criticism. Billy might have been better advised to talk about how the Navy could control the airplanes and could have their own Naval air force. And, of course, this is what actually happened. If Billy had really paid attention to the Navy's hot button and underlying need to remain important and viable and had integrated this kind of dialogue into his scheme, the Navy might have played nicer with him.

John Kilcullen knew that Bill Murphy had a good sense of humor and was against his idea of Dummies on seemingly logical grounds. So John used Bill's humor button and competitive nature to create a little seam in Bill's armor just wide enough to give his Dummies idea a chance.

Human Hot Buttons

These kinds of buttons are always based on some "need" that is based on emotion. And when a rational approach doesn't work with a blockhead, you may find an emotional approach a more viable option. You can see some common examples of the need-emotion relationship in the following.

Human Hot Buttons

Need	Emotion
To be in control	Fear of losing control
To be important	Feel good about oneself
To be liked	Feel accepted
To win	To feel superior
To create	To feel self-satisfaction
To give to others	To feel unselfish
To say no	To feel powerful
To feel safe	Fear of risk-taking

Blockheads are not always malleable, but if you can understand their needs, then you can often use these needs to your advantage to create an opening for your idea to move forward. For example, pilot studies allow people who are risk averse to feel safer in that they do not have to commit to something entirely. Pilot studies also give blockheads who fear losing control more control because they can pull the plug or change things if the pilot is not going well. Having people help shape your opportunity if it is clearly hooked to corporate strategy can engage the need for both self-control and power, and even creativity.

As you can see, fear is often behind a blockhead's irrational resistance to innovation. This fear is irrational because it is based on emotion rather than logic. When introduced to change, most people are afraid of four things:

1. Loss of job
2. Loss of competency
3. Loss of informal network
4. Loss of face

Clearly, innovation can cause *job loss*. Machines are doing more and more of what humans do. Just look at our UAVs (unmanned aerial vehicles) or drones that are doing a lot of the work in the wars in Afghanistan and Iraq. These unmanned aircraft are being flown remotely by twenty-year-olds stationed in the United States. It is not lost on fighter pilots that at some point in the future, we may not need manned aircraft flying off of aircraft carriers. In fact some of these smaller UAVs are now being launched by SEALS out of their backpacks. While pilots may lose their jobs, there will be more workers needed to build these drones and to maintain them. So there may not be a net job loss, but that doesn't matter to the pilot.

Loss of *competency* happens when we ask people to work in new ways that they are not used to. The sailor who loads powder and fires the deck gun will have to learn new skills for the rail gun. There are always mistakes made when learning, and thus, there is predictable loss of competency in the early phase of an innovation's implementation.

Most of us rely on the organization's informal network to get things done. We don't learn this right away unless we have a boss like the KCI kid had at J&J. Innovation often causes changes in the organization's structure and thus a change in both the *formal* and *informal* networks. The Navy now has a very cool new ship called the LCS (littoral combat ship). *Littoral* means "shallow water." The ship only has a draft of 17 feet, and can go 40 knots (50 mph) over water. Look out, pirate ships. But even cooler is the fact that the ship is sort of a LEGO ship. It is configured in modules that can be changed in and out, thus creating a different ship with a different mission without spending a lot of money. A plug-and-play concept if you will. Forty percent of the crew will operate the ship from shore through remote electronics. This ship will require significantly different manning, training, and equipping, thus creating changes in Navy structures, processes, and command and control. So it is no wonder that others don't embrace our innovative ideas as much as we would like them to.

Some blockheads don't have hot buttons that you can use or find. In such cases, you will have to rely on some other Innovation Judo principle. For example, Walt Pullar, whom you met at the very beginning of this book, was a Navy SEAL for twenty-seven years until he retired a few years ago to start his own business. Walt faced a few higher level commanders in his career who were risk averse, and because Walt often had to move quickly, especially in crisis situations, he could not wait for all his bosses to push his requests up the chain of command. Some of you know how frustrating it can be to try to get a decision inside a hierarchical bureaucracy. Walt was brilliant at taking the risk-aversion need of his boss and making this fear an asset. He would make sure that he was on firm ground to make the decision himself (you will see that he often knew the rules better than his boss) and used speed to get things done, often making any reversal of his decision by his bosses very difficult. But as Walt will tell you, you can't do this too often, only for the really important things or you could become a Billy Mitchell.

Roadblocks

ORGANIZATIONAL HOT BUTTONS

No matter what innovation landscape you find yourself in, it is always wise to hook your innovation to one or more of these organizational hot buttons. This can create an instantaneous opening as well as give you leverage, because you are wired into an important *organizational need*. Organizational hot buttons are almost always linked to some numerical performance indicator. If there are no numbers associated with this indicator then it is probably not that important. It makes no difference whether we are talking about public or private sector organizations. They both have to manage to some sort of metric from return on investment or stock price in the private sector or budgets and polls in the public sector. If you can figure out what metrics are currently hot, then it is best to translate your innovation into one or more of these metrics to give you a chance to get your idea heard with greater attention and immediacy.

COST CUTTING/COST CONTAINMENT

Most organizations I have dealt with in the last eight years are pursuing some kind of cost-cutting or cost-containment initiative. And this means that they have to do more with less. Most people complain about the lack of resources, but I am actually a fan of keeping this kind of pressure in an organization. Without pressure, innovation does not happen. We are only moving into hybrid and electric cars because of the cost of fuel and the uncertainty in the Middle East. John Kilcullen would not have come up with his idea for Dummies until he was down to his last $200,000 from a $1.5 million stake, and dry cleaning would not have been invented had a husband not been afraid of his wife's wrath for spilling red wine on her white evening gown. Some sort of pressure is requisite for innovation to happen. General Langley was given $100,000 to invent the first airplane, and when the Wright Brothers beat him to it with almost nothing in the way of assets save for their bicycle shop, he complained to his bosses that if he only had more money then he would have beaten them to it. Necessity is always the mother of invention.

In the *leverage* principle section, I talked about the importance of aligning any innovative idea to the organization's strategy if not directly, at least tangentially. Since cost cutting is so ubiquitous in today's business environment, you should align your opportunity with the company's cost-cutting measures in addition to the potential revenue generation side of the financial equation. In wacky organizations, there is often a lot of nonsensical activities going on that don't add value. In my last book I talked about the 5C's virus that often infects an organization. This is checkers, checking checkers, checking checkers syndrome.

We are all aware of the damage that IEDs (improvised explosive devices) have done to our young men and women in the armed services especially those caused by explosives set to go off under our Hummer trucks. We finally created a much safer vehicle called the MRAP, which has a snowplow-shaped undercarriage that redirects and reflects the energy from one of these IEDs away from the vehicle and its participants. But it was taking us too long to build them and ship them overseas due to the manufacturer's capacity and the ability of the government's procurement system to act at the speed of combat. So eventually we created a new fast-track way to get these vehicles ordered, built, and shipped to the front lines. Pressure forced the military to create a newer, more effective process that wound up preventing thousands of injuries and deaths. Notice that this organizational innovation got great receptivity because it not only aligned with the military's strategy and mission in the Middle East, it also saved lives, one of the most important and embedded values of all the American military people I have ever met.

We often think about innovation as requiring an investment, yet oftentimes innovation involves a rearrangement of what is already there that results in less costs. This is especially true when it comes to organizational innovation as opposed to S&T (science and technology). I am actually a fan of continuous cost cutting in both the private sector and the public because cost cutting creates pressure to do things better, cheaper, and faster with greater effect. Innovation is unlikely to occur without this cost-cutting pressure.

Most really good salespeople have either understood this connection innately or learned it along the way. In fact many companies train their salespeople to go beyond what the potential customer says he or she wants to what the customer really needs. This is particularly true if the salesperson meets resistance. Bad salespeople keep pushing their agenda, good salespeople are more interested in understanding the customer's agenda so that they can find that opening that connects what they need to what you need. The probability of a successful sale goes up dramatically when you can understand and meet or redirect the customer's needs.

Corporate innovators also need to be salespeople. You will need good selling skills to get your idea approved, but more importantly you have to make sure that your selling acumen does not overshadow your credibility. When you meet resistance to your ideas and you have to go to people's hot buttons, you will always have to do so with right-mindedness. I once worked with a saleswoman in the executive education business. She was very well trained in the steps of selling, but customers always found her lacking in credibility because they felt that she wasn't really listening to them. Potential customers felt that she was just following the company's salesperson manual, going through the motions, like asking the terribly overused question, "What keeps you up at night?" Not personalizing her sales pitch would probably always generate the same answer from her clients, "You keep me up at night, when I think you are going to be visiting my office with the same old line."

If we cycle back to Galileo, it is clear that the pope had an incredibly strong need to keep himself in power and the earth to be the center of the universe. When faced with Galileo's data, fear took over and the pope could not handle the reinvention of his presumed world. Behind most innovation resistors, there is an element of fear.

EFFICIENCY/EFFECTIVENESS

In today's competitive, resource-constrained environment, innovation that is clearly aligned with both efficiency and effectiveness is just as likely to get approved as are innovative products and services. I tell my students that we often think of innovation in terms of products and services, but organizational innovations that help the company do things better (effectiveness), faster (more efficiently), and cheaper with fewer assets are music to the executive's ears. Lean Six Sigma is now becoming more of a destination than a toolkit, but the toolkit, when used properly can create both effectiveness and efficiency. It is generally more effective in finding cost savings and efficiencies in business than in innovation, but because so many organizations are using it, it is smart to align your idea with it. The purpose behind Lean Six Sigma is to utilize highly trained teams to identify and remove both costs and errors in the company's business processes from manufacturing to customer service.

One of my clients was trying to get an innovation off the ground in her business, and after making little headway, she talked the company's Lean Six Sigma guru into taking it under his auspices since identifying inefficiencies and errors can often identify new business opportunities for those with a keen eye. Once this group was aligned with the company's Lean movement, the idea was implemented.

BRAND ENHANCEMENT

Another way to get traction for your idea if it is facing roadblocks is to align it to brand enhancement especially if your organization has a strong brand identity. Steve Paljieg's creation of the Kimberly-Clark mompreneurs website did not face a lot of roadblocks because it was seen as directly enhancing the company's ability to reach its current and future customers, and because the brand was trusted so much mom entrepreneurs were not afraid of the their ideas being stolen. Keep in mind that this does not always work. More than a few people at IDG thought John Kilcullen's Dummies idea would actually hurt the brand so John was better off aligning his idea with new business development and revenue generation.

WHEN NUMBERS TALK, ROADBLOCKS WALK

One of the mistakes that corporate innovators often make in their pitches to stakeholders is that they start with their idea, their rationale, and their analysis, and then only at the end do they bring out the numbers. Start with the numbers and the value proposition first if you anticipate organizational roadblocks. I talked early about "a compelling value proposition," and corporate innovators should start with them. When your idea has truthful and compelling numbers attached to it, you are much more likely to see roadblocks weaken. Numbers talk louder within the public and private sectors these days, and starting with the value proposition is much more likely to be the opening you need to garner the attention that will get your idea moving forward.

The language of for-profit organizations is clearly finance. Innovators won't get very far up the chain of command without developing a fair amount of literacy in this language. And you have to ensure the company that your idea is an opportunity that creates financial value for the company. As I told you earlier, every opportunity must have a value proposition, and in the private sector this means money in some form for the organization that will be potentially derived from your idea. If you can't predict, within some margin of error, the economic value your idea will create, then you only have an idea not an opportunity. Aligning your idea with revenue generation is clearly a must. Brands have a value on the accountant's balance sheet so even brand enhancement can be boiled down to creating economic value. "Show me the money" was as true for Jerry Maguire as it is for the innovator.

The Red Sea of roadblocks can part very quickly when executives see an innovation that can help raise the company's stock, which is not surprising given that so many senior-level executive pay rises are directly related to it. This book was not intended to be a primer on organizational levers that affect stock price but if you just Google "Company factors affecting stock price," you will find a wealth of information that might help you align your idea with financial information that will benefit the company and you as an Innovation Judo master.

Numbers are also effective "openers" in the public sector as well. There are two number items that are most relevant in the public sector today: reducing costs and managing assets more efficiently. I currently spent a lot of time on the Monterey Peninsula because of my work at NPS. We have lots of small towns in this area, and every one of them has a separate fire and police department. One great idea recently arose regarding the possibility of merging these small-town fire and police departments under one regional organization. Why have all these small-town police chiefs and fire chiefs, and why duplicate assets across all these communities? In addition, this consolidation could create greater coordination and communication among these townships, which would be especially helpful when fighting California's huge forest fire problem.

DON'T BE FRIGHTENED, IT'S JUST A PILOT

Another extremely important way to create an opening is to utilize a "pilot project" or "trial" approach that I talked about earlier. Pilots are very useful in Asylums and Jungles where trying something new or radical is often met with a no since it is so hard to bring about change in these landscapes that want to preserve the status quo. But small experiments, pilot programs, and trials are using the word *lecturette* instead of *lecture*. *Lecturette*, which I often use to describe one of my upcoming lectures, doesn't seem to scare students as much as the word *lecture*. It sounds lighter, more fun, less deadly, and certainly less permanent. Although the event may still be a lecture, it is often received more positively simply because of my word choice.

Pilots by their very nature are less expensive than implementing the full idea. What a pilot does is create an opening for the development of greater leverage. If you get positive results, the fulcrum under the teeter-totter begins to change position, reducing the naysayer's risk. Risk taking in large established organizations is not necessarily a coveted attribute. Most companies say they want risk taking when what they really want is risk management. Pilots are a great risk management tool. In my field, entrepreneurship, we often say, "Pay a little, learn a lot." This is what venture capitalists do when they give entrepreneurs seed capital. The term *seed* is perfect. Give the idea a little "water" to see if the seed will start to germinate.

If you are contemplating some sort of large-scale change or organizational transformation, pilots are a great way to overcome resistance to change. As of this writing, the United States is in a major maelstrom regarding changing health care. This change scares many people, because it came out of a binary decision making process; vote yes or no! In fact, there have been pushing and shoving matches in town halls because of the public outcry over the passing of this bill due to uncertainty and lack of clarity around what this all means to us in terms of personal impact.

Think about how innovators might have handled all this. First they would have asked, "Why risk it all on one major throw of the dice?" Wouldn't it be better to take a few pieces of the new plan and implement them, thus paying a little and learning a lot while simultaneously soothing the fears of millions who feel the changes will be irreversible and who aren't sure of the consequences of the new plan? It would be much better to take a group of hospitals and doctors and try a number of pilot programs to see what works and what doesn't work first. Even better, take four Democratic states and four Republican states and use them as laboratories. For example, allow them to create insurance competition across these states to see how it works. Or enact some changes in medical lawsuit caps and then assess the impact empirically. Healthcare pilots would have allowed us to have fact-based discussions instead of heated, emotionally driven opinion discussions.

This pilot strategy doesn't work if the ship is clearly sinking, in which case you do have to get everybody off now. But many organizational change initiatives or transformations have major opportunities to utilize the pilot strategy approach as leverage. And if one pilot fails, it doesn't mean the whole project is doomed. We can take what we learned from one pilot and do it differently in the next until we get it right. And as I said, pilots not only involve the development of leverage, they create a small, time- and resource-constrained opening to test-drive your idea. Innovation is always risky because it involves something new that is yet to be proven.

My nephew Scott is in the sales rep business and had lived in Cleveland most of his life. In the last couple of years, of course, cities like Cleveland have lost a lot of manufacturing jobs and were hard-hit by the latest recession. So Scott decided that he needed to look elsewhere for employment where the long-term prospects for job security and career growth were better. So he found a job in Florida that looked more promising and took it assuming his wife, teenage daughter, and younger sons would immediately see the logic behind this move and be overjoyed by the concept of moving to a warm climate. Now why anyone would want to stay in the Cleveland winters when they could move to Florida is beyond me, but the rest of the family disagreed with Scott's decision. The teenage daughter had a boyfriend, his wife had family in Cleveland, and of course the younger boys had their friends, so none of them wanted to move.

Scott finally called me to ask for advice as to how to overcome their resistance. I told him to call the move to Florida a pilot. They would go for a year and, if they did not like it, he promised to move back to Cleveland as part of the deal. This is not exactly what the family hoped for, but it was better than the thought of permanently moving, so they finally agreed. Well you can imagine what the situation was a year later. The daughter quickly found a new boyfriend and friends, the two younger boys enjoy playing baseball year-round, and Scott enjoys his hobby of fishing in much richer waters. They aren't coming back. His wife was the last to get on board with the move, but since the family seems happy, and Scott's happy with a better job, she has acquiesced to their change in lifestyle and has now landed a job that she enjoys.

The beauty of pilots is that they allow for rapid failure and fast learning while mitigating the risks. The problem with a capital budgeting mentality is that it puts upper management into a thumbs-up or thumbs-down decision-making mode. With pilots the thumb can be sideways since a commanding decision does not have to be made, and the consequences of failure are less. The Dummies example I spoke of earlier is why IDG is such a successful company. They gave John Kilcullen a little bit of money to see if his idea looked like an opportunity. If he could show that the Dummies concept was a real opportunity, they were willing to provide some more capital. If not, they were prepared to pull the plug with very little cost or risk to the company.

IDENTIFYING, CREATING, EXPLOITING SEAMS

Creating or exploiting seams in the organization's fabric provides a great way for innovators to move forward despite the obstacles, especially in hierarchical and heavily rule-bound, process-oriented organizations. Large hierarchical organizations present especially difficult challenges for the corporate innovator. These organizations are not only complex; they are also typically built around a strong command and control structure with many rules that often wear out or run out would-be innovators. I recently spoke with an exasperated government innovator who continued to have repeated unsuccessful jousts with government officials who would not take action on his great idea even though they agreed with its merits. First, none of them was willing to make the decision at their level. In addition, they would have to navigate a lot of rules and regulations in order to get his idea approved, and none of them wanted to take the time or effort to do so.

In my executive education talks and working with middle-level managers, I often hear them lament, "I can't be an innovator in my organization because it is so risk averse and you risk getting fired for bending the rules, let alone breaking them." This of course is certainly a good excuse for not innovating, and I have some sympathy for these comments because it is difficult to innovate in rule-bound organizations, but it is not impossible. Rules, of course, are necessary, and I would never suggest that an organization not have some rules, but unfortunately, oftentimes, well-intentioned guidelines become ill-intentioned rules that prevent innovation and rapid adaptation to change.

But, for the Innovation Judo master, rule-bound organizations also provide wonderful openings for innovators to get their ideas going because they are able to exploit the seams between rule one and rule two. Or, they are able to find one rule that negates another. Not only are there seams and inconsistencies in rules; there are often narrow but highly exploitable seams where one person's authority ends and the other's begins. So instead of bemoaning rules and regulations that you see as roadblocks, you might be able to find narrow pathways between or around the roadblocks that you can navigate to your advantage. To be good at finding these small openings, you will need to know the rules at least as well as, if not better than some adversaries.

Walt Pullar, who I mentioned in the beginning of the book, was an expert at finding and exploiting seams, but he would never describe himself as a rule breaker. However, one of his life-saving innovations required him to walk a fine line between his authority to implement this innovation and a counterpart's authority to stop it. Walt refused to back down, and so his counterpart decided to escalate this disagreement up the chain of command. Because Walt felt that he was on the right side of that fine line, he began to implement his innovation before the final decision. As you read more about Walt, you will see that he was able to exploit these authority seams in several critical situations throughout his career, but always with right-mindedness.

You can also use one rule to counter another rule. For example, a few years ago I bought a new state-of-the-art Motorola cell phone. It was the first cell phone to use a version of Microsoft Windows. Unfortunately, the phone had many bugs. The first phone got locked up after only two months. Since it was under warranty, AT&T sent me a new phone the next day. The new phone wouldn't even turn on. Clearly, there was more of a problem than either AT&T or Motorola anticipated. So I called AT&T customer service to complain and order a different kind of phone. Of course I got an unknowledgeable customer service representative who said that these new phones were recalled by Motorola and that she had no knowledge of when the problems would be fixed; she said it could be weeks or months.

So I asked her to send me a new phone, but not the Motorola version I had. She apologized and said that I would have to wait for the phone since I had a contract with AT&T for that particular phone. However, she did offer to send me a different phone—for more money. Not satisfied with this answer, I asked her to put me through to her supervisor. The supervisor gave me the same answer and an additional option. She said I could call the refurbishing department at AT&T and see if they had a refurbished Motorola that I could get. Although I thought it should be her job to make the call, I did call refurbishing. Refurbishing told me that they could not authorize any sale and that I would have to talk to customer service. I was now in a cycle of wackiness.

I know that many of you can sympathize with my situation and have dealt with this customer service black hole. Although I was irritated, I decided to see if I could outsmart them. I found out that one of AT&T's policies is a guaranteed return of a new phone within thirty days of purchase if you don't like it. So I called customer service at AT&T and told them that I would now buy a new phone from them every month and return it on the thirtieth day for a new phone until they sent me an upgrade for free. When I explained my plan to the customer service representative there was stunned silence. I could tell that her wheels were spinning. Finally, she said, "I guess that would be all right because it doesn't violate any policies." My plan must have had some effect as I received a new upgraded phone three days later. As you can tell from my story, I used one rule to negate another one. My knowledge of AT&T's return policy not only created an opening for me to get a different decision; it also gave me leverage and counterbalance—all elements of Innovation Judo.

PRINCIPLE 5: SPEED

The Need for Speed

Speed on the highway kills, but speed in martial arts and Innovation Judo is one of your best friends. When I was in my college Judo course, I was pretty hard to throw. I lifted weights so I was relatively strong compared to others in the class and I had the ability to get people on the mat and use grappling techniques to my advantage. But there was one kid in class who I could never beat. He was shorter than me and weighed thirty to forty pounds less, but he was fast. He would keep his body away from mine so I couldn't get a real good hold on him, and then like lightning he would break my defenses in a flash and over I would go. He had good technique, but his real advantage was his quickness. I have no idea whether he could run faster than me in a road race, but he was able to close the distance between us in a millisecond. Let's look at several ways in which speed can help you overcome roadblocks and blockheads.

Idea to Opportunity

In principle 1, *discipline*, I talked about the importance of following the opportunity process, but I did not mention speed. If you anticipate potential roadblocks and blockheads you will want to move the idea through to the opportunity phase very quickly. I have seen a number of good ideas derailed because the innovator took too long to determine whether the idea had enough opportunity characteristics to make it worth pursuing. It is critical that you get to a one- or two-sentence sound bite for your idea as soon as possible. First, this forces you to come to grips with what the core essence of your idea is and for whom. Without quick distillation, you risk having a very diluted and ill-conceived idea that both you and the listener will have trouble understanding and thus attending to. Make sure that you can write the value proposition down verbally and numerically:

V= B/C or Value equals benefits over costs.

To help you do this, use my opportunity template at the end of the book and make sure that the people for whom you are trying to create value (usually the potential customer—internal or external) give quick feedback so you can rapidly hone this value proposition. This sounds easy but it's not, and I would revise this value proposition until you can articulate the value you intend to create and for whom or you will remain unfocused and plodding.

I was on a panel of other entrepreneurs and innovators recently listening to innovators pitch their ideas to us. We can be pretty brutal as most of us have relatively short attention spans. With over 60 percent of the participants we had to work hard to get at the real essence of their ideas. All the presenters were good at giving us a thorough diagnosis of the problems or challenges they were trying to fix with their new ideas, but only a couple of people had developed a clear, crisp, memorable value proposition that told us the who, what, why, and how much. With one presenter, I turned to a fellow panelists and whispered, "Do you get it?" He shook his head and said, "No"; then he quietly queried the other three panelists, and apparently none of us got it. We could only conclude that the would-be innovator probably didn't get it either.

Fail Fast, Fail Often, Succeed Sooner

Earlier in the book, I talked about IDEO and *ABC News*'s challenge for the company to build an innovative shopping cart in just five days. IDEO's ability to have met this challenge successfully was dependent on their willingness to fail fast and often so that they could succeed sooner. They created lots of designs and mock-ups, many of which failed so that they could get to the successful design quicker. Thomas Edison was quoted as saying that his lightbulb didn't fail, he just found 1,000 ways it didn't work. These flash experiments as I like to call them are extremely important for innovators facing roadblocks and blockheads. Small failures don't frighten people as much as failures that come with making large decisions.

Suffice it to say, that IDEO would not be a global brand with offices around the world if it did not have a pretty good handle on what it takes to innovate. Note that the cart, even though

IDEO built a prototype, was a great new idea but was never taken through to the opportunity process to determine its potential as a commercial success. And that was not what the challenge was about. IDEO was only asked to innovate the shopping cart, not to commercialize it.

But in the video you see that one of the company's mottos is "Fail Fast, Fail Often, Succeed Early." Speed is the underlying theme of this motto, and Thomas Edison was known to utter similar advice. Innovators need to combine ideation with model building and experimentation to understand if they really have a good idea or a good opportunity. Real innovation always requires failure or the idea is probably not very innovative.

Failing early and fast often allows you to keep the risks small so that any one particular failure will not kill the idea and it allows you to shape your idea in ways that simply thinking about it or talking to customers about it can't do. And you are not innovating if you are not learning from these mistakes. I meet too many corporate innovators who want to bet the whole enchilada on one big trial, which is very dangerous. Can you imagine the United States building the whole space shuttle and then trying it out for the first time? There was lots of experimentation and testing before the first shuttle ever lifted off, and even then we clearly did not anticipate all the risks, but we mitigated a lot of them.

Be Quick to Reshape/Pull the Plug

While IDEO never tried to commercialize that shopping cart, it did take it out to a supermarket to get some feedback from the store owners and employees and to demonstrate to *ABC News* how the mock-up might work. The mock-up had a lot of innovations in it as part of the *investigation* phase of the 7I model.

Now IDEO never took this idea or the prototype any farther in terms of opportunity assessment. But at the end of the video, I ask my students if the shopping cart is a good idea or a good opportunity. About 70 percent of the class will say, "It's an opportunity." Actually, it's not. It certainly is innovation, but we then have to ask the opportunity questions:

1. Can we make it for a competitive price?

2. How many people will buy it for how long? (Durable)

3. How much margin do we need to cover the cost of development and make a profit? (Sustainable/Defensible/Value Creating)

4. Will store owners be willing to switch given their investment in current carts, and do they see the current carts as suboptimal, but "good enough"? (Value Creating)

The IDEO video was made over ten years ago, so I then ask those students who said the cart was an opportunity, have they seen any of these in supermarkets. Only a small minority of participants say they have seen perhaps one or two of these innovations commercialized. For example, some carts do have the four rotating wheels, but not everyone likes this concept especially if you have had the fun of pushing a luggage cart with these wheels down a ramp at Heathrow Airport. They make you look more like a drunken sailor than a world-class traveler.

If I were in charge of commercializing IDEO's prototype, I suspect I might have pulled the plug pretty early. I don't think this cart had strong opportunity characteristics. Now parts of this shopping cart design are catching on like the handheld scanners. I have seen these in stores in Europe and some in the United States. Perhaps this is more of an opportunity than the actual cart. This is the shaping process. Almost never does the original innovation appear in its initial form in the marketplace if due diligence is undertaken in the opportunity assessment process. If IDEO were to actually turn this into an opportunity, it should quickly take the employees' and store owners' feedback, redesign it, and then take it out to the people who would actually pay for it and ask them if and how much they would pay for such a cart. IDEO only asked for improvement suggestions, not purchasing intent. The sooner you can get your idea, or actually a prototype, out to the intended customer for feedback, the quicker you can either reshape the opportunity or pull the plug on it.

Just for fun, let's take this shopping cart challenge out to a large cart manufacturer, not to IDEO, and ask it to develop a prototype of an innovative design in five days. This would probably never happen in this time frame, and you can imagine a typical scenario: The design engineer would probably have to meet and schedule design work followed by fabrication, assuming he or she could get the head of engineering to agree to work on this project, which would probably have to be discussed in an executive-level committee where the marketing people would have to debate its merits and then go do some sort of rigorous and always expensive marketing analysis, and then the idea would have to be blessed by the CFO (chief financial officer) as worth investing in as opposed to some other opportunity. To be sure, this is the worst of all scenarios that I could paint, because it has *slow* painted all over it. But many organizations work this way, and since opportunities open and close quickly, you could see this idea arriving too little, too late, at too much cost.

Speed is essential for innovation. IDEO knows this as did Edison. Fail fast, fail often, learn quickly. Imagine for a second that marketers, engineers, customers, finance people, and production people all have to get behind an opportunity. Notice, I used *opportunity*, not *idea*. Some companies have built such innovation structures and processes and can collaboratively fail early, fail fast, and learn together. This type of approach enhances speed dramatically, assuming you can get these various folks to collaborate, which is whole different story.

Innovation Judo then becomes very important in slow landscapes. Shortcuts and workarounds are essential in these kinds of environments, and this is what Innovation Judo masters bring to the party.

If Jim Repp had stayed with the traditional Chrysler route at the time where he just suggested to marketing that they had a great opportunity to sell a mass-produced off-road Jeep (scenario one), the Rubicon would never have seen the light of day. As you will see, he tried this and was rebuffed. So he bypassed all this rigmarole, found a few passionate like-minded souls, built the Jeep in his garage, and took it into market testing at Jeep camps with no permission or sanctioning from the company. He was in need of speed and was unwilling to have his dream suffocate under the weight of bureaucracy and infighting.

If after going though the idea to opportunity process and deciding that your idea is not an opportunity, pull the plug! This is not always easy for innovators who love their ideas, and of course you don't want to pull the plug unless you have thoroughly gone through the opportunity evaluation process. But if not enough people care about your idea, for long enough, and are willing to pay you enough, move on to something else. There is one caveat to this advice, however. If your intuition tells you that you have an opportunity even though you can't prove it, you should get five other people to believe in it as passionately as you, or one paying customer. The best opportunity evaluation does not override the importance of the pocketbook.

Dash into an Opening

Whenever you can create or identify an opening to push your idea farther along the pathway to creativity, rush to and through it. Openings can open and close quickly, some may last for only a few seconds. Chris Kluckhuhn, my Coast Guard Innovation Judo master, was having trouble getting his life-saving situational awareness technology an objective and timely hearing. He needed a push from one or more senior admirals to help him move the idea along, but you don't just walk up to a lieutenant commander and say, "Hi, Admiral, have I got a great idea." You can set up a meeting, but you have to go through many aides who surround the typical admiral. If the idea is important enough, you may get an appointment, but you have to be careful that your immediate boss gives you the okay.

Chris attended the yearly Coast Guard expo where there was more than one chance to rub shoulders with Coast Guard admirals who would stroll through the booths to see what innovations people were working on. In these encounters, the aides are not around and you can make sure that your boss is having a coffee at Starbucks. Chris has a chance encounter with an admiral who was going down to the Hurricane Katrina site, so Chris, as a pilot, offered to give the admiral a ride in his plane instead of the admiral having to go commercially. Chris did this because he is a nice guy, but he also did it because he wanted to see if he could get this admiral to be an advocate for his idea. This invitation and acceptance only took seconds, but the payoff was huge. He put himself in a place where many openings could appear, and when he saw one, he went for it. But think of how many would-be innovators might be in that social situation and never look for nor take advantage of such an opening. Innovation Judo masters, especially if they need speed, do this instinctively.

Ask Forgiveness, Not Permission

Many of you have probably heard the old business school adage, "It's better to ask forgiveness than permission." While this is not always true and can get you in a lot of trouble if you break a law, acting instead of soliciting can be an incredibly important Innovation Judo move especially in complex and wacky organizations. Walt Pullar was able to save a life because he organized a SEAL rescue operation on the high seas, and he was not willing to wait for permission. He acted, found a seam in the decision-making process, and boldly moved ahead before the bureaucracy could stop him. Today, a man owes his life to Walt and his SEAL team because of speed, not just in tactical deployment, but because Walt did not ask permission twice. When he saw decision makers dragging their feet on his first inquiry, he did not wait to ask twice.

Knowing whom to ask is equally important. As a kid I learned pretty quickly which parent to solicit permission from and on what subject. Sometimes it was mom especially on the domestic side and dad on the adventure side. Mom was always afraid of us getting run over on our bikes, but dad was more permissive. So I would ask him, not my mother, if I could ride my bike up to the park, along some speedy highways. By the time my mother found out that I had been to the park, it was too late and then the argument was between them, not with me. A subcomponent of speed is knowing whom to ask for permission based on permissiveness. Also, having superiors fighting with each other about who has the right to make the call gives you time to get stuff done before their wrangling ends.

Embed Quickly

Officers in the Navy move to a new position about every eighteen to thirty-six months. This doesn't give them a lot of time in a complex organization to find their way to the restroom, let alone transform anything. This rapid rotation is great for training leaders but not so great for creating and sustaining any kind of organizational change. Then, likely as not, a new commander comes in wishing to make his or her mark quickly and thus may disregard what their predecessor has done unless there has been a through and detailed change of command briefing between the incoming and outgoing leaders. Fortunately, there are usually senior civilians in these organizations who stay for much longer periods, but some of them become pretty weary of these constant changes that are hard to sustain and just hunker down and focus on their day-to-day tactical activities. This in not just true of the Navy but also for many for-profit organizations that cycle through rapid leadership changes and turnover. It can also breed complacency in those subjected to the latest "soup du jour."

The savvy Navy commanders who want to make significant changes and want them to stick know that it is important to embed these changes in the organization as quickly and as deeply as they can so that reversing them is not easy. Of course this is a double-edged sword if the changes are good. VADM (Vice Admiral) Mike Vitale (retired) ran all the shore installations for the Navy from Boston to Guam and beyond. It was a big job. About halfway through this tour of duty, he came in with a big agenda to transform his operation using innovation as a tool to generate greater efficiency and effectiveness. Since CNIC (Commander, Navy Installations Command) is asset intense, a big part of Mike's job was to figure out how to do things better, faster, and cheaper with less assets. He trained all his people in the use of innovation as a tool to help him do this. But he knew that he only had eighteen to thirty-six months to bring about significant changes and didn't want them easily unraveled by the next commander.

As part of his strategy, he and his team borrowed a retail model from industry, upgraded their computer and IT systems so that they can now get dashboard readings of CNIC's performance worldwide, and they are outsourcing some functions that the Navy thought only the Navy could do. Mike and his team knew that they not only needed better IT, but also that once these systems were installed they would not only prove invaluable from a performance transparency perspective, they would be hard to dislodge down the road. Embedding support systems for your innovation quickly can make it hard and perhaps unwise for people to try to remove them. When Walt Pullar saved a yachtsmen's life, he had already put the process and asset allocation so far down the path that it would be very difficult for any of his superiors to reverse it.

PRINCIPLE 6: UNBALANCING

One of my favorite moves in the martial arts form of Judo is the foot sweep. It's a tricky move because of the need for precise timing, but it can be very effective in knocking an opponent off his feet. As an opponent starts to step forward, you quickly kick his foot out from under him just before it hits the ground. Since his weight is now over this foot, you have essentially removed the leg on which his weight was about to rest. The opponent is immediately off-balance and falls to the ground with a little tug on his uniform as you can see in the picture at the beginning of this section. As I said, it is a trick to get your timing right, but an opponent who is off-balance and now on the ground is much easier to control.

Unbalancing is a core principle of Innovation Judo as well and is especially helpful when dealing with blockheads who may stand in the way of innovation. Remember earlier I talked about John Kilcullen dedicating his first Dummies book to the CFO who actively tried to get the Dummies idea killed. This is an example of unbalancing as it most certainly made his boss think more deeply about why John would dedicate a book to him even though he was against the idea.

Unbalancing stops an opponent from coming at you just long enough for you to get an advantage, and this is true of Innovation Judo. In John's case, unbalancing the CFO gave him just enough time to give his idea a chance to breathe and temporarily lessened the CFO's outcry against the book idea. You can unbalance innovation opponents in several ways.

Surprise

I tell my students that I like surprises on my birthday and at Christmas, but not necessarily at work as many surprises in organizations often have something negative attached to them like losing a big customer unexpectedly, finding out a shipment has been lost, someone quitting, etc. Surprises can also delight, and delightful surprise is the friend of the corporate innovator. Innovators who demonstrate that they can create the same or better performance using fewer assets is a delightful surprise.

One of my corporate innovators surprised his company by bringing in a customer who was willing to invest in his proposed innovation even though his own company was hesitant. This is a delightful surprise. As you can see, these surprises can unbalance negativity about your idea and temporarily, if not permanently, neutralize the opposition. Another one of my Innovation Judo masters took his boss out to a company in another industry who had implemented what his boss said couldn't be done. GM wanted its newly formed Saturn division to build cars in a more innovative way by using teams and a mechanized moving assembly line rather than the typical one-man, one-job line approach. But this innovative approach to building cars was seen as a threat to the union as it would change job content and potentially affect the pay for skills. So GM flew key plant supervisors around the world with the union stewards to see this approach being applied in Japan and Europe to great effect. The union stewards were very surprised to learn from their union counterparts in Germany, where unions are especially strong, that this change had no adverse impact on them and that the work changes actually made the production workers' job more interesting. When the trip ended, the union agreed to help GM implement the Saturn concept. So what are your options for using surprise when the need for Innovation Judo arises?

Jim Repp, the brains behind the Jeep Rubicon, got together with a few other "Jeep Lunatic Fringe" colleagues from Chrysler and secretly built a high-end off-road Jeep in their garage using aftermarket purchased parts and some purloined parts from Jeep. They then took their Jeep, which looked like Chrysler's stock Jeep, out to off-road competitions and beat Chrysler's best Jeep but also the ones modified by individual Jeep owners. Of course they did this in front of several Chrysler executives who could not understand why this one Jeep was better than all the other ones they made. Not only did Jim surprise these executives, he also created an incredible opening to talk about his dream of having the company mass-produce this kind of vehicle for Jeep "Lunatics" like himself. Jim also used a number of other Innovation Judo techniques, which you will read more about in Chapter 8, "Mastering the Maze."

- *Underpromise and Overdeliver:* Too many company innovators fall into the trap of talking too much about their ideas to others before they have done the necessary homework. It's easy for you to fall in love with your idea, and there is great temptation to start enthusiastically jabbering about it to anyone and everyone within earshot. Your enthusiasm for an innovation that you only have in your mind is an invitation for idea stomping by others. Your idea isn't even half-baked, so why let people call your baby ugly before you have a chance to let the baby mature a little bit before showing it off? Venture capitalists who listen to a lot of entrepreneurial pitches get very nervous when they hear too much exuberance from the entrepreneur who promises the world if the venture capitalist will only invest. The same is true for the innovator. Falling too much in love with your idea without doing the disciplined work of opportunity identification often leads the innovator into overpromising, which makes it pretty hard to deliver on lofty expectations.

  Overpromising and underdelivering is also a surprise but not a good one. You quickly get a reputation as a blowhard and will thus have even greater difficulty getting your next idea heard. But underpromising and overdelivering is a great surprise for most large organizations as they don't see it that often. It is a little like customer service. If companies make lofty promises, they better deliver or they get even more dissatisfied customers. Because innovative ideas need proof that they will work, it is always best to be conservative in your predictions and then overperform.

- *Foot Sweep Criticism:* I sit in on countless innovation presentations. Some are very good, but the majority are lacking in a very important factor: self-criticism. I think most of us have seen the famous hockey stick curve that many innovators use to try to sell their ideas. Figure 6.2 shows this infamous curve with time on one dimension and financial returns on the other. With innovations that are significant we expect to invest for a period of time before we start making money and then my how that curve goes vertical over the next few years. At least it goes that way in the presentations.

  When you foot sweep an opponent in the martial arts Judo you are literally knocking the pins out from under him. With potential innovation critics, you must do the same thing. You must be your own worst critic and think through all the risks that you could face in trying to implement your idea before someone else does. Because you have found these soft spots and highlighted them first, it not only shows that you have gone through the opportunity process, but also that you have spotted your idea's potential flaws and have developed risk-mitigating strategies for all of their potential arguments, stealing the critics' thunder. It also increases your credibility as an innovator.

  The most embarrassing moments I have witnessed in innovation discussions or presentations is when innovators are blindsided by an oppositional argument that they never saw coming. It makes them not only look unprepared but surprised in the wrong way. It is best to off-balance your critics instead of you being put off-balance.

- *Apply Shock Therapy:* Sometimes bad surprises are extremely effective against both roadblocks and blockheads, but manufacturing these surprises requires some careful thought and planning. KCI, the company I talked about earlier, contracted my consulting firm to conduct a strategic planning program for its senior leaders. I mentioned its V.A.C. product earlier that helps mend serious wounds through not only antibacterial materials but also through negative pressure, keeping air and thus infection away so the wound can heal. KCI also makes therapeutic surfaces like mechanical beds. KCI was very well positioned in its V.A.C. business because it had a proprietary product that allowed it to be the sole vendor in a specific medical reimbursement category. Thus, if you wanted a V.A.C. product, KCI was your only choice.

Fortunately, for the customer, V.A.C. is a great product, but unfortunately for KCI it had made them less customer-friendly because frankly they didn't have to be. This is not to say that KCI people were uncaring or uninterested in the customer, but they had become a little jaded as to the competition and a little complacent even though several competitors were trying to break into KCI's dominant market position with one going so far as to launch a lawsuit challenging KCI's assertion that their product could be the only vendor in that specific category.

As we do with most of our executive education programs, we conducted a needs analysis with internal managers and potential program participants, but we also went outside KCI to talk with some of its customers. We found out that customers were delighted with KCI's products but not necessarily its service. However, internal KCI folks thought they were doing a pretty good job at customer service. When we presented our initial finding to senior management there was quite a bit of pushback and denial about the negative customer relations feedback especially from the folks in the marketing department. So we realized that we had not really cracked the shell of denial, and that KCI could be in serious trouble if its competitors were able to crack KCI's proprietary status especially if the competitor could offer better service and friendlier customer relations.

KCI needed a jolt to get it innovating again around new products and services because the king of the hill complacency was not only eroding KCI's innovative spirit, it was creating a cadre of customers who would switch to someone else if they could. So we created the architecture for our four-day strategic planning program and arranged to bring in a medical doctor who told us that he loved KCI's product but hated them. We asked him to come in as a guest speaker to talk about his perceptions of the company as an outsider and user of its products. We thought he might sugarcoat some of his comments, but he let the group have it with both barrels. When he was done with his diatribe against the company, gaping mouths turned to grimaces, which then turned to snarls. After he left, the group turned on us saying, "How dare you bring in someone who says that we are arrogant and that he hates working with us." So the group's initial reaction was to blame us as the program designers for allowing this to happen. But after the initial venting, a couple of people mentioned that he was not the only one and that they had heard similar comments. Even though they didn't like hearing it, it might just be the shock they needed to rethink the whole business from products and services to customer relations.

The KCI leaders picked up the gauntlet and eventually turned the organization's customer reputation around. They brought in some new people from the outside, hired a new CEO, and began investing heavily in new technologies eventually buying a genetic engineering firm to fold into their portfolio of healing products.

As you can see, we took some big risks, but the risk of the company not changing was even bigger.

When you read about Russ Sabo, you will see that he also used shock therapy to get his executive team to acquire a very innovative and strategically valuable company about which they had been dragging their feet. Russ's move was one of the most inventive Innovation Judo moves I had ever heard of, and his story was in part why I decided to write this book.

Power Shifting

- *Negate Blockers/Increase Promoters/Transform Blockers into Promoters:* Innovators in many of the companies with whom I work complain about their innovation stalling. The idea gets off the ground, it starts to show some traction, and then along comes the inevitable roadblocks and blockheads. While they may not be able to kill the innovation outright, they can slow it down to a bare crawl or keep in limbo, neither moving forward or backward. Limbo is a bad place for the innovator because given enough time, most people will lose interest and ideas will die.

In such cases you will need to try to increase motion by changing the forces that are keeping your idea in limbo. To help you do this, we can reach back in history and look at the works of Kurt Lewin, a German/American psychologist (1890–1947) now considered by many to be the father of social psychology (Lewin, 1951). He developed a theory of change known as Force Field Analysis. This model has stood the test of time and actually underpins a number of modern theories of change that we see in the current literature. While his theory was specifically aimed at helping introduce and stabilize change, it is also quite pertinent to innovators trying to move a stalled idea along.

Lewin posited that all organizations are affected by two sets of forces: Driving forces push the organization toward change while resisting or restraining forces prevent the organization from moving forward. So, according to Lewin, executives who desire organizational change would be well advised to carefully analyze the forces for and against change, thus allowing them three choices to enable the desired movement in new directions. When the forces for change equal the forces against change, the organization tends to stay in equilibrium. To increase movement in the right direction you can either increase the driving forces, reduce the restraining forces, or transform the restraining forces into driving forces. Lewin referred to this assessment as Force Field Analysis. Figure 6.2 shows a typical chart that allows managers and executives to analyze forces for and against change by labeling the arrows for and against change and increasing their length and thickness to denote the strength of the forces.

This model can be applied to stalled innovation as well, but you will need to look at driving and restraining forces through a slightly different lens. This model is quite applicable as it stands for those of you working in the Land of Oz. You should be able to easily identify the logical forces and their relative strengths. For example, the need for new products or loss of market share are certainly driving forces for the development of new products. And the restraining forces might also be logically explored and could include such arrows as limited investment funds, needed operational capacity, and retraining of employees. This is how Lewin's model was intended to be used.

Force Field Analysis Model

Driving and restraining forces in equilibrium

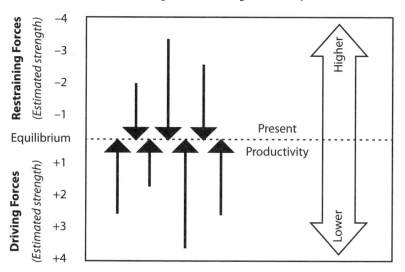

For those of you needing Innovation Judo to move your idea along, you will need to translate restraining forces into two subsets, roadblocks and blockheads. As you remember, roadblocks tend to be structural barriers and blockheads refer to people. Your analysis will be less logical since you will have to rely on your knowledge of how your organization actually works and your intuition as to where and how you will be stalled. For driving forces you will of course have to list yourself, and any others who are on your side or promoters of your idea both internally and externally. You can then estimate the strength of these forces and denote them by the length and thickness of the arrows, and select the best Innovation Judo principles to apply in three possible scenarios. Increase the promoters (could be the CFO or a customer), decrease the strength of the blockheads, and turn a roadblock into a promotional tool.

These tactics help you unbalance the situation, at least long enough to get your idea moving again. Lewin said there are three stages of change: unfreezing, transitioning, and refreezing. He presents a number of things that managers can do to get people uncomfortable with the status quo, get them moving in the right direction, and then cementing their new position through reinforcements. This part of Lewin's theory is much less applicable to innovators since innovation is not so easily staged. Even though there are stages in the opportunity process, innovation requires constant learning as to what works and what doesn't and adaptation to this new learning and its implications. But the unfreezing part is applicable as you saw from my discussion of the concept of surprise. This can be a very effective tool especially for creating openings that may or may not stay open for long. You just need them to be open enough to get to the next hurdle. Unbalancing is an essential principle of Innovation Judo. All of my Innovation Judo masters found some way to unbalance their opponents just long enough to keep their ideas alive.

PRINCIPLE 7: REDIRECTION

Redirection of an opponent's energy is different from *unbalancing*. Redirection means that the opponent's energy and force remains intact but goes away from you, not toward you. You redirect their energy for your purposes, not theirs.

My college Judo instructor would sometimes do a class about street fighting. I often wondered how the sport of Judo might be used if I found myself in a real situation of self-defense. For example, what if someone came at me with a knife or tried to punch me or hit me with something? Would all this practice help me protect myself? So, the instructor would give us all a chance to practice our moves under some of these simulated situations (no real weapons of course). One of the first things he taught us was to not back up if someone comes at you with a knife but to move sideways at an angle. For most of us, our initial reaction was to start back pedaling and then try to turn and run. This is not a bad move if you are sure you can outrun the attacker, but if not, you would likely make yourself defenseless to a stab in the back. Moving sideways at an angle makes sense, especially the more we practiced it. The attacker has put his energy into moving straight at you. Stepping sideways forces him to follow your unanticipated move and adjust his direction, and thus his energy. From a physics point of view, you will move faster sideways than he can since you started your move first. As the attacker would start his turn, you could grab either his arm or shoulder and pull on him as he was turning, thus increasing his speed of turn, and then with a jerk, you could often pull him off his feet. To do this move successfully you clearly have to practice being attacked from various directions in order to get your timing and moves down. But the change in your direction is a very effective move to throw the attacker off his game temporarily to give you a chance to get him on the ground and either finish him off with a kick or turn and run like hell.

Redirection in Innovation Judo can also be a very effective self-defense if you are faced with direct and aggressive assaults on your innovation. Redirection can be accomplished in a number of different ways, but here are a few good suggestions.

Feigning

I can think of no sport where feigning is not an essential element. Football players juke; basketball players pretend they are ready to jump, then wait for the defender to pass by before they actually jump; and baseball players feign stealing a base just to throw the pitcher off. The goal of feigning is to always "fake out" somebody or some group: looking like you are doing one thing when your real intent is to do something else. In football, players actually call a fake pass a fake pass or a fake punt a fake punt. These fakes are intended to redirect the opponent's energy in a different direction, giving your team the advantage. An Innovation Judo master may also have to feign in order to give his or her idea a fighting chance. Russ Sabo faked a trade magazine article to redirect his boss's inertia into action. Jim Repp and his team built a fake Jeep so they could surprise a senior executive into signing off on the Rubicon project.

Faking, of course, has its dangers. Most people don't like to be faked out because it makes them feel foolish, but sometimes the benefit for the company and the innovator outweigh the risks. As in sports, the positive effects of feigning are temporary, and if the same move is used too frequently it becomes predictable. The basketball player who always fakes jumping will eventually cause his counterpart to wait, and the baseball player who always fakes stealing not only becomes predictable, but will also wear himself out in the process and is an easier target for a pickoff. So you will need to see feigning as a temporary fix to a blockhead or roadblock and should use it sparingly to avoid both predictability and pissing people off.

Feigning can give you more time for your innovation because folks think you are working on one thing when you are actually working on another. You may want to do this when there is a fear of intervention. Bob Ballard, the world famous oceanographer, innovator, and adventurer, is probably best known for finding the *Titanic* at the bottom of the Atlantic Ocean. Lots of people had looked for the *Titanic,* but Bob was the only one who found it. I was in a seminar where Bob gave a talk and was impressed with his depth of knowledge, his futuristic orientation, and his cutting-edge views of our world underwater. But he shocked all of us by revealing some now unclassified information: Bob wasn't actually looking for the *Titanic.* This was a cover story. He was actually working for the U.S. government to help find two sunken nuclear submarines. All the hoopla about the *Titanic* drew people's attention, especially the Russians and Chinese, away from his actual mission. He told us the finding of the *Titanic* was actually serendipitous as he was funded by the government to fulfill his primary mission of preventing these sunken subs from being found and/or recovered by our adversaries. If the Russians or Chinese knew that he was looking for subs, they would have had ships near him hoping to beat him to the punch. This is a great story of feigning. He was also not bothered by the pesky press except for adoration regarding his quest for the *Titanic.* You can imagine the press he would have gotten if they had known he was looking for subs with nuclear payloads at the bottom of the ocean. The environmentalists would have had a field day.

The Rail Gun

Captain Bob Hein of the Navy helped get funding for a break-through Navy weapons system called the "Rail Gun" by combining three of the seven Innovation Judo principles including *redirection.* It is truly a technological wonder. For hundreds of years, gunpowder has been used to launch ordinance rounds be it from a revolutionary war musket or a deck gun on a battleship. In World War II a number of U.S. ships went down, not from a direct hit on the ship but from the explosions caused when huge bags of gunpowder in the ship's magazine caught fire. This type of weapon necessitates loading tons of explosives on a ship, and there is always a danger that if an accident happens or al Qaeda gets lucky with a rubber boat attack and hits one of our ships' magazines, then hundreds of sailors would die. In World War II, if a Japanese dive-bomber was lucky enough to send a bomb through the deck and hit the powder magazine, the whole ship was gone. There is always some danger in handling and storing these big bags of gunpowder on a ship due to the risk of an unintended explosion outside of the gun's chamber or a misfiring within the chamber. Over the years countless sailors have been injured or killed due to misfiring or mishandling.

But what if you didn't need gunpowder? Well maybe you don't given the arrival of the rail gun. The shell is propelled into space not with gunpowder but by causing dramatic changes in the polarization of electrical currents running along a rail on which the shell sits. Despite the excitement and successful prototype demonstrations behind this concept there is still resistance not only because it involves radically new technology but also because of the huge investment it will take to bring this rail gun through to actual implementation on ships. It will require a change in training, a new model of bombardment, new technology still unproven compared to literally decades of magazine-powered shells, and a refitting of ships to accommodate this new technology.

This innovation originally emanated from the ONR (Office of Naval Research), but this organization can only take this concept so far without the funding and involvement of the folks who decide on what the Navy's weaponry requirements are and at what cost. The decision to pick up the funding rests in large part with OPNAV, especially a subgroup called N86 who are responsible for our surface warfare fleet. If these folks, stationed at the Pentagon, don't think the Navy requires a rail gun then it probably won't get funded beyond its infancy stage. And as I mentioned earlier, for those of you who have not ever visited the Pentagon, it is a city within a city. And with any city, it has a fair amount of politics and bureaucracy, thus getting innovative things to happen requires more than logic. It often requires Innovation Judo.

Captain Bob Hein

I first met Bob when he attended our NSLS (Navy Senior Leaders Seminar) at the Naval Postgraduate School in Monterey. As I was describing my work on Innovation Judo, I asked if there were any people in the audience who had ever engaged in this organizational sport. As you can imagine, many of the class participants did not raise their hand, either because they did not actually practice Innovation Judo or they were hesitant to admit it. Not Bob, he raised his hand immediately and said, "I've got some stories for you!" When I found out his story involved the rail gun, I was even more interested because my sponsor was ONR and I was aware of the work it had done on this system, but I had not talked to anyone who might actually have to fund it or use it. Bob had a direct role in helping it get funded, or not.

The reason that Bob openly admitted to being an Innovation Judo expert is that he is the kind of guy who likes to get things done, and with the Navy job rotations happening every one to three years on average, he did not have time on his side. Like many of his colleagues Bob did a rotation at the Pentagon with OPNAV, the staff that supports the CNO, the Chief Naval Officer in charge of the whole Navy. This is great training for officers who want to advance because they get to see the Navy behind the Navy. These are the folks who have to work with others in the Pentagon, the different military branches, and a plethora of governmental agencies in the discharge of their duties. Many are active-duty officers who are now assigned for a couple of years to mostly desk jobs. They do critically important work, but it can be a real slog due to the complexity of the Pentagon and the inherent politics involved in any governmental agency.

But Bob seemed to survive and thrive in that environment and was quite keen to tell me his rail gun story. When he found out about this innovation from ONR and others, he was very excited about helping it become a Navy requirement so that it could get proper funding, although he found out very quickly that not everyone shared his point of view. In fact, many people were against it for the various reasons that you would expect: too costly, too radical, and what's wrong with what we have now? He faced numerous roadblocks that would not yield to logic. So he turned to Innovation Judo.

While the rail gun doesn't require powder to work, it does require significant amounts of electrical energy to create the polarization effects in the rails. And these power systems don't exist today so they will need to be developed as a requisite for the rail gun to be operational. If Bob were to help keep the rail gun idea alive, he would have to get significant investment for upgrading the power supply systems in our current ships. Most of the these ships have four diesel engines and three gas turbine electrical generators in order to run everything that needs to be run. The batteries and capacitors necessary to handle the rail gun would fill a small warehouse. And many of our ships are already at capacity. Bob knew that there was very little chance he would get much interest in upgrading these power systems for the potential use of the rail gun unless he got clever. He describes investment in HEC (hulls and electrical capabilities) as "not very sexy" to most of the people at OPNAV. He had to capture another source of emotion and interest and *redirect* them to his advantage. Right now there is a requirement to reduce fuel usage by 6 percent over the next six years, which comes right from the top. And as the old saying goes, "What interests my boss fascinates me." One of the ways you can save on fuel usage is to increase the number of electrical power supplies on the ship from say three to five and run the diesels less. And now we have the possibility of powering the rail gun and saving on fuel as well. Truly a win-win and a great example of using redirection in service of a truly radical idea that could be a game changer.

Notice that the potential performance increases are significant and the personal danger goes down dramatically, as there is no gunpowder on board a ship that is outfitted with rail guns. So Bob was successful in getting attention and funding for this important work by harnessing his idea to a new value around energy and positioning his innovation not only from a safety perspective, but also from a long-term financial one as well. He then used the rail gun not as the end goal, but also a means to obtain other goals that seemed much less radical, like saving fuel. Not a bad example of feigning with right-mindedness.

Pulling
THE DIAGONAL SLICE

I was recently asked to address a group from OSD (Office of the Secretary of Defense) regarding the implementation of an innovation program. The folks at OSD had already decided that they needed new ideas on how to run the organization especially given the expected budget cuts they were about to face. As with most organizations that embark on this "idea gathering" path, there is a real rush to organize the structure and processes first before divining the intent. So, they found my comments helpful as there was some confusion from some of the team members as to the intent questions. Are we really looking for cost-cutting ideas, technology, and/or risk sharing? Defining the intent obviously informs the kind of ideas you are looking for and is thus an important first step that links to all the others, like idea evaluation and opportunity identification.

There was a lot of excitement and enthusiasm in the group for doing this innovation work so they had the passion for it. I have no doubt given the motivation and talent in the innovation team members that they will get some good processes and procedures up and running. And they will no doubt get some good ideas in the pipeline for review. But with many such endeavors, there is a good chance that the enthusiasm of the team will not be shared by the rest of the employees. After all, this is the government, and it is a bureaucracy, and cynicism among government employees is not unheard of. So this group's challenge is not in constructing the pathway for idea generation it's getting employees to believe that the organization really cares about their ideas and that they will act on some of these ideas.

I have talked a lot in this book about the challenge of getting an innovation up and running but not much about shaping an implementation process. I have seen many great innovations derailed even though they got off to a great start because there was no feedback loop built into the system. If the innovation either isn't working or isn't working in the right ways, no one is willing to pull the plug or admit it. This is especially true if they had something to do with the genesis of the innovation. Also, opportunities almost always have to be reshaped at the implementation phase, and this often tells you that your original idea needs to be modified due to current realities that you may not have initially seen.

But once an innovation is given the okay by senior management, very few folks are willing to question its direction. The now-famous space shuttle *Challenger* disaster is a chilling testament to the unwillingness of people to identify and communicate potentially fatal flaws if something has gone far enough down the line. One of the best ways to redirect certain organization-wide innovation is to develop what I refer to as a diagonal slice of the organization that has the mandate to communicate the progress of the innovation be it good, bad, or ugly.

This diagonal slice works best when it is set up after the intention phase of an innovation is determined. This slice can be part of the Infrastructure phase of the innovation cycle. Thus, it can create a very interesting two-way street for the innovator or

The 7I Model of Innovation

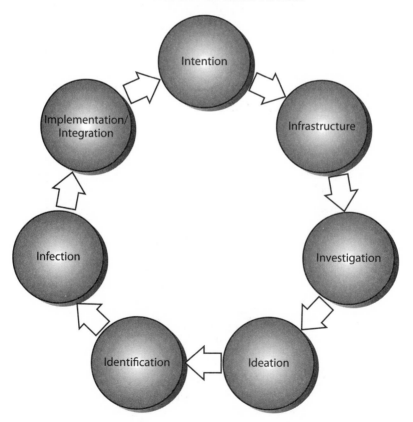

for the team tasked with innovation. It allows you to monitor in real time how the innovation is doing through all phases. And because the diagonal slice of the organization has representatives from not only different levels but also different functions, it provides multiple perspectives on progress, while providing you with ambassadors back in the organization who help sell your idea as well as pick up early warning signs when it is offtrack.

Diagonal slice works most effectively of course with innovations that are generally large scale and impact many parts of the organization. It can also work on a smaller scale with a unit or small function, but it is best when it creates a feedback loop to senior management if they are the ones pushing innovation. This look helps you and management identify roadblocks and blockheads so that they can be dealt with proactively and offensively, not reactively and defensively.

Here is what this slice looks like.

Diagonal Slice of the Organization

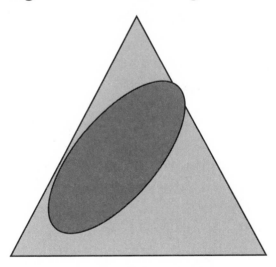

For illustrative purposes, assume that the triangle represents a generic hierarchical organization and the oval represents the innovation team as a feedback loop through all stages of the innovation process. Note that the model gives you different levels of organizational feedback along with different functional perspectives as well. Since the slice is diagonal, team members don't have to worry about being stifled by their direct supervisor. The diagonal nature brings people in from different levels and different functions, but never a boss and his direct report from the same function.

Also, you will see that this slice takes advantage of the many folks in the middle of the organization who are both the best sources of innovative ideas and potentially the biggest blockers as well. The beauty of the diagonal slice is that you get a wide organizational perspective of how your innovation is doing. Senior leadership are notoriously out of the loop when it comes to understanding what is going on throughout the entire organization unless they actually visit every part of it. Also, they tend to go to their direct reports for information, and these people tend to tell the boss what he or she wants to hear.

Very rarely have I seen this feedback loop employed in any organization that embarks on wide-scale innovation. I am currently working with a large organization that has just put together a middle management group as a font for innovative ideas. This is actually a good idea since most of the best ideas come from the middle of the organization. But this group is floundering and there is no feedback loop to the top, thus it continues to flounder. People stop coming to meetings, or they come late and leave early. There is a lot of wasted time and discussion, and very few are willing to tell the senior executive who spawned this group that the group needs redirection.

Here are a few things to keep in mind when building and selecting people for successful teams:

1. They must be liked and respected by their peers.

2. They are not afraid of you or their boss.

3. They are passionate about how things can work better, cheaper, faster.

4. They are not afraid to fight the status quo for something better.

5. They are not allowed to discuss the meetings or get approval for ideas brought up in the meetings from their direct bosses or peers.

6. No attribution is allowed when people leave the meetings. (You can't attribute comments made in the meeting to a particular person when talking with others outside the group.)

7. The group meets at least once a month and very few excuses, including their bosses calling them out, are allowed.

8. They have homework to do for each meeting.

9. Meetings must be fun.

This diagonal slice is really useful in redirecting negative forces. It has top-level support, it involves truth telling, and it creates ambassadors to the rest of the organization. I was asked by a large retail food manufacturer to develop an innovation program that involved real new business opportunity development. The class was taught over a number of months to a group of handpicked employees whom we thought had both innovation energy and entrepreneurial spirit. This group was a diagonal slice consisting of members from the strategic planning staff, to high-potential Stanford grads, to an accounts payable clerk, and a secretary. We used this group to not only identify new business opportunities but also to report directly to senior management if they encountered major roadblocks or blockheads that could prevent their new opportunities from being tested and implemented if they showed promise. Instead of trying to predict cultural and personal impediments to this initiative, we moved forward and let the obstacles pop up. I think this is a much better approach than simply guessing.

We also put this in place for an even more important reason. Many company leaders say they want innovation but are they really willing to remove the things in their organization that kill innovation? That is the real test of whether senior leaders are serious. So we used this diagonal slice as a test of the company's commitment, and we all agreed that if we ran into a barrier to innovation that they were not willing to either remove or modify, then we would stop the program because the company was not really serious about innovation.

I often recommend this diagonal slice approach to my clients because it very quickly and visibly tests management's commitment to innovation. And if management is not willing to remove the barriers, then they should just stop talking about innovation and cut back on investing in it. No harm, no foul. There is no reason to disappoint employees by asking them to engage in initiatives that the company is not serious in pursuing.

As you read the black-belt profiles in the following chapters, it is helpful to refer back to the quick guide on the next page to help you spot the use of these principles in action and assimilate them into your innovation toolkit. I have listed each principle with its associated tactical applications. While all the Innovation Judo masters described in the following profiles utilize leverage, for example, their tactical implementation is different based on their particular landscapes, just as yours will be.

7 Principles Quick Guide

Discipline
- ☐ Preparation
- ☐ Passion
- ☐ Bring opportunities
- ☐ Patience
- ☐ Self-control

Leverage
- ☐ Corporate values
- ☐ Customer
- ☐ Competitor
- ☐ Referent power
- ☐ Strategy
- ☐ Informal network
- ☐ Dote on quotes

Redirection
- ☐ Feigning
- ☐ Pulling

Circling
- ☐ Walk around opponents
- ☐ Walk around ideas
- ☐ Circle the wagons
- ☐ Brand enhancement
- ☐ Pilots/Prototype

Opening
- ☐ Hot buttons
- ☐ Cost cutting/Containment
- ☐ Efficiency/Effectiveness
- ☐ Numbers
- ☐ Seams

Speed
- ☐ Idea to opportunity
- ☐ Fail fast
- ☐ Quick to reshape/Pull plug
- ☐ Dash into openings
- ☐ Forgiveness, not permission
- ☐ Embed quickly

Unbalancing
- ☐ Surprise
- ☐ Underpromise/Overdeliver
- ☐ Foot sweep criticism
- ☐ Shock therapy
- ☐ Power shifting

At the end of each profile, I have summarized a number of Judo principles and associated tactics that these masters have used in pursuit of innovation. I have not tried to be all inclusive and instead have focused on some of the more salient ones. But in your reading, you will note others. It is a good self-test to see if you can identify them for yourself and will help these principles to stay in your mind. Not all the tactics are utilized by these four practitioners and the ones you use could be different, but trust me, they are all potential weapons in the quest for turning creativity into cash. In Appendix C, you will find a brief planning tool to help guide your personalized approach to Innovation Judo.

Part III Becoming a Black Belt

In Part III, you will meet a number of real-life Innovation Judo black belts who have been successful at innovating in their respective organizations by customizing their approaches to their particular organization's innovation landscape.

Stephen Paljieg found himself operating in a Maze landscape at Kimberly-Clark. Although this innovation landscape usually requires less emphasis on Innovation Judo, Stephen still had to call on some of the principles to get his "Mompreneur" idea through to fruition.

Walt Pullar, a Navy Seal, worked in the Jungle of a military/ government environment, and you will see how complexity and wackiness can be a 1-2 knockout punch for innovation without some Innovation Judo savvy. It is easy to get lost or eaten in a jungle unless you are well-armed against innovation predators. Walt found Innovation Judo principles essential for disarming barriers to innovation, especially when lives hung in the balance. Without Walt's Innovation Judo skills, there is no doubt that numerous lives would have been lost.

Jim Repp, the engineer and driving force behind the development of the Jeep Rubicon, found himself in an Asylum environment at the former DaimlerChrysler organization and had to reach deeply into his bag of Innovation Judo principles to get this innovative vehicle to market, despite all the politics and marketing experts who said it would never sell. Without self-defense skills, Asylums can easily run out or wear out the best of innovators.

And you also will meet Russ Sabo at Eaton Corporation. Although Russ worked in a seemingly Oz-oriented landscape, he still had to rely on some valuable Innovation Judo skills. In his story, you will hear one of the best and most clever examples of disarming I have ever run across in my research. It was risky, but it paid off for both Russ and Eaton.

CHAPTER 7

Operating in the Land of Oz

PAVED IN YELLOW

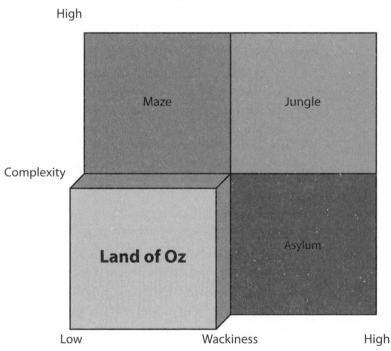

A Dangerous Intersection

When complexity and wackiness are relatively low, you are operating in a more favorable environment for innovation. This doesn't mean that the environment is inherently innovative, but logic works, political gamesmanship is relatively low, and at least you know who you can discuss your ideas with, and you usually don't face as many oppositional forces as in the other landscapes. The Land of Oz can also be built within the other landscapes to counterbalance both wackiness and complexity, but this takes a purposeful strategy, top-level involvement, and a strong level of organizational commitment to keep this "landscape within a landscape" alive. In Chapter 11, I will offer you some long-term solutions that involve the building of Oz landscapes, but Innovation Judo skills may still be required even if you already live in a landscape with Oz characteristics as you will see from Russ Sabo's story.

THE SLOW ROAD

In Russ's case, the hierarchy at Eaton was clear. He knew the key decision makers, and he had a straightforward path to their door as required in his job description. Plus, the company was interested in innovation. So his challenge was not the company's willingness to innovate, it was its ability to make the decision-making process fast enough to capture this new business opportunity that Russ and his team had identified in his role as business development manager. Russ didn't face blockheads in his quest for innovation, but he did face a roadblock in the slowness of the decision-making process due to risk aversion. As a result, he had to resort to one or two Innovation Judo principles in order to keep his idea alive within the corporation. Unlike Jungles, Asylums, or Mazes, Oz landscapes do not usually require the serial use of Innovation Judo principles but rather their application in a measured way relative to a fairly specific innovation. And this was the case for Russ.

Russ's story is very special because of his creative use of Innovation Judo principles and some would say willingness to take a great risk by setting an ingenious trap for the key decision maker and funder of his proposed innovation. Not only did he set the trap, but he also closed it in front of others. Fortunately, his networking skills and relationships with the people in the organization allowed him to get away with it. Remember, this might not work in your organization, but it is certainly an example of utilizing unbalancing, surprise, and redirection in helping his company take a needed step in new product creation.

Land of Oz Profile

Russ Sabo, Business Development Manager, Eaton Electrical Components

Russ doesn't look like a cowboy, but his roots are surely western, and if pressed, he's able to do a little kicking with those boots as you'll see. He was born in Cheyenne, Wyoming, and was lucky to have a father who taught him a great deal about the art of networking and relationship building.

After working at Eaton, Russ moved on to Harbor Research and then started his own consulting practice. He is now a Partner and President, Business Strategy Lead, of Bessemer Alliance. Russ has more than twenty-five years' experience in new-business creation with major corporations. He brings to his clients a background anchored in both "on-the-street" customer-facing roles and a diverse range of new-business development experiences that have allowed him to successfully steer many new ventures through the icebergs of corporate politics.

I think the biggest thing I take from my father is that he was an amazing listener and he was really, really good at moving across any level. So he could be talking to somebody who was on a factory floor, or he could be talking to a rancher, or he could be talking to the general manager of the Fish and Game Department. These are the types of people he sold his machines to when he worked for Monroe Business Machines.

He was from Pueblo, Colorado, so he definitely had a western mindset. I didn't see him in operation that much in business per se when I was little boy, but my father was very, very good at managing his time. He loved to fish. So in the spring and the fall, that's when we would fish, and he would structure his business around that. He didn't fly, so he drove to cover his sales territory, putting on tens of thousands of miles a year on a car, and he would take me along, when he could.

Where I watched him interact with others I grew to understand how important proactive relationship building could be. We would often drive by a ranch and he would just stop the car and literally go knock on the door. He would meet the wife or he would meet the rancher and he would strike up a conversation by asking if they knew any good fishing places in the area. Or he would get a tip—because the University of Wyoming was a big customer of his—by going to the university's biology department, or he would go to the Game and Fish Department and he'd talk to people about fishing to find out where the best trout streams were, etc. And they would tell him to go out and talk to Mr. Ryan on the Platt and maybe he'll let you fish.

So imagine the impression that made on a little six- or seven-year-old boy. We would go to these places and he would sit down and have conversations with people and listen very carefully to them and always treated them with the utmost respect. They'd let him on their property, where they wouldn't let a lot of other people. He built these extensive relationships and made sure that he was trusted by doing things like always closing the gates he would go through so the cows wouldn't roam around.

I think back on that a lot. That was a wonderful gift that he gave me. I call it the gift of gab, the gift of listening. My father always used to say, "You never know unless you try." I didn't realize these things *until I was probably in my thirties and started reflecting back on my career successes.*

This early education at his father's side gave him the underpinnings for a successful career in sales, business development, and consulting. Despite moving out of the West and working in big jobs for some well-known organizations like Emerson Electric and the Eaton Corporation, he has never lost that humble, down-to-earth, authentic aura to his persona. If Russ makes a commitment to you, you can take it to the bank.

But, he also has that twinkle in his eye that tells you he is not above some good-humored mischief, and that is what led me to profile him in this book. In fact, it was his mischievous nature and his ability to utilize a couple of Innovation Judo moves that really captured my attention when I first met him in one of my executive education seminars.

Russ graduated from Marquette University with a joint degree in engineering and theology reflecting both his practical side and his inquisitive nature. He started working for Leroy-Somer, a French company, to help build a distributor network for its products in North America.

Back then I was twenty-six, and I thought it was normal for me to call on the president and go have these conversations and just negotiate. Isn't that what you're supposed to do? I didn't know any better. I probably always had a little bit of that in me anyway. I liked to buck, you know, the status quo.

So I developed a very unique skill set of understanding channels and distributors and behavior. The French company during that time, they were dying to get something in North America. They bought a distribution channel. It was a $200 million acquisition and about that time the fourth largest power transmission distributor in the United States, a company called King Bearing in California. It was a very nice company, but the French tried to use French management methods and business style to sell their products, and they were failing miserably.

So they said, "You know, we've got this kid from Wyoming who's up in Canada and the distributors seem to like him. Maybe we should put him down there in charge of marketing of those products." So they sent me down there as the manager of the European products working inside of that distributor. I had a team of people there. I under- the French and I understood Americans, and we grew the business dramatically.

Leroy-Somer eventually merged with Emerson Electric, where Russ worked in channel management, eventually moving on to a role in the strategic planning area due to his extensive network and ability to see the business from many different perspectives. After seven years he was recruited to Eaton Electrical as the director of business development for the components division. He was also tasked with the building of its e-commerce strategy.

That's Been Tried Before, and It Didn't Work

I can't tell you the number of times I have heard this or a similar phrase or something like it used to stomp on an innovation. It's an obvious and easy way to decertify someone's idea, and on the surface this argument has some logic. But if you look more closely you would most likely discover that the people were not the same, the idea was not exactly the same, and the situation was not the same. So, don't be put off when people use this idea killing phrase.

Nonetheless, you must hear it because your idea will most likely face resistance unless you can prove that things are not the same or you utilize Innovation Judo. And this is the approach Russ Sabo used to get the Eaton Corporation to produce an innovative new product called Home Insight, which is now available at retailers like The Home Depot and Lowe's.

As a business development manager, Russ was always looking for ways to grow Eaton's component businesses, and because of his innate orientation as an innovator, he liked to look at big ideas in unproven spaces. And as an innate collaborator and network builder, he engaged in mind sharing across a wide spectrum of internal and external stakeholders including Eaton people, consulting firms, external R&D organizations, and industrial design firms. Much of Russ's success over the years came from his ability to broker the capabilities of others, and his new position in business development gave him a great opportunity for pulling a diverse, talented group of people together in the service of innovative new products and services.

Once such ideation session resulted in the idea of a new product that Eaton might develop for the home owner. This product would leverage some of Eaton's existing capabilities but would require new investment dollars in building additional capabilities. The idea, which the group initially dubbed "Home Heartbeat," would allow home owners to check their home's vital signs through telemetry from anywhere in the world. The system would have to involve the placement of sensors at strategic sites within the home and the development of some computerized brain that would read the data and then transmit them to the home owner either passively or proactively.

Did I leave the lights on? Is there a break in security? Is there water in the basement? Is the house warm enough to prevent pipes from freezing? Can I put the AC on before I get home to make sure the house is cool? As the ideation group thought about the answers to these questions, it became increasingly excited about the possibility that this new product could fundamentally transform this business.

I looked around and I said, "Well, we have this residential business that wants to be more than it is today, because all they manufactured were circuit breakers and load centers." Those are those boxes that sit either in your garage or your basement where the electronic fuses, you could call them, are set up. That's what you go reset when you leave the iron on for too long. I said, "Maybe we should think about expanding their product scope through some kind of new innovation." I got the VPMG at the time and said, "I think I found this company, Maya, that might be able to help us think differently about products." Everybody said, "Well, let's do an ideation—we call them innovation—session." I have worked with Maya before and liked its approach to new product development, which looked at the process through three different disciplines simultaneously: engineering, design, and human factors.

So I brought the people from Maya together with the CTO of the business and some other folks to have this session where we innovated several concepts. We came out with this concept that we thought had merit. It was what if you had a dashboard you could carry around that was like idiot lights for the home. Like typically the single largest investment people have is their home. Maybe there are some key things that I might like to track about my home. Interesting idea. Everybody got excited enough about it, and the entire team developed this and called it Home Heartbeat. That was the name of this product, like I can get a pulse on my home. They decided the idea had merit, but it would also have some challenging requirements. You've got to be able to get into this for less than $300 and to have a working system so that the consumer who goes into Lowe's or Home Depot or Best Buy could say, "Hey, I want to try this." And it needs to be easy enough to install so that anyone can do it. It would have to involve really simple things like peel-and-stick sensors and be very simple in the way it communicates to the home owner.

Eaton then had some concept testing done with a sample of home owners to see if this idea had any merit with actual consumers. The testing firm came back to Eaton and said, "Are you guys thinking about doing this, because in our measurement scheme, this is way up in the charts in terms of attractiveness to the consumer." Despite these positive concept data, many at Eaton were still gun-shy for a couple of reasons. This kind of consumer-level product was relatively new to them, and they had tried to do some things before with this market segment and had failed miserably.

> Everyone's going, "Wow, that's good." But we'd never been in this kind of consumer-level product market. We tried a couple of times and failed miserably, because we don't know how to get the product to the market. We don't have channels, we tried that before. They had also seen some others fail in this market as well—there was an IBM initiative called the Smart Home back in the late 1990s, a lot of money and a lot of marketing. They tried to build a smart load center. They had their engineers design it, and it was the most kludgy (complicated) thing that you ever saw. That was one of those $5 million experiments that failed. Everyone in the residential business had scars from those past failures, and like from war, they said, "Well, we're not going to do that again." People were just really kind of reticent about saying, "Let's go do it."

So the project was in danger of stalling but Russ's gut along with the data told him there was a real opportunity here.

> I said, "There's a risk, but this is something that we should pursue." I was emotionally committed to it because it just felt right. So some extraordinary measures would have to be taken to overcome the roadblocks to this opportunity.

He had the right people in the room, and he had taken the logical steps to get them there, but now logic would no longer work. The real challenge now was to see if they had just an idea or a real opportunity. And this would require a significant investment.

> All this conversation had been going on for a while. By that time, I got to be good buddies with the CEO at Maya, Nick, and I was at the Maya offices a lot. I started to actually just hang out there because I liked the place so much, and I would work from there instead of working from my own office. And the CEO said, "Come here. I want to show you something. Just imagine if you had this box." And he started pulling

out these stereolithography models that they had done on Home Heartbeat. "What if you had a thing that sat on your keychain that looked like this? What if the sensor looked like this?" These were models, like foam core–style models, but they were in plastic. I said, "That's interesting." He said, "Don't you think if we show this to the guys that we can get them to be excited?" I said, "Yeah, well, this is interesting." And then he said, "What about this?" and he pulled out a magazine and it had this Home Heartbeat thing on the front cover. I said, "Now, that's interesting."

They had gone through the trouble of making a fake cover to a magazine. I said, "Okay. Now, Nick, let me explain to you exactly how we're going to get it funded. What I want you to do is I want you to go home this weekend, because you've been involved at least from the beginning, and I want you to write me an article, a two-page fake article, and I want you to embed it in Metropolitan Home, *and we're going to call it 'Levitan Introduces Home Insight.'" I just named it right there, the product. Metropolitan Home *was a magazine that all the executives in the residential business read every Monday morning like clockwork when they first got into their offices.*

So the folks from Maya went to the newsstand, they bought copies of Metropolitan Home. *They took a picture of the cover, razored it off, went into Photoshop and changed the title, and glued it back on. "I want you to make me three of these." They asked what I was going to do with them. I said, "I'm going to take these and I'm going to put a little Post-it Note on them and I'm going to put them on the desks of the general manager, the marketing manager, and the product line manager, and I'm going to say, 'Levitan beat us again.'" That's what we did.*

I went in on a Saturday, because I knew normally these guys would go in on Sunday mornings, and I put it on each desk. I went in on Monday and I told my controller friend Paul, "I just want you to know that Dave Talman, the GM, is going to probably explode this morning. He's going to be coming and telling you that we've got to get the lawyers, and these assholes." I told my boss, Bill Van Arsdale, "Bill, you've got to play with me here. This is what I'm doing to Talman." Talman was the target for me. It was his decision to fund. He had the signing authority; he had the budget.

As predicted, the shit hit the fan. He picked up the phone and he called the marketing manager and said, "Those blankety-blank-blank guys at Maya. We'd better call the attorneys. That stuff looks just like the idea we had. Someone's stolen it." He went into, like, Patton mode. He's kind of that type of person anyway. Very commanding and goal-oriented. He called his team together for an emergency staff meeting and read them the riot act for not being bold enough to take this forward.

On Tuesday, Talman's demanding, "What's happened? I want to have the other lawyers on this. How much in patents have we filed?" Nick calls me and says, "Russ, this is getting kind of serious. Everybody's all wound up."

I said okay. I literally walked into the marketing manager's office, since he and I were friends. He was just getting ready to dial the attorney, and I put my hand on top of his on the phone and said, "Rufus, it's a joke." And Rufus, looked at me and said, "You asshole." He put it all together and just smiled and said you're wicked or evil or something like that. I said, "You've got to let this go." We let it go about one more day. Everybody knew but Dave.

But Russ wasn't done yet. He had to add a little more drama to the scenario to really make the message hit home. So he added yet another twist to his well-choreographed play.

By Wednesday, now we're three days into this, four counting the week-end. Dave was pretty much frustrated because the lawyer thing wasn't happening fast enough; everyone was dragging their feet. So he said, "I want to see Nick." We're going to have Mexican food someplace in a strip mall. He arrives, and I'm there and Nick is there and Rufus is there. I just said, "Nick, what's going on here? I can't believe that this has happened! You know, did somebody leave your business and take our idea with them?"

Nick says, "I don't know. I'm really confused, because I called the number that the magazine said to call to get more information on this Levitan product. This is really puzzling to me."

At that point I said, "Rufus, what's this number? Let's call it? What's Nick talking about? Dial it up." Talman says, "Let me have the phone and listens to it." It was an 800 number: Eaton's customer service number. The message comes on, "Welcome to . . ." Eaton was in a brand-shift change, and the product at that time was called Cutler-Hammer. So it said, "Welcome to Cutler-Hammer. For more product information, dial 1-800—"

Talman is looking and listening. He goes, "You guys won't believe it!" He thought that somehow Levitan was having people call Eaton, because he was just so emotionally convinced that they had stolen our idea.

I looked at him at that point. He looked at me. I said, "Dave, it's a joke." And he's a little hard of hearing, so I said it a second time: "It's a joke, Dave." Then all of the pieces fell into place and he connected the dots. He was normally the kind of person that pulled pranks and did things to other people, rarely having other people prank him.

He looked at me and said, "I don't know when it will be, where it will be, or how it will be, but I will get you." So we laughed about it, but he went off and wrote the check for $500,000 to commission some serious prototyping and real product development, which led to the launch of the product that can now be found in Best Buy under the name Home Heartbeat.

The key fob idea became part of the design and was key to the system. Owners can place sensors wherever they like in their homes like in the basement. Then you activate the fob, and it automatically identifies the sensor, allowing you to name it utilizing a scroll function. It allows you to key in 100+ sensors. Then you can scroll through the list, call up a sensor, and get a read for temperature, humidity, etc.

Russ's story is now legendary at Eaton.

Judo Application Summary

It is important to note that in Russ's part of Eaton, Land of Oz was the predominant innovation landscape. He had good relations with all the players and his ability to play a prank with real meaning was the shock therapy needed to unbalance the failure to make a decision. It is not clear that such an open, potentially embarrassing prank would work in an Asylum or Jungle landscape as clearly the risks for Russ would be dramatically increased. In Asylum cultures, when someone says they are going to give you pay back, they are probably only half kidding. Nonetheless, Russ's story is still helpful! because he was able to apply several Innovation Judo principles to get the desired effect. Let's analyze them:

- Unbalancing
- Leverage
- Redirection
- Speed
- Opening

UNBALANCING

You can only imagine the joy that Russ and those on the inside who knew about his trick must have had in anticipation of the trap being sprung on Dave Talman. Up until the newspaper incident, Dave and his team had felt pretty good about not moving quickly to endorse Home Heartbeat. After all it was risky, others had failed in what looked like similar products, and the team did not even contemplate the possibility of someone scooping the idea. But we have all seen cases of leaders who have dragged their feet just a little too long only to be outsmarted by a competitor.

Not only did the mock news article surprise; it also shocked. It might be interesting to read about the introduction of a new product into your general market, but when it is a direct competitor that just came out with a product you were already thinking about actually bringing to market, then it's personal. Add to that, the possibility of industrial espionage then it gets really personal. Russ built these two elements of unbalancing into his plan to dramatic effect.

Power Shifting I spoke earlier about the need to increase the driving forces or reduce the constraining forces when a system is in equilibrium (Lewin). Russ only used his "prank" when he felt they were not making progress on this idea despite some good market research data that said consumers wanted a product like this.

He needed to increase the driving forces and used Maya's expertise to help him. It was senior management who were hesitant due to some understandable risk aversion. Russ didn't target the whole team although they all got the magazine. He targeted one person in particular, Dave Talman, the person who could authorize the funding. He also knew Dave as a practical joker himself and as a friend. He also had to know Dave's personality in order to somewhat predict his reactions.

> *It probably wouldn't have worked as well on a different type of person. Dave had the emotional quotient as part of his personality, and that was the key to making it work. If you had somebody who was cool as a cucumber, who basically didn't care about stuff, it would have not worked at all. Because he is an emotionally and extremely passionate person, I knew I just needed to jack him up another 10 degrees in the right direction.*

LEVERAGE

Russ's little charade also worked well because of the huge leverage he was able to get by showing that a competitor had likely stolen Eaton's idea or at least beat them to the punch. Most competitive executives do not like to be bested. It bruises their egos.

Russ showed them what would likely happen if they didn't move on this opportunity. Even though the story was a sham, it was also in the realm of possibility that a competitor could come along and scoop the idea.

Redirection

Once Russ got the boss all fired up against the competitor, threatening to bring in lawyers, it was not difficult for him to turn that energy into another more productive direction especially when the boss was relieved that the story, which could have been true, wasn't. So instead of anger directed at Russ, he was relieved and thus much more interested in getting behind the idea.

SPEED AND OPENING

Since Russ is such an astute observer of people, it didn't take him long to realize the importance of *Metropolitan Home*. All the key players who he needed to influence read this magazine without fail when they would come in on Sundays. This magazine gave him the opening he needed, and with help from Maya, he was able to move into this opening and substitute his mock magazine for the real one.

7 Principles Quick Guide Self-Test

Reread the preceding profile and look for the use of other Judo principles that I have not referred to in the summary. Place a check mark beside each tactic which you can identify.

Discipline
- ☐ Preparation
- ☐ Passion
- ☐ Bring opportunities
- ☐ Patience
- ☐ Self-control

Leverage
- ☐ Corporate values
- ☐ Customer
- ☐ Competitor
- ☐ Referent power
- ☐ Strategy
- ☐ Informal network
- ☐ Dote on quotes

Redirection
- ☐ Feigning
- ☐ Pulling

Circling
- ☐ Walk around opponents
- ☐ Walk around ideas
- ☐ Circle the wagons
- ☐ Brand enhancement
- ☐ Numbers
- ☐ Pilots/Prototypes
- ☐ Seams

Openings
- ☐ Hot buttons
- ☐ Cost cutting/Containment
- ☐ Efficiency/Effectiveness

Speed
- ☐ Idea to opportunity
- ☐ Fail fast
- ☐ Quick to reshape/Pull plug
- ☐ Dash into openings
- ☐ Forgiveness, not permission
- ☐ Embed quickly

Unbalancing
- ☐ Surprise
- ☐ Underpromise/Overdeliver
- ☐ Foot sweep criticism
- ☐ Shock therapy
- ☐ Power shifting

CHAPTER 8
Mastering the Maze

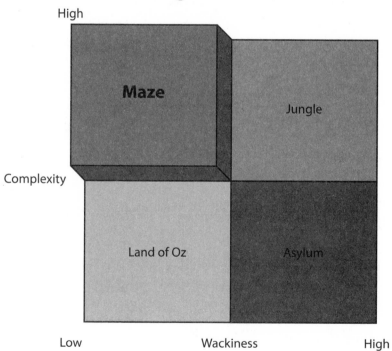

A Dangerous Intersection

Maze landscapes tend to be high in complexity and moderate to low in wackiness. Companies like ABB and General Electric are complex but not particularly wacky. GE in particular is good at reducing wackiness because of its focus on clear goals, specific financial targets, and corporate values that are for real. For example, GE will fire even the best performer if he or she does not adhere to GE's values. And having worked for them as a consultant I can attest to this. GE still has some wackiness as all organizations do, but people are so busy trying to reach their performance targets that they don't have a lot of time left over for political intrigue or manipulation.

The challenge for innovators in the Maze landscape is not so much defending against wackiness but trying to figure out how to navigate their way through a highly complex set of relationships, reporting structures, and informal networks that are hardly ever written down on paper. Complex organizations often choose or have grown into some sort of matrix organization or matrix hybrid to get their work accomplished by leveraging this complexity and probably adding to it. Those of you who work or have worked in a matrix-type structure know the challenges. When a matrix works, it usually works well, but it can also be fraught with frustrations due to the inherent haziness around lines of authority, individual responsibility, and ultimate accountability. Most "matrix organizations" usually have you reporting to at least one solid-line boss and one dotted-line boss. Theoretically, the solid-line boss has more authority over you, but you are also expected to please the dotted line boss who will also weigh in on your performance appraisal. Note, I said *theoretically*.

Complex organizations are by definition difficult to understand, let alone navigate. That is why it takes a lot of time for new employees to get on board, just finding the restrooms let alone understanding how all this complexity fits together. Acronyms often abound, and the newcomer is challenged to learn this corporate speak as quickly as possible. Being a relative newcomer to the military and defense industry, I am always in conversations where acronyms are used as helpful shorthand for communications, but if you are not in the know as to what these acronyms stand for then you can quickly get lost. I have to admit to still not knowing a lot of them, but I do ask for definitions when I absolutely get lost in the lingo. You have to be careful when revealing how much you actually don't know, and you don't want to be a pest. It's funny that when asked, some of the old-timers don't know what the letters stand for, but they know what the acronym means.

Complex organizations are often filled with old-timers who can give you insight into how to get things done within all this complexity and they are the best at acronym translations. When I was a psychology student, I was forced to read an article about how rats learn to run mazes, and, like people, some rats are much better than others especially under conditions of punishment. I am not sure we should extrapolate this finding to people, but those folks who are not "maze bright" as we called the rats will probably not be that successful in a complex organization.

Innovation Judo skills come in handy in Maze organizations, not because you are trying to thwart purposefully malicious people, but because you are trying to get visibility and then a critical mass of people to help you move your idea along. In addition, there may be numerous potential blockheads, not because they lack an innovation orientation but because they are part of the network of people that you need to influence, and you don't exactly know how to get to them. As you can imagine, Innovation Judo principles like *leverage, openings,* and *speed* become useful allies in navigating through these murky waters.

COUNTERINTUITIVE BUT NOT COUNTERPRODUCTIVE

Innovating in the different landscapes can require different approaches, and in the Maze some of these strategies are actually counterintuitive. In our next profile, Steve Paljieg would actually advise against inclusiveness and teamwork in getting an idea off the ground. You would probably never get this advice from any other book on innovation because they tend to treat cultures as monolithic. Steve is a very savvy innovator who has worked at two large, complex organizations, P&G and Kimberly-Clark, and believes that inclusivity can actually help kill not help the innovator, especially in a Maze. Too many cooks can spoil the broth especially when trying to come up with a uniquely innovative dish, especially in its early phases. Teamwork in the traditional sense is not always as good at enabling innovation as conventional wisdom may have you believe.

Maze Profile
Steve Paljieg, Kimberly-Clark
Senior Director,
Corporate Growth &
Innovation

Huggies MomInspired
Launches Second Year

Nurturing Babies and Innovations

Huggies MomInspired Grant Program Launches Annual Search for
Best New Products Inspired by Parents and Babies

DALLAS, May 6, 2013 – Is your little bundle of joy your greatest source of inspiration? This Mother's Day, Huggies is celebrating innovative parents by encouraging them to apply for the Huggies® MomInspired®

Grant Program. Four million babies are born each year and more than 84 percent of "mompreneurs" said they developed their big ideas *after* becoming a parent[1]. The Huggies MomInspired Grant Program – now in its fourth year – is here to help turn those dreams into a reality.

Just as Mother's Day draws near, applications can be submitted starting <u>today</u> at www.HuggiesMomInspired.com. Huggies will award $15,000 grants to up to 12 people to explore and grow their innovative product ideas that help make parents' lives easier. Winners will receive business advice from Maria Bailey, author, radio and TV personality and founder of BSMMedia.com, as well as support from Kimberly-Clark.

"The Huggies MomInspired Grant Program was created because we saw the need to help fund women-owned businesses and start-ups, but the grant is open to anyone who has an innovative baby or child care product or idea – it is not limited to only Moms or women," said Kelly Stephenson, Huggies senior brand manager. "We are looking forward to adding a new group of creative winners to the Huggies MomInspired family and giving them the opportunity to grow their innovative ideas and businesses."

Apply Now:

- **Who:** Anyone with an original, innovative and viable new product idea to help make life easier for parents; must be 21 and older and reside in the United States
- **How:** Log onto www.HuggiesMomInspired.com and submit application, including the idea and business plan
- **When:** May 6, 2013, through July 31, 2013
- **Why:** For the chance to receive $15,000 and advice to help start or grow your business idea

MomInspired Success Stories:

This year's grant recipients will join 32 others who have continued to develop their winning ideas, products and succeed in small business – from faucet accessories to help little ones wash their hands to wall-mounted diaper dispensers that create a quick and mess-free diaper changing environment.

A past winner, Lauren Levy, continues to experience success with Magnificent Baby – a clothing line that uses special Smart Close magnetic fasteners to make dressing and changing baby faster and easier. Since winning the grant, her business has tripled in sales every year and is now carried nationally in more than 3,000 boutiques and department stores and in more than 15 countries.

Romy Taormina is a 2011 grant recipient for Psi Bands, award-winning acupressure wrist bands for the relief of nausea associated with morning sickness during pregnancy. They are now sold at more than 13,000 major retailers across the country.

For more information about all the grant recipients and the program, visit HuggiesMomInspired.com. Grants will be awarded in fall 2013. (Reprinted with permission from Kimberly-Clark.)

This promotional ad from Kimberly-Clark invites mothers around the world to put forth their innovative ideas and fledgling start-ups for possible seed funding by Kimberly-Clark in Kimberly's quest developing new products for their global markets. Steve Paljieg, the brain trust behind mom inspired describes their mission in the following way.

"Our hope is to help these mom inventors jumpstart their journey, empowering them with the funds, confidence, and resources to realize their dreams and share their unique perspective on parenting challenges," says Steve Paljieg, senior director, corporate innovation for Kimberly-Clark. "Who knows how to solve child-rearing problems better than the moms who live them every day?"

In 2010, the Huggies brand invested a total of a quarter million dollars to financially support the twelve inaugural grant recipients who submitted inventions at every stage of development, ranging from a spill-proof training cup, to a device that relieves the stress and pain of child vaccinations. The program also pledges to further encourage their business success by allowing them access to educational and financial resources from within

Kimberly-Clark and third-party marketing experts. The program is now in its fourth successful year, but it was not easy to get this idea implemented, especially in a very good but conservative large organization like Kimberly-Clark.

Open Innovation

MomInspired is yet another example of the increasing trend toward open innovation. Open innovation (Deloitte, 2009) is a philosophy backed up by action that says, "We as an organization don't have all the best ideas in this increasingly complex and demanding world. Thus, we have to move from 'Proudly Invented Here' to 'Proudly Not Invented Here.'" In fact this last phrase comes from P&G, which now requires that 80 percent of new product ideas come from people outside of P&G. Many companies are now adopting this approach for getting the best ideas from "anywhere and everywhere." The kind of attitude is now quite operational as a result of the Internet, the advent of social networks, and the ability to communicate with anyone around the world in a nanosecond. Health and Human Services, ONR, the CIA, and others have also moved to open innovation as part of their portfolio for idea gathering and problem solving.

In fact, ONR, with the help of researchers at NPS, has funded a multiplayer war game called MMOWGLI (Massive Multiplayer Online Wargame Leveraging the Internet) that allows thousands of people both inside and outside the military to offer ideas on how to best deal with different situations like piracy. Literally thousands of people can sign on to this platform and present their ideas for which they gain points. The Navy hopes to gather information this way, which would not be possible in face-to-face meetings, to help it solve many ongoing problems.

MomInspired is an example of open innovation and can lead Kimberly-Clark into very different types of innovation that cannot only add to the value of the Huggies brand, but could also lead Kimberly-Clark to completely new and different business opportunities. But more importantly, MomInspired allows Kimberly-Clark's employees to increase their intimacy with and knowledge of their target market in ways that no customer surveys or interviews could.

The Value Proposition

As you might have already guessed, the idea for MomInspired was SteveInspired, with the help of his small group of innovators at Kimberly-Clark. As he explains,

> MomInspired was developed under the Huggies franchise. We use external "mom" innovators to broaden our brand promise. We typically give a number of $15,000 grants per year and plan to up the number over the coming years. Kimberly-Clark gave a total of $250,000 in seed capital in the first round and we plan on doing a couple of rounds a year up to $500,000 per year just in the United States alone. We then want to extend the grant process to other countries as well.
>
> We look at these grants as initial seed capital to help take an interesting idea to the next level. We don't intervene but try to act like coaches and business advisors on how to start and manage a small business. We have contact with these entrepreneurial moms at least quarterly to discuss how their businesses are growing and developing and help them assess how these ideas are received in the marketplace.

Since many of the moms that Kimberly-Clark give grants to are not businesspeople, Steve and his team are pretty open about how the ideas are presented. Some moms come with business plans that may be partially executed, but many others come in various stages of maturation.

> Plans range in depth. Some moms, more than half, have a patent application or some sort of small online business, but others (40 to

50 percent) come in the form of "I have an idea and am sending you a jpeg with the idea sketched out but no business plan." We capture them at varying levels of maturity in what we call our innovation funnel. Then we evaluate these ideas to see if they have the capability to

- *Extend the Huggies brand promise—To resolve the everyday chaos of being a mom and to create a better relationship between mom and baby.*
- *Ideas have to come from moms who are or have been emerged in the experience of motherhood.*
- *The ideas have to relate to our target audience.*
- *They have to take us to "places and spaces" the company does not naturally gravitate to. Huggies is only involved early on in a baby's life, so it only covers a small corner of the motherhood experience.*

Mompreneurs have several choices in how they want to partner with Kimberly-Clark. Some mothers may want to retain the rights to their businesses and grow them to significant size in which case Kimberly-Clark would most likely take an equity stake. Some moms choose to simply sell the rights to their idea exclusively to Kimberly-Clark, who would then continue developing the idea. Finally, a mom could develop a business with dreams of cashing out at some later date. The only thing that Kimberly-Clark asks in this case is the right of first refusal to buy the business.

Kimberly-Clark is a very sophisticated consumer goods company and consequently has developed very sophisticated consumer analysis techniques. MomInspired has given it another very innovative way to become intimate with its customer base in ways that it has not done before. As Steve says, "There is a real ROI for Kimberly-Clark in giving out these grants because the investments are small but give the promise of huge returns for the company and its customers."

We can get huge benefits from this program, such as the following:

1. *Real knowledge value from the market. We wager a small amount for the mom's particular innovation to see what happens. Most of our resources are dedicated to Huggies diapers, and it would be expensive and difficult for us to convince the company to make big investments in tangential spaces. So we get a real high-quality learning experience in these market opportunities with little bits of seed capital. We can then watch and participate with them in the knowledge they are building.*

2. *Low-cost execution with a very simple business agreement on the website regarding expectations. We guarantee confidentiality and that the IP (intellectual property) is theirs, but we want right of first refusal if they are anticipating the sale of the business. Or we might ask for equity, or just buying the idea. In essence, we are buying an option as the business expands. Who they sell to is their business, but we would like the right of first refusal.*

3. *Opportunity to give commercial potential on a global basis due to our ability to scale.*

4. *Passion. We don't have to try to manufacture passion for an idea within the company, we can capture the passion that these mompreneurs already have about their ideas. Most have a great desire to share their idea with other moms around the world, and we have the assets and capabilities to make this a reality for them.*

I first met Steve while doing a round-the-world tour with Kimberly-Clark as a keynote speaker on innovation for their Global Marketing University. Steve has been with the company since 2006 and is currently a Senior Director, Corporate Growth & Innovation. His title tells you something about his orientation toward innovation along with his nearly twenty years of experience innovating at P&G. He knows a thing or two about innovating in large, complex organizations and with MomInspired, he has hit another innovative home run.

If you are not familiar with Kimberly-Clark, you are probably familiar with one or more of their global brands including Kleenex, Scott Paper Products, Huggies, Kotex, and Depends. In addition to its consumer goods products it is also involved in medical care products including disposable gowns, latex gloves, and sterilization solutions. The Dallas-based company was founded in the United States in 1872 and has around 57,000 employees worldwide.

MomInspired, however, is very different from Kimberly-Clark's traditional focus on brands. It taps into new moms, some of the world's best innovators, for its inspiration. Moms by necessity have to innovate if they are to survive. From using pots and pans as toys, as my mother did, to childproofing doors, new moms often have to improvise on the spot to manage their unpredictable and sometimes chaotic environment, and they are very open to sharing their ideas and solutions with other moms. Steve and his team were quick to understand the wealth of innovative ideas moms possessed that Kimberly-Clark could capitalize on by helping moms become "mompreneurs." In addition, Kimberly-Clark's resources could make a mom's in-home innovation available to others around the world.

Steve-isms: Lessons for the Corporate Innovator

After meeting Steve and talking with him about how he was able to be a serial innovator in two large, successful, and complex organizations, I quickly realized that he also knew a thing or two about Innovation Judo. He has thought a lot about how you innovate in large organizations, and he was happy to share some of these insights in my interview with him. Steve is a very unassuming, down-to-earth person, but behind his humility is a brain that is not only constantly churning out new ideas, it is also thinking astutely about how to get these ideas accepted by the organization. He is very organizationally savvy or Maze bright. How appropriate since he has to innovate in a Maze environment.

As Steve and I were conversing about his life as an organizational innovator, I jokingly told him that he should write a book about innovation because he has been able to boil down a lot of his lessons learned into some fairly simple but powerful suggestions, many of them representing his expertise as an Innovation Judo master. He is especially adept at working in Maze organizations like Kimberly-Clark, which has multiple dimensions of product, brand, function, and geography. Because of its strong historical values and customer-centric focus, Kimberly-Clark has remained relatively free of Asylum-like behavior. Kimberly-Clark is very big on analytics and thus a majority of its decisions are fact-based rather than politically based. That doesn't mean that the company doesn't have politics or some Asylum behavior. All large companies do. But since it tends to live its values, the Asylum orientation is minimal.

Near the end of the interview with Steve, I asked him what lessons he had taken away from his work as an innovator not only at Kimberly-Clark but at P&G as well, and I was immediately struck by how he has utilized Innovation Judo principles throughout his career to help his employers not only innovate but also generate economic value from these innovations.

You will see how Innovation Judo principles underlie a number of his insights.

1. **Top-level sponsorship.** At P&G, Steve was fortunate to report directly to then CEO A.G. Lafley even though he was only in middle management. But since innovation was a hot topic for Lafley, and Steve's job was to help innovate, he had frequent meetings with not only Lafley but the CFO and CIO. He said that they were all great coaches and he was extremely fortunate to

work under their tutelage. Not only did he learn a great deal, but there is nothing like at least one senior-level supporter of innovation to help open doors.

At Kimberly-Clark, Steve was again fortunate to work for CMO Tony Palmer who had the vision to have a group whose mission it was to take Kimberly-Clark to places it would not ordinarily go. Tony is a grand master when it comes to marketing and brand strategy and tactics, but he is also an innovator, and his support of this skunkworks of eight people, called the Corporate Growth and Innovation Team, gave the group the legitimacy to pursue different places where Kimberly-Clark did not have a strong presence. Notice I said *legitimacy*. The approach and tactics for innovating were left up to the group. Legitimacy only gives you the right to formalize the entity, not the capabilities to succeed.

2. **Build the team one person at a time—just in time.** Steve and I agreed on all his lessons, except this one. I was a little taken back at first because this edict seems so counterintuitive. But the more he spoke, the more I realized how important this approach can be especially to innovators in a Maze environment. I often get asked to consult and coach innovation teams that have already been organized. It sort of goes like this: Company A needs to innovate around *X* where *X* could be a product, service, brand, etc. And, of course, it makes sense to put a team together to do this. The team's job is then to go through the 7I model I presented to you in Chapter 2.

Steve's view is that entrepreneurs often succeed because they are very clever about building their team only choosing those who can really add value and only when the time is right for that particular individual to join. And you don't generally know who can help you at the beginning of a new idea because you have to test it with others to get their reactions and passion before you add them. What if you get a blockhead, simply because you think you should add that person to your team because of title, function, or position? Let the idea determine the team membership using a "just in time" mindset.

Nowhere on the Kimberly-Clark organizational chart would you find a team that is assigned to and working on MomInspired. We don't have a formal team but more of a federation or constellation of experts who volunteered their services to make this idea come to life. We made the process of building the team one at a time as a process of self-association. No one was asked or directed by their immediate supervisor to be on a team to do this work. Only when I thought I needed some legal advice on MomInspired did I call up the legal department and say I would like to do this and get your point of view on this. And legal would connect me to someone who might be interested. Something really powerful was working here. People approached this idea as kind of entrepreneurs themselves. They weren't told to go and work on it but saw the value themselves and then negotiated a little with their bosses to get some time to work on it. The dynamic of this was very different. I just got the people I needed at the time I needed their expertise to move the idea along, and through this process I knew that they had passion for the idea because their help was voluntary. Most people try to build the team in preparation for the destination; I build it for the way points.

3. **Be clear on decision rights**—Sometimes we invite people into a decision-making process, not because they can actually make the decision but because we think it would be politically prudent to do so. I have a colleague who does a lot of consulting work in organizational change, and he has his students go through this huge and complex stakeholder mapping exercise just to make sure that they have not forgotten anyone who has a stake in the change. A stake is not necessarily a decision-making right.

Steve has a very different take. Don't worry as much about stakeholders when it comes to innovation, worry about who actually has the decision-making rights regarding your innovation and know specifically when and how these rights can be applied in the innovation process. In fact, he believes it is a mistake to invite people into the decision-making process for political reasons because they can slow things down, even though they can't make the final decision. You may want to inform the nondecision makers, but you can also ignore them as well. Steve knows that sometimes including these folks might backfire, but he is willing to take that risk in order to make sure that a good idea gets implemented. And in Mazes, getting even is less likely to occur than it is in an Asylum or a Jungle.

You could quickly develop a cast of decision makers who would weigh in. The real trick is to just find the three to four people who you need to put in place to be the key decision makers and help support the idea versus working exclusively in the corporate decision-making tree (formal chain of command). Map out just a few of the key decision makers and then use them just in time. Then when I go to the naysayers it is just to inform them because it has already been blessed by the key people. So we tell them what we are doing not to ask their permission to proceed with the idea.

You need to be very clear on who to address and on what basis and what their decision-making rights are. You can ask those with the critical decision-making rights to share their thoughts on how you are navigating the ideas through the organization. One advisor said, "Let's see how far we can get before anyone knows that we are doing this." How do we change our culture from everyone participates to only those we really need so we can speed the pace of innovation?

4. **Avoid box checkers.** Box checkers can be extremely problematic for the innovator. These are the people who want you to cross all the t's and dot all the i's before they are willing to pass an idea up the chain of command. Innovation is a messy process and does not lend itself to this type of box checking mentality. The purpose of prototyping and fast failures allows you to learn what works and what doesn't work. Box checkers either don't understand that ideas take time to evolve or they

are asking you to check all those boxes as a delaying tactic for the purpose of wearing you out, or waiting you out. If your direct boss is a box checker, try to follow Steve's advice and get a higher-up to sanction a trial of the idea or keep it under wraps. Develop proof of concept and then present. It's hard for someone to ask you to go back and check all the boxes if you already have compelling proof of concept.

Box checkers make it much more difficult for the innovator especially in the early phases. They want certainty at gate one but you only really want to address one of their questions as gate three not one. Your idea has to look like something before it gets a fair hearing. I can get a lot more support with just a one-page business plan that captures the essence of the idea.

5. **Link to strategy/speak the native tongue.** While Steve's group was tasked to take the brand to places it wouldn't ordinarily go, he was always careful to communicate that MomInspired, although very different from typical brand marketing, was still part of the Huggies strategy because it was just another way to extend the brand promise. Since brand management is so embedded in Kimberly-Clark, it would be hard to sell an idea that was not considered part of brand management. While MomInspired may wind up taking Kimberly-Clark into some very different businesses, the idea would probably not have seen the light of day if the idea was positioned as creating innovative new businesses as opposed to extending the brand promise. Brand is important to Kimberly-Clark, and Steve had to stick with this focus in order for his idea to get a fair hearing.

We know we will eventually have to get firm approval, but let's get it crafted enough so that it can get a fair shake so that people can appreciate it. As much as you want to tease out the idea, you want to understand the needs of your internal audience for your innovation, and then put something in front of them at the right time in the right way to get a receptive audience.

6. **Pull from the top, push from the bottom.** Getting an idea adopted and implemented in a Maze is a little like pushing a stone uphill. The destination is clear, but you need some leverage in order to give enough oomph to get to the top of the hill before it can pick up its own energy on the down slope. Steve believes that you need to get some push from the top as well as pull from the bottom to get an idea rolling.

It took me half of the year to develop the idea. The project team was just me, but only when we got to some concrete stuff did I start to reach out to others. Only a handful of people helped get it off the ground.

What I have become adept at is doing innovation from the bottom but getting the pull from the top that helps negotiate the middle levels. With this help, you could quickly see how the person who owns the North American family business for Huggies would feel about this.

7. **Pitch it in a page.** The culture at P&G was that of a "one-page memo," and this is where Steve learned the discipline of boiling even the most complicated "big idea" down to one page. P&G's philosophy was that if you couldn't say it in a page you didn't understand the real essence of your idea so why should others waste their time in trying to figure out what you were saying. When Steve first came to Kimberly-Clark, the modus operandi for introducing new ideas was "death by PowerPoint" so it was a big adjustment for Steve. When Tony Palmer, the new CMO, came on board from Coca-Cola, he also brought the one-page mindset. For all his MomInspired selling within Kimberly-Clark, Steve only brought a one-page description. Of course he had backup material if asked, but he rarely needed to use it.

When Tony, my new boss, came on board I gave him my idea in a one-page memo. He looked surprised and said, "Thank God, I finally found someone who can give me just one page." It's also important to get to this one page quickly. First it helps you understand, then it helps others understand.

8. **Don't let lack of resources stand in the way.** One of the truths about innovation is that if you had all the time and resources in the world, you probably would not be innovative. Innovation usually germinates from a lack of time and resources. Not that resources are bad, but people get truly innovative when they have to do something without something. Opening a beer bottle without an opener. If you always had an opener with you, then you would probably never improvise. And so it is true with resources. Constrained resources, not abundance, is the catalyst for real new ideas. When Steve worked for P&G, he wound up developing an internal venture capital group that reported to a venture board. They came up with a great new idea but did not have the resources to pull it off.

We got to a point on a project for the venture board where we said we love the idea and we want to advance it but we did not have the resources to do it. So we went to one of our vendors and came back with $5 million to underwrite the development cost. We then developed the product, commercialized it, and rewarded the vendor with a sizable piece of the action based on the performance of the product in the market. Going it alone today is pretty difficult. It was a really new experience for P&G to say we can't do it ourselves, but we constructed a model where vendors could participate in a new business development project.

9. **Don't let process substitute for progress.** I believe that many American businesses are process obsessed. Since the arrival of Lean Six Sigma there is too much talk about process black belts and not enough questioning about whether all these processes lead to progress or just bureaucracy. There are numerous books on the processes involved in organizational innovation and not enough talk about measures of progress, especially the right measures. Although it does let us know our ideas are moving along, we should use the process to help but not to substitute for progress.

As of this writing, I am on a plane headed back from an innovation summit held in Washington, D.C. Most of the participants were in one or more of our prestigious government science and technology centers. I volunteered to be on a breakout team that tackled the challenge of how to measure innovation. It was interesting to see how many of the people in my group thought that the number of patents they produced was a measure of innovation. It may be a measure of intellectual capital creation, but it is not a measure of progress. The real measure would be how many patents actually turn into implemented ideas that wind up creating value for a customer of the lab. But, of course, what gets measured gets done, and if we are measuring patents instead of real progress, then not much might be getting done.

And more importantly, Steve believes that a lot of passion gets hidden or eroded in the processes, but it is the progress that excites the innovator and those who will support the innovation.

10. **Passion can be read as overconfidence.** Earlier in the book, I told you how important passion is for innovating. Without passion for an idea, you or others probably won't have the motivation to overcome the roadblocks and blockheads that will eventually stand in your way. But Steve reminded me that sometimes you have to lever back on your outward display of passion if you think others will see you as being overconfident. Kimberly-Clark is a fairly conservative organization run by very thoughtful people, but a display of too much passion could indeed be read as over the top and therefore suspect.

I recently got a call from an entrepreneur who wanted me to help him pitch his idea to my bosses in D.C. His idea was a good one, but his passion, combined with his frustration, really turned me off. He was so passionate that he even threatened to go directly to my boss if I wasn't willing to be the go-between. This kind of passion is scary, and I ran in the other direction as fast as I could.

Judo Application Summary

Working in a Maze has its special challenges for the innovator, but the good news is that it can and often does work on logic. For example, Steve was able to identify the decision makers, make a one-page pitch, and ignore others who didn't have decision rights without much fear of retribution because he convinced enough of the right people and he had done his homework.

But he still had to rely on several of the Innovation Judo principles I talk about in this book.

So let's take a look at the ones he used.

- **Leverage**
  - *Informal network*
  - *Top cover*
  - *Referent power*
- **Speed**
  - *Idea to opportunity*
  - *Embed quickly*
- **Unbalancing**
  - *Foot sweep criticism*
  - *Power shifting*
- **Discipline**
  - *Bridled passion*

LEVERAGE

The Informal Network The real decision makers in a maze are not hard to identify. Unlike Jungles, they are often the people who have the formal authority by right of their job descriptions to make certain decisions. They are responsible and accountable. In Jungles, the real decision makers are hidden, and their power may have nothing at all to do with their titles. Steve went after the real decision makers at Kimberly-Clark one at a time so that he could utilize one person's support to win another's support. This is an excellent example of using leverage to create more leverage. Steve kept adding people to his side of the teeter-totter until he had enough people on board to lift the rock.

Top Cover/Referent Power With most innovators, it's nice to have someone near the top who cares about innovation and wants you to succeed. Kimberly-Clark had recently hired a new chief marketing officer who was a keen advocate of innovation, and MomInspired clearly caught his attention. Steve used that support to help him get more top-level support, which helped give him a lot of power to fend off naysayers—and there were definitely some naysayers.

SPEED

Idea to Opportunity He was also quick to get his idea from fuzzy concept to clear and concise in a one-page memo. He didn't run around to a bunch of people throwing around half-baked ideas, but took the time to edit his idea down to an easily understood and communicated document. This document provided not only the essence of the idea but the business case behind it. Try doing this for yourself in one page. I can tell you from experience it's not easy. You have to a lot of research, talking with others, and looking at technology to be able to really come to grips with the innovation you are trying to sell to others. I wish more people were trained to do this as it can increase the speed of innovation for the individual and the organization. Many ideas die simply because they take too long to develop or they cannot be easily explained to others, or the innovator doesn't actually understand his own idea very well.

Unbalancing This Innovation Judo principle is typically less used in Mazes than it is in Jungles or Asylums, but Steve did use some of Lewin's Force Field Analysis when he talked about pushing from the top and pulling from the bottom so that he could overcome resistance from the middle, which is where most resistance resides regarding innovation that will create significant changes.

DISCIPLINE

Steve also utilized discipline. He carefully identified the decision makers, presented an opportunity rather than just a half-baked idea, and took the time and energy to carefully seek out and influence others in the organization who could get excited about his idea and were willing to give their time and energy in support. He was also very disciplined in making sure that his show of passion was appropriate to the Kimberly-Clark culture. It has somewhat of a conservative feel to it, and Steve was very adept at modulating his passion in the service of persistence rather than hyperbole.

Note that some of the other principles of Innovation Judo were not as useful in Steve's case. Unlike Russ Sabo, there was no need for shock therapy, and in fact shock therapy would probably have worked against him at Kimberly-Clark or P&G. He also did not have to utilize opening or circling to advance his idea. He just had to work the system in a methodical manner.

7 Principles Quick Guide Self-Test

Reread the preceding profile and look for the use of other Judo principles that I have not referred to in the summary. Place a check mark beside each tactic which you can identify.

Discipline
- ☐ Preparation
- ☐ Passion
- ☐ Bring opportunities
- ☐ Patience
- ☐ Self-control

Leverage
- ☐ Corporate values
- ☐ Customer
- ☐ Competitor
- ☐ Referent power
- ☐ Strategy
- ☐ Informal network
- ☐ Dote on quotes

Redirection
- ☐ Feigning
- ☐ Pulling

Circling
- ☐ Walk around opponents
- ☐ Walk around ideas
- ☐ Circle the wagons
- ☐ Brand enhancement
- ☐ Numbers
- ☐ Pilots/Prototypes
- ☐ Seams

Openings
- ☐ Hot buttons
- ☐ Cost cutting/Containment
- ☐ Efficiency/Effectiveness

Speed
- ☐ Idea to opportunity
- ☐ Fail fast
- ☐ Quick to reshape/Pull plug
- ☐ Dash into openings
- ☐ Forgiveness, not permission
- ☐ Embed quickly

Unbalancing
- ☐ Surprise
- ☐ Underpromise/Overdeliver
- ☐ Foot sweep criticism
- ☐ Shock therapy
- ☐ Power shifting

CHAPTER 9

Assailing Asylums

A Dangerous Intersection

Innovating in Asylum landscapes is tricky because they are often fraught with politics, jealousy, silos, and revenge. And, of course, there is NIH (not invented here). As I said in the chapter on wackiness, most organizations don't desire to be wacky but the way they are set up and the approach of key leaders often conspire to set up this kind of atmosphere.

Nonetheless, Innovation Judo can be a valuable ally as it was for Jim Repp especially when he worked in DaimlerChrysler. I did quite a bit of consulting and executive development programs for this company and I liked the people a lot, but I also had a great deal of empathy for them because it was not easy to get things done, especially across organizational boundaries. I recognized this when I did my first executive program for them. My contact in HR at the time was not in her office when we ran into a technical problem with the projector and sound that needed immediate attention for the program to continue. When I couldn't find her, I asked the person in the next desk over, also an HR person, if she could help. I was quickly informed that it was not her job, and she brusquely turned back to her work. Fortunately there were a couple of engineers in the class who were able to sort the problem out, but my experience was not unusual at the company, so I quickly learned whom I would get help from and whom I wouldn't. Chrysler at that time was also quite political. We had several debates about which employees should be in my class together. Should a first-level manager be allowed to participate because it might offend another manager who was one grade above him? And we once debated where we were going to hold a meeting as one manager insisted we hold it in his office because he felt more important, even though another manager's office was more convenient.

Despite wackiness, Chrysler was still able to turn out some great cars like the Jeep Wrangler, the Chrysler 300, and the

Dodge Viper. It also turned out some losers like the K-car that even the senior executives were ashamed to drive. But one of its consistently loved and revered brands is the Jeep Wrangler even though they were often troublesome mechanically until just a few years ago when they started focusing on quality. After finishing this book, and prompted by Jim's story, I went out and bought a new Jeep Rubicon. It is a terrific vehicle and the best Jeep yet. Good thing I didn't find a story involving the creation of a Maserati.

The following is the story of Jim Repp, an engineer and Innovation Judo master extraordinaire. He was the product developer who got the Jeep Rubicon built against some pretty big odds. This very successful vehicle, and now the brand's poster child, would never have seen the light of day had Jim and his "Lunatic Fringe" team not applied a number of Innovation Judo principles including *openings, surprise, discipline, leverage,* and *redirection.* Jim's story reveals how these principles can be used for your own company's good even though no one thinks your idea is a good one.

When I use DaimlerChrysler as an Asylum example, I am not saying the company is in any way bad. Chrysler is a great American company that has rebounded a number of times from near-death experiences and has made some great cars over the years, such as the iconic Jeep, the Chrysler Town and Country, Dodge trucks, and the inimitable Dodge Viper. But like many large established companies, silos and politics begin to erode the fabric of the organization. It doesn't mean that good products can't be made, only that the innovator has more hurdles to go over. Jim's story is about insular silos that often develop in large complex companies that start to create a certain NIH (not invented here) mentality that then becomes a symptom of wackiness (illogic).

Asylum Profile
Jim Repp, Jeep Brand Engineer

I first met Jim when I was teaching a course on innovation for DaimlerChrysler (now Chrysler). The course was for director-level managers, and we were trying to encourage greater innovation and entrepreneurial thinking within the company. As with most large companies, the topic of innovation is often met with a certain amount of skepticism. Some employees voice concerns that the company is too big and bound by too many rules or that managers don't listen to their ideas, or that risk taking is actually discouraged rather than encouraged.

So to counter these attitudes, I often look for internal company innovators who represent proof that innovation can happen within their walls. Jim was one such case. The Chrysler HR manager suggested him as a possible guest speaker in my class as he was the innovator behind the Rubicon, one of Jeep's most successful new product launches.

Jim was perfect. He is ebullient, slightly irreverent, and has energy oozing from every pore. He is not afraid to take on tough challenges and doesn't mind a tussle or two with the organization's hierarchy. He is also a Jeep nut, and part of the "Lunatic Fringe" surrounding the Jeep Wrangler, one of America's most recognized and revered car brands.

Jim is now the Vehicle Development Manager for Jeep at Chrysler Corporation. This picture is of Jim in his Jeep going over the Moab Rim in Utah. His love affair with the Jeep Wrangler continues, as does his innovation of Jeep products.

The Lunatic Fringe, as Jim calls them, are the hard-core Jeep Wrangler enthusiasts who like to do extreme off-roading. They push their vehicles to the limit over terrain that would scare most of us to death, and as far as major dents, dings, fenders torn off, or transmissions ripped from the bottom of the Jeep while trying to surmount a rock, well these people see these as badges of honor. Jim considers himself a member in good standing with this group, but he also has his feet firmly planted in the automobile industry, where he has worked for more than twenty years.

I profiled Jim in this book because he is also an Innovation Judo master par excellence. The Jeep Rubicon would probably not exist today if Jim and his passionate core team of Jeep enthusiasts at Chrysler had not practiced this art. The Rubicon, named after one of the most difficult off-road trails in California, is arguably the best stock off-road vehicle available today. It can do things that not even the ordinary Jeep can do when it comes to off-roading. It has a unique suspension, special axles, a heavy-duty transmission, and other rugged features that enable drivers to take it places that even hikers might find daunting,

But the Rubicon would have remained a figment of Jim's imagination had he not been able to practice his Innovation Judo skills in overcoming a tremendous number of barriers, both organizational and individual, that conspired to kill the idea.

Jim graduated from Bowling Green State University in Ohio with a degree in manufacturing engineering, and after a couple of jobs in different industries, he was enticed to follow his boss over to Chrysler to work on the Jeep products. He was always a car nut and had owned a couple of Jeeps so he was happy to work in the product development area on both the emerging Grand Cherokee and the languishing Jeep Wrangler products.

In the late 1990s Jim was in vehicle development for the original Grand Cherokee. He started the second generation of the Grand Cherokee and did some work on the Wrangler as well. Chrysler had a big marketing splash in 1996 for the Wrangler, but then let it languish due to redirected attention in different areas of the business. He eventually lobbied with his boss to become the vehicle development supervisor for Wrangler, because

I wanted to come back. Wrangler was kind of languishing—it launched, it was good, but it wasn't really getting any attention. Chrysler had developed some off-road packages for the Grand Cherokee and the Cherokee, and I wondered why didn't they want to offer a package for the Wrangler? That just bugged me because I'm kind of a four-wheeling freak. So I went back to Chrysler with the intention to do some type of an off-road package for Wrangler. That was really my original goal for going back there, and eventually I wanted to get the company to pay more attention to the Wrangler program. We jokingly referred to the Wrangler as the redheaded bastard stepchild of the corporation. No one even cared about it, and no one was really working on it much. It had very little visibility. It was in life-support mode. It had mediocre sales over three years, and there just wasn't that much excitement over it.

Jim pulled together a small team of other Jeep enthusiasts to help work on some of the Wrangler's quality and performance problems with the mission of improving its quality and customer appeal. He was also able to get his group to move to their own lab away from the mainstream operation so that they could concentrate on the Wrangler's problems. But in the back of his mind, he really wanted Jeep to build a high-end, best-in-class off-road Wrangler that anyone could buy. His intuition told him there was a market for this kind of mass-produced vehicle because of his experience in off-roading contests and meets. A lot of off-roaders would buy a stock Wrangler and then put in anywhere from $3000 to $12,000 in modifications to make the Jeep really handle difficult situations. Since these folks were amateur car builders, they would often put in the wrong components or do things that could actually make their customized Jeep more dangerous, and often these modifications didn't give their Jeeps the hoped-for performance capabilities. Some amateurs put the wrong size tires on their Jeep, or they had the wrong shocks on that made the Jeep less agile.

So why didn't Jeep already make a modified Jeep for the market so these folks wouldn't have to build their own and sell it for a price less than what the modifiers were paying? Plus with Jim's automobile engineering experience he knew he could build his dream Jeep by knitting all the right components together at the time of manufacture. Because of his years in the industry, he knew Chrysler could build it to or beyond current safety requirements for such vehicles.

Giving Birth

One Friday afternoon at 3:30 Jim and his team were having their regular staff meeting, but this time, as Jim said, something happened that made it a very different kind of meeting.

> *So we have our staff meeting at 3:30. We kept talking about what we can do to sell more Wranglers, and we've got to do some packages. And of course you're always working with marketing to do those little tweaks—you can build a couple thousand special packages and call them spring specials. Little things to get marketing blurbs and some attention.*
>
> *And at about 5:30, we started to write the list of those incremental changes that none of us were particularly excited about. But one team member said to another, "What if you could build your dream Wrangler? What would it look like?" We then changed direction and started listing all these different dream components—locking axles, affordable PKs, rocker protection, bumpers, tires—all these things*

that we would aspire to have on a production car, which were effectively things we had done to our own Jeeps, our own personal stuff. Because one of the other team members, Dave Yeggee, was a Jeep nut as well, we were both in tune with this idea. He probably owned at least eight or nine Jeeps at the time and I had two. We started discussing how he modified his and how I modified mine. It was an interesting balance between Dave and myself. Dave was much more the off-road modification guy. I was more the reality guy. "So let's put our ideas together and get it into production. Let's find a realistic compromise," guys.

After we made the list, at about six o'clock, we read it back, and all three of us basically laughed hysterically because there was no way in hell Chrysler would let us get that into production. It was going to be over a million dollars. So it's like, "Yeah, we're going to do that," and we just chuckled and walked away.

And that was the birth of the Jeep Rubicon concept. But they knew that the road from idea to implementation would be as obstacle-laden as the physical trails that their dream Jeep would have to navigate if it ever became a reality. There was no interest for this car at Chrysler, no strategy or budget had been allocated, and here were a small group of engineers trying to tell Chrysler marketers that they knew more about the market potential for this kind of car than they did. Nonetheless they knew the 7,000 to 8,000 Jeep Lunatic Fringe folks who attended Camp Jeep each year very well because this was one of the few times engineers were allowed to come face to face with the customer.

This is when the Innovation Judo skills started to kick in. Jim and his team knew that logic would not prevail, plus their logic had no proof of concept that people would actually buy such a vehicle from Chrysler despite the very palpable passion within the Fringe. It was only their intuition and knowledge of these niche customers that made them believe there was a real market for this product out there. Plus they knew that in a silo like Chrysler, it would take some real discipline, surprise, leverage, and the right openings to make the Rubicon a reality.

Then we knew we had to try to transition this idea to upper management if it was to have a chance of survival. We would have to be clever. Dave and I decided that we're going to build a little stealth car, a stunt car sort of, a little project vehicle. We sometimes call them mules because they look like any other Jeep on the outside, but we hide the other specialty things on the inside so no one can tell the difference. We then acquired, shall we say temporarily borrowed, some parts from the company and bought some stuff with our own money. We traded for parts. We did all sorts of stuff. We were building it—Dave builds the first transfer case over the weekend in his garage. One of the axles was built in somebody else's garage. Then we got braver and started bringing these parts into the plant located in Toledo, Ohio, and started doing the prototyping work because basically we had very little supervision.

To maintain our normal jobs, everything had to be clicking. There were normal programs coming along, obviously you're very busy with that stuff. This Jeep work was all done after-hours. We started working on this project car at five or six o'clock at night, and we'd stay in the office until nine, ten o'clock. We'd come in on Saturdays and put in seven or eight hours. The mechanic started coming in on his own time for free. The union guy was helping us. So we were just basically project building under the radar. Of course, meanwhile we're still talking to the managers and saying, "Wouldn't it be a great idea if . . ." We knew in our hearts that this is what customers would buy. Convincing management this is what customers wanted was a little more challenging. And of course there's a business case that you have to prove to the corporation, so you have the white shirts with the ties in the company, and they say, "Well, it's kind of a cool car, but it's crazy, why would I do that? I've already got the best off-road vehicle in the world, it's already the best." Yeah, but we can make it better.

Fortunately, Jim and his team had a great opening to see if their idea was a real opportunity or just a dream. Every year Jeep sponsored an event called Camp Jeep where Jeep lovers could come together and compete on some of the toughest off-road trails you can find in the United States. These events bring thousands of people together so Jeep owners can mingle with people from Chrysler, and they allow engineers to come talk directly to the customers without any influence from the marketing department.

> So one of the ways we went about it is we built these mules as we called them. And we built a couple of these secret vehicles and began sneaking them around showing them to people. We'd have these big executive trips and go to the Rubicon Trail and teach a little bit about four-wheeling at Camp Jeep. We would build stock vehicles, a couple of Wranglers, a couple of Grand Cherokees, and then we would include one of our mules in the shipping without telling anyone. Of course it looks like a normal Wrangler, but when you get in it, it's like, "Wow, this car never gets stuck. This car's easier to drive. How come this car can go up that mountain while the others get stuck at the bottom?" And we start to demonstrate what a four-wheel transfer case is, what a locking differential is, what the differences can be, how the bigger tires can help, and how having different air pressure in the lighter construction tire makes a huge difference in off-road capabilities.

Opening, Speed, and Leverage

Jim is a gregarious guy who has no trouble schmoozing with anyone at any level in the company. He noticed that the executives who would come out to Camp Jeep got pretty excited about off-roading because most had never done this before, at least not with the extreme Jeep enthusiasts who really know what they are doing. Plus these trips would usually last two days a day to drive out to the remote area, an overnight camp-out, and a day getting back.

When the executives got out on the trail, they got kind of excited about four-wheeling, because they don't usually do this kind of stuff, and then they find this one car, our mule, and they go, "Wow, that thing does everything. What is that?" And you have time to sit with them while you're camping out in the woods around the campfire having a beer, because basically you have to camp because it's in a pretty remote location. It's a good time to interface, and you're teaching them about what the car can do. And you can have a very intense uninterrupted conversation with an executive in this kind of remote setting.

Jim also identified a young woman in the marketing department who was new to the company, thus potentially more open-minded to their Rubicon project. They invited her to come out to Camp Jeep, and she showed up in high heels and makeup. They told her she couldn't get out of the car because she would probably sink up to her knees in mud, but they made their point, eventually turning her from skeptic to advocate.

These outings with executives were particularly helpful. Jeep customers would often surround one of Jim's mules after it outperformed all the others under extreme road conditions, and they would ask him how they could get one like it. When you start to get customers who want a product that isn't even on the market, you know you have a real opportunity not just a good idea. This was not lost on Chrysler's executives who eventually gave Jim a formal green light to bring this concept into production with full company backing. Jim also learned a lot during these trail rides as well that would prove important to the company, especially the marketing department. He noticed that there were actually two extremely diverse and distinct customer segments at opposite ends of the spectrum, not just the Lunatic Fringe.

There were the guys who knew what the Rubicon is, and they were going to use it—they were going to go out and four-wheel the hell out of it; and then there was the box checker rich guy. I've got to have it.

It's the coolest looking thing since sliced bread. He's buying the image. The other guys are establishing the image.

Patience and Discipline

Despite the formal go-ahead, Jim and his team ran into multiple roadblocks and blockheads.

We did an official kickoff to look at some of the content that would be in the production model. Well, of course, that came out and it was Chicken Little. The sky was falling. "There's no way we can do that. There's no way you can do this. What are you guys, crazy?" It had gone through engineering, the dynamics of the handling guys, and the lawyers, and they all went ballistic. Now you have to partition off each individual group, you have to talk to them, and you start to work with them and you start to explain what you're doing. You have to demonstrate that it works. You have to have a lot of salesmanship. There's an awful lot of one-on-one discussion about working with people individually.

And you have to let them vent. You have to let them talk. If they freak out, then you have to point out tactfully how they're wrong and you're right. We used data to fight perceptions. Let's go run the test and I'll show you it works. Here are the numbers that says it works. I mean every time you turned around it was a roadblock. You know, the handling guys were concerned about these types of tires and having a taller vehicle. The impact guy said it would never work because it was taller and it was going to change the way the airbags fired. The lawyer said there was too much liability off-road. You can't have a locking differential because of on-road manners.

There had to be hundreds of issues that people threw in our faces, and we just partitioned each one and individually took it on and started to work.

So eventually we do the program. We get it developed with a lot of angst. I don't need to bog you down with the details of every little component possible, because it was a lot of work. I mean it was just literally like climbing Mount Everest. Every time we'd turn around, there was another rock to climb over. Because as production comes closer, you have to get all those issues organized so you can launch. It was becoming very difficult to do all that at the last minute, and we were running twelve to fourteen hours a day. Of course, no overtime. We just did it. We worked the weekends. Whatever it took to get this program launched. It had become a work of passion at this point. Our passion was the whole platform. They're running way outside their normal realm. We're completely out-of-control from a corporate control standpoint, but we're rocking. We're excited about the project. We're going.

But the great thing was, when we realized we're going to launch this. We're friends with all of the four-wheel community. Rumors are out there that they're seeing these weird wheels and different axles on the cars. But it looks like a regular Wrangler. We didn't badge it. If you looked real close you could see a few differences. And when we'd go out on a public trail to test it, we didn't tell people what it was. We just said we were a bunch of Jeep guys. We never told them we were engineering. We tried to hide the manufacturer plates. We'd always have other cars in front and other cars at the back.

There were all kinds of rumors floating around in the four-wheel-drive magazines. And, of course, we can't say anything because of corporate confidentiality—you want to have the PR launch, you want it to remain secret. But the rumors are out there, and the magazines are starting to write about this one like a year and a half before it came out. Because they felt that we were up to something, but of course we can't tell anybody. We won't tell them anything because that's not our job. Our job is to keep it quiet. The PR's job is to launch the vehicle to the press, not us. We'll support them from a technical standpoint, and we're friends with the PR people, but we're better friends with the four-wheeling editors. So we're walking this fine line. You can't tell them what you're doing. They're respectful, but they're always trying to learn something. But you never tell them anything.

After two years, the Rubicon was officially launched in Utah at an off-roading event attended by 8,000 to 10,000 people. Marketing estimated that only 2,000 to 3,000 Rubicons would sell in the first year. By the end of the year sales were over 12,000. Fortunately for Chrysler, Jim and his team had told the suppliers to make sure that they build parts for at least 10,000 cars, but of course, they didn't mention this to either finance or marketing. They were so sure they had a winner, that they were willing to take this risk potentially hanging themselves out to dry.

Judo Application Summary

- **Discipline**
  - *Preparation*
  - *Passion/Patience*
  - *Self-control*
- **Leverage**
  - *The customer*
  - *Top cover*
- **Unbalancing**
  - *Surprise*
  - *Power shifting*
  - *Shock therapy*
- **Redirection**
  - *Feigning*
  - *Pulling*

Let's take Jim's story apart from an Innovation Judo perspective. He faced both roadblocks and blockheads and had to utilize a number of Innovation Judo principles to defend his idea. As you could tell from his account of the process, very few people were compelled by his dream, and marketing was actually against it. Clearly NIH was working as well as the silo mentality that often exists in Asylum landscapes. Jim and his team also faced a big bureaucracy of people whose first and easiest response to his idea was to say no. But perhaps the biggest roadblock was on the wackiness side. Large organizations need to have specialists or you would have everyone doing everything and getting in each other's way. This differentiation of skills and focus is necessary and most often results in the functional organization designs that we are all familiar with. Engineers have to go to school a long time to be good at their specialty as do accountants and production folks. Marketing people normally get most of their training in the function as they learn by doing.

The goal is that these various functions listen to and cooperate with each other so that the organization is both differentiated in terms of specialties and also integrated in terms of cooperative interactions, but in Jim's case it was clear that people in the marketing function could not accept an innovative idea from an engineer because he was just an "engineer" and how could he possibly have the customer insights that they did? Additionally, marketing folks often rely on statistical surveys, data analysis to parse the customer into a multitude of different categories. How could Jim's personal insights and intuition as a member of the Jeep Lunatic Fringe ever outweigh their scientific approach? Innovators often face this problem. Since innovation is often about the unproven, you have to resort to nondata tactics like Innovation Judo to get your idea heard. Let's see which of the Innovation Judo principles Jim used. In Asylums, it's very important to be disciplined and steadfast in your approach. It's easy to get worn out and discouraged when people say no without the facts. Jim not only did his behind-the-scenes Innovation Judo work; he also did his out-front persistent and data-driven logical work.

DISCIPLINE

Preparation Early on, the Rubicon team predicted that it would run into roadblocks and blockheads. The team members left their seminal first meeting laughing hilariously, feeling that there was no way in hell the company would let them put all this stuff into a Jeep. Although they started to share this idea with others in the company, they didn't just talk; they built. This is critical because there was no proof of a market for the Rubicon, so they had to demonstrate that they had an opportunity, not an idea. Having hoards of off-roaders mob the mule demonstrated that there were a lot of potential customers with an unmet need who were keen on the Rubicon idea. They also demonstrated that with their designed-in components this Jeep could outperform other off-road vehicles including Chrysler's, and at a price point that individuals who tried to modify their own Jeeps could not match.

The team spent a lot of time planning its assault on the Asylum. Note the steps that they went through:

- Develop the design.
- Build the mules.
- Prove the concept on the trail.
- Use Camp Jeep as the focal point for proof of concept.
- Divide and conquer naysayers.
- Anticipate resistance and fight it with data.

Passion/Patience It took over two years from that Friday meeting for the first Rubicon to roll off Jeep's assembly line. Without extraordinary passion, the Rubicon team would never have been able to sustain their march toward the realization of their idea. Yet they balanced their passion with a disciplined plan of attack. And, they were very patient. Instead of losing their tempers at the naysayers, they took a lot of time to speak with people individually, and used data and observation to allay their fears.

Self-control Frustration with complexity is different than frustration with wackiness. Under conditions of complexity, you and I must become good detectives uncovering people and places we have to go through in order to get our ideas heard, but there is a pathway that exists and we must discover it unless someone gives us the map. With wackiness, there is no road map since wackiness is not logical. Fortunately, Jim is a pretty sage guy, and his years with Chrysler gave him a great deal of experience working the system and self-control when dealing with frustration. Although Jim would tell you that he had to spend some time encouraging his own team, in helping them deal with the frustration of wackiness especially the slowness in finding and creating openings, the NIH, and the bureaucrats' no as first response.

LEVERAGE

Top Cover Jim realized early on that without executive support his idea would be easily squashed. Inviting the executives out on the trail was all part of the team's strategy to co-opt the executives into formalizing the secret attempt to develop the Rubicon. Most middle-level employees don't have that much opportunity to interact in a prolonged manner with the senior-level executives. Camp Jeep was the perfect tool for this interaction and a chance to sell the idea. Three days on the trail provided an incredible venue for having this interaction. You will see that Innovation Judo masters are quite adept at finding or creating these opportunities. Chris Kluckhuhn, the Coast Guard innovator, used a plane ride to New Orleans after Hurricane Katrina to get this kind of time. Senior leaders, who are behind your innovation, give you incredible leverage as well as top cover. And remember that this co-opting of senior management is done under conditions of right-mindedness. We are not "sucking up" to them for self-promotion purposes; we are trying to engage them in the innovation process for the good of the company.

The Customer The customer, of course, can be one of the biggest leverages that you can utilize, assuming of course that your organization cares about the company. Jim's love affair with his concept is admirable but not as compelling as having hundreds of people at Camp Jeep and other off-road events literally salivating over the mule after it just climbed a mountain that no other vehicle could. And if you can get an executive there to see this, or in Jim's case some skeptic from marketing, then there is no doubt that your idea has the beginnings of opportunity written all over it.

UNBALANCING

Surprise The building of the secret mule(s) in Jim's garage was a key to their success. First, it gave the team a chance to actually touch the idea. For some reason, innovators need a tactile feel for their idea. Just looking at it on paper or even on a CAD/CAM display does not suffice for actual touch and feel. That is why prototyping is so essential. You really don't understand your idea until you can play with it. Building the mule helped the team members understand what worked and what didn't, and they got a feel for how much various off-road options would cost and what kinds of advantages in performance they could achieve. For example, some expensive modifications had very little effect on improved performance while others like tires had a lot.

Keeping it under wraps was also essential to the team's success. This prevented interference from management before they could really demonstrate that they had something worth looking at. Ideas are easily killed when they look ugly, and the Rubicon team wanted to make its idea work before presenting it. The team's ability to really test the mule and make modifications allowed it to surprise everyone. They built a good surprise, which is an important part of their approach. If this mystery Jeep had been unveiled too early in its development and fallen off the side of the mountain rather than climbing it, they probably would have doomed their idea forever.

Shock Therapy Notice that Jim and his team also maximized the shock value by making the Jeep look ordinary and then put it through its pace at Camp Jeep, the best possible theater for gaining maximal attention from both Jeep lovers and Chrysler executives. Many organizations formalize a skunkworks organization for this kind of prototyping out of the spotlight. It's too easy for people to take a look at a half-baked idea and see only what doesn't work versus the potential of things that could work. It is a little like keeping a newborn in the hospital for a while to make sure that his or her immune system works properly enough for the rigors of the outside world. Jim's garage as skunkworks served this purpose admirably.

Power Shifting In an earlier chapter, I spoke about Kurt Lewin and Force Field Analysis where the innovator can increase driving forces for his idea, reduce restraining forces to his idea, or convert restraining forces into driving forces. When the Rubicon project was finally greenlighted, Jim still heard many bureaucratic nos.

While data don't usually help that much in Asylums, they did in Jim's case because of the sheer amount of tests and data they could put together about the Rubicon's performance. For example, the lawyers were against a high-end off-road vehicle due to liability concerns, but Jim was able to convince them that with the right design and attention to weight, balance, and antiroll warnings, they could mitigate these risks. But it took a lot of data to do this.

REDIRECTION

Feigning Feigning or faking out was another Innovation Judo principle applied in this story. While management thought Jim and his team were working on the small tweaks ordered by marketing, they were actually using much of their time instead to build the dream machine. While marketing thought they were doing the minor modifications, they were also doing major ones, but the untrained eye would not easily detect this specialty work.

Pulling Redirecting negative energy against your idea can either convert this energy to your advantage or neutralize it. Jim's ability to pull that young marketing rep's energy in his direction was extremely helpful to the project. She was quite skeptical and perhaps a little overconfident given her young age and inexperience. When they took to the trail with her in high heels and a business suit, they were able to get rid of a lot of that overconfidence, and they cleverly unbalanced her by taking her out of her comfort zone where smart talk could not get her out of a mud hole. So first they unbalanced her, and then they showed her the salivating potential customers crowding around this yet unmade Chrysler product. This made her into an advocate. All of the engineering data and vignettes about the Jeep Lunatic Fringe would have had little effect on her initial attitudes. It was the actual experience, and its unbalancing nature, that won her over.

7 Principles Quick Guide Self-Test

Reread the preceding profile and look for the use of other Judo principles that I have not referred to in the summary. Place a check mark beside each tactic which you can identify.

Discipline
☐ Preparation
☐ Passion
☐ Bring opportunities
☐ Patience
☐ Self-control

Leverage
☐ Corporate values
☐ Customer
☐ Competitor
☐ Referent power
☐ Strategy
☐ Informal network
☐ Dote on quotes

Redirection
☐ Feigning
☐ Pulling

Circling
☐ Walk around opponents
☐ Walk around ideas
☐ Circle the wagons
☐ Brand enhancement
☐ Numbers
☐ Pilots/Prototypes
☐ Seams

Openings
☐ Hot buttons
☐ Cost cutting/Containment
☐ Efficiency/Effectiveness

Speed
☐ Idea to opportunity
☐ Fail fast
☐ Quick to reshape/Pull plug
☐ Dash into openings
☐ Forgiveness, not permission
☐ Embed quickly

Unbalancing
☐ Surprise
☐ Underpromise/Overdeliver
☐ Foot sweep criticism
☐ Shock therapy
☐ Power shifting

CHAPTER 10
Jousting with Jungles

A Dangerous Intersection

High

Complexity

Maze

Jungle

Land of Oz

Asylum

Low   Wackiness   High

Innovating is always challenging but never more so than in Jungle landscapes. Combine high wackiness and high complexity and you have a deadly cocktail. Jungle landscapes never happen intentionally—nobody would want to create such an organization or a part of their organizational design where it takes people a year to find anything unless you ask the right person, but nobody will tell you who that is. If you are looking for a Jungle there is no better place to look than in the government or a government-related entity. Government entities are by definition political and complex.

Military organizations are the offspring of legislators and thus prone to both complexity and wackiness.

There are many extremely dedicated people who serve our country every day who have great insights about how to run things better, cheaper, faster, and less expensive. But, Jungle landscapes have a tendency over time to sap our natural proclivity to be creative. They can wear us down, wear us out, or just make us passive responders to the tasks at hand. And bending or breaking rules can get us in real trouble. Breaking a rule in the private sector can get you fired; breaking a rule in the government or military can get you jailed since many of the rules in government are laws. So it takes a particularly talented Innovation Judo master to innovate without breaking a policy that is backed by a law. But there are some people who can innovate in these environments without breaking laws or rules, who actually use rules and policies to neutralize others. You will read more about Walt Pullar's skills in doing this and Chris Kluckhuhn, from the Coast Guard, who not only used rules against rules but did so ethically, honorably, and for the greater good.

Jungles are not just the purview of the government. There are plenty of Jungle landscapes in the private sector as well. Just take a look at Enron. Large and complex and the pressure to show profits and look good financially caused the senior leaders to cook the books, eventually bringing themselves down along with a lot of their shareholders as well. This is the epitome of wackiness: pushing so hard for short-term results that you risk the future.

You can find wackiness in almost every company, but it is endemic to larger organizations that have had longer life spans and thus more time to engender wackiness. When I mentioned Greiner's work (1992), I talked about the hangover or fragmentation effect from earlier manifestations of the organization. As organizations grow and change, they often leave residual traces or fragments of the old organization behind even though their functionality is no longer effective. Wackiness is part of life in corporate America, the real question is the degree of wackiness that you have to face as an innovator.

Despite the challenge of Jungle landscapes, some innovators still succeed because of their ability to outsmart and outmaneuver their own organization's complexity and wackiness using Innovation Judo skills. They represent a critical and often unrecognized asset quite necessary for these organizations. One such innovator is Walt Pullar, a former Navy Seal and now a CFO of RMGS, Inc. and a private consultant.

When I started looking into the Innovation Judo concept within the military, a number of people mentioned I should talk with Walt, and I am glad I did. He gave me some great new insights into how Innovation Judo can be used in Jungle landscapes especially in the government and the military without violating rules or putting your career at risk. But, as I said, many private sector companies also have Jungle landscapes so these skills are applicable as well.

Jungle Profile
Walt Pullar III, Former Navy Seal, CFO of RMGS

From 1962, when the first SEAL teams were commissioned, to the present day, Navy SEALs have distinguished themselves as an individually reliable, collectively disciplined, and highly skilled mari-time force. Because of the dangers inherent in special operations, prospective SEALs go through what is considered by many military experts to be the toughest training in the world. The intense physical and mental conditioning it takes to become a SEAL begins at BUD/S (Basic Underwater Demolition/SEAL) training, which is conducted at the Naval Special Warfare Center in San Diego, California. Candidates must complete a mentally and physically demanding six-month basic training course, three weeks of parachute training, and a fifteen-week advanced training period prior to becoming a

Walt is the CFO of RMGS, Inc., a service-disabled, veteran-owned small business providing services to Department of Defense, Department of Homeland Security, and Defense Threat Reduction Agency. RMGS, Inc. is the recent 2013 recipient of *Inc. Magazine's* list of 5,000 (ranked #144) fastest growing private companies in America. Walt also supports a number of clients as a private consultant, specializing in special operations opportunities. In addition to heading up Walt Pullar Consulting, he also serves as Chief Financial Officer for RMGS Inc., a firm that supports military and homeland defense organizations.

SEAL and earning the Trident—the warfare pin insignia of all SEAL operators.

The Navy's Special Forces (SEALs) provides a versatile, responsive, and offensively focused force with continuous overseas presence. The major operational components of Naval Special Warfare Command include Naval Special Warfare Groups 1 and 3 in San Diego, California, and Naval Special Warfare Groups 2 and 4 in Norfolk, Virginia. These components deploy SEAL Teams, SEAL Delivery Vehicle Teams, and Special Boat Teams worldwide to meet the training, exercise, contingency, and wartime requirements of theater commanders. With approximately 5,400 total active-duty personnel—including 2,450 SEALs and 600 Special Warfare Combatant-craft Crewmen (SWCC)—NSW forces are busier than ever answering "911 calls" from around the globe. NSW also calls upon a 1,200-person cadre of reservists.

I hadn't met any Navy SEALs until I interviewed Walt. He of course represents the best of the best in the U.S. military. Only about two out of ten SEAL recruits ever make it through the initial BUD/S training. These are not guys who just come in off the street, they are the best the Navy has to offer. These are the guys who have worked hard to become SEALs. They are the best runners and swimmers, they have above average IQs, and they are physically strong. But Walt will be the first to tell you that mental toughness trumps physical toughness every time. It is really the SEALs' ability to focus on the mission and shut everything else off that is the secret to the group's incredible success. Cold, lack of sleep, pain, a hostile enemy, or a hostile territory are all parts of the job and hazards of the job for a SEAL, but the mission is the goal.

Walt recently left the SEALs after twenty-seven years to start his own consulting business. But as he says, you really never leave the community, so he now helps companies tailor products and solutions for SOCOM. Their requirements are unique and they need people like Walt who can help bridge the gap between the special operators and private industry trying to supply them with mission-specific capabilities and technologies.

Thanks, Lloyd

Walt was born in Buford, South Carolina, the son a marine who retired a full bird colonel. So Walt knew what military life was like, constantly moving and adapting to new environments. Thanks to Lloyd Bridges and the TV series *Sea Hunt*, Walt became enthralled with the idea of becoming a sea diver. His dad encouraged him to follow his passion and told him about a special group in the Navy called the SEALs who did this for a living. Walt was hooked and in high school decided he had to become a SEAL.

> *Dad had served with the SEALs, and he used to tell me stories about their exploits, which really piqued my curiosity and interest in becoming a SEAL. I set this as a career goal. In 1975 I started Duke University and enrolled in the Navy ROTC program on a scholarship so I could get a commission and become a SEAL. At Duke I started in engineering but wound up getting my degree in zoology. I was into sports like soccer and skiing, and was a big swimmer, but had no "legal" diving experience until I joined the SEALs. By legal, I mean I wasn't really licensed to dive, but I had some friends who let me go out with them a few times.*

Walt graduated in 1979, got his commission and started SEAL training the next month. He was actually lucky to have gotten in because his application had been lost, and he only found out about that when he made a follow-up call.

> *You have to have desire, balls, and luck to be a SEAL. I applied but hadn't heard anything back. I called Margaret my detailer (akin to a personnel rep) and found out that my application was lost. Fortunately my dad had a SEAL friend, Norm Olsen, a great officer*

who was instrumental in forming the SEALs. I contacted him and asked if he could help. He wrote a letter, and suddenly they found my application. If Norm had not sent that letter I am convinced I would not have had a twenty-seven-year career as a SEAL.

Since SEALs are a unique lot, I asked him what it takes to be one. As you will see, it takes much more than physical strength or stamina.

I am not sure that I would be selected today because competition to become a SEAL has gotten so much more intense. A lot more people know and admire the SEALs and there are a lot more applicants today than there were in my day. But the abilities to succeed once you are selected haven't really changed that much in thirty years. What we say now is that we look for adrenaline junkies. These are the people who like to parachute, rock climb, do extreme skiing—someone the average person looks at and thinks are crazy. I loved to ski. That was my adrenaline fix. Brains are important, and SEALs have above-average IQs, but the thing that is common among SEALs besides athletic ability and the need for that adrenaline fix is their focus on getting the job done. It is mental discipline more than anything else. Clearly there is a physical side, but it's the mental side that determines whether or not you make it through BUD/S training and become a SEAL. In BUD/S training, they use the physical side to challenge your mind. I am convinced that the people who make it through have the mental discipline to get through each challenge event to move to the next by compartmentalizing these events. They are able to just focus on the next task and not worry about all the things they must accomplish to get through.

A lot of guys in my class were stronger and more athletic than I was but less capable of willing their bodies to go through the exercises. The SEALs have consistently had a 70 percent dropout rate in the BUD/S training. Study after study has been done to find out how to improve this percentage, but the success factors haven't changed. It is as much about your mental ability to deal with the physical challenges. Instructors used to say it's mind over matter: "I don't mind and you don't matter." SEALs have an unusual ability to focus on getting the job done despite everything else going on around them. Successful people break the mission down into challenges taken one at a time or as we say, "Eat the elephant one bit at a time," despite being asked to do things that no sane person would do.

In addition to mental and physical toughness, SEALs have to be proficient in weapons, demolition, first aid, and communications. While a platoon has specialists in each of these areas, the team members have to know enough about each other's jobs to do them all if necessary, whether it's putting in an IV, slapping on a tourniquet, or using the radio. Walt's specialty was leading, or "herding the cats" as he likes to say. Most SEALs are enlisted, and even some officers give up their rank to enlist as a SEAL.

My job was to get the best out of the people assigned to me. One of my key skills is the ability to quickly size up an individual and then help him play to his strengths. Class structure is much less obvious in SEAL teams. It is much more about each of us having a job to do and trusting in the others to do their jobs. I had to rely heavily on the judgments, knowledge, and experience of my people in order to lead. They are the experts, I just had to help manage the integration of this expertise and keep the mission in focus.

SEALs don't complete missions forever either because they can no longer physically or mentally meet the challenging demands of the job or they get promoted to higher level management jobs in the Navy. In Walt's twenty-seven-year career he had eighteen to nineteen assignments. In his last five years with the Navy he moved four times. His last job with the Navy was as resource sponsor for the SEALs, and he worked on the OPNAV staff at the Pentagon. Before that he worked as both a project manager and in acquisitions in jobs that kept him connected to SOCOM in a support role.

Jungles and Judo

SEALs by the nature of their jobs have to be innovative. When you are in covert ops you have to be ready for many contingencies, and often the best-made plans have to be modified or abandoned in real time. There is nothing quite like being shot at to bring forth both the spirit and the incarnation of innovation. But as troops get away from the battlefield and get promoted into more management and administrative positions, their world changes dramatically. Most of our military officers do a tour of duty at the Pentagon as part of their career development. Although working at the Pentagon is a great experience, many are happy to leave because the Pentagon is the epitome of both complexity and wackiness. Complex because it is the hub and spoke of most of our country's defenses made up of multiple government divisions and groups, and wacky because it is also highly political. If you want to have a good breeding ground for political behavior, have lots of people competing for the same or limited resources and then add in congress, a politically appointed body, as the oversight group, and you can predict a fair amount of wacky behavior.

Walt worked in the Pentagon and can attest to both its complexity and its politics. Going from the battlefield to the bureaucracy can be quite a shock for the average warfighter. Innovation is admired on the battlefield, but it can be admonished in the bureaucracy. Yet Walt has done his fair share of innovating even against the odds, and Walt is not a rule breaker or a rebel. When I interviewed him, two particular stories stood out in my mind as good examples of Innovation Judo.

> *If you are too much of an outlier it can affect your career. So you have to pick your battles carefully and make sure you know the swim lanes (borders of authority).*

Nonetheless, Walt is good at picking his fights and especially adept at utilizing openings and seams to get innovative things done in the face of both roadblocks and blockheads. And he does so by not breaking the rules but by knowing the rules better than others, especially the limits and bounds of his authority versus others.

Hey, Man, It Saved My Life

SEALs rely on their equipment to help them complete their missions, and they become quite knowledgeable about what works well and what doesn't. Walt was aware that the Mitch helmets issued to the SEALs prior to 9/11 had some level of ballistic protection and limited integrated communications abilities, but they were not nearly as good as they should be for the dangerous operation that SEALs could find themselves facing. Especially troubling was the limited ballistic protection that these helmets afforded. Walt was on a team of people in the acquisitions area responsible for testing and upgrading the equipment used for Special Forces.

Pre-9/11 there was no sense of urgency for upgrading these helmets except in the Special Ops groups. And since I worked closely with them, I knew that these helmets did not provide sufficient protection. We had done some testing on the new helmet prototypes, and with the exception of a few statistical outliers, the helmet that we were developing was two to three times better than the old one. But some of the testers refused to pass the helmet because of these outliers and were holding up our ability to get them into the field. They told me I couldn't field the helmet yet because it wasn't ready. I argued that the product was significantly better and we needed to field it, even if all the bugs weren't worked out. My decision was that even though it wasn't perfect it was good enough, and I would rather risk the possibility of saving lives than waiting for perfection. The chief of the testing office for SOCOM was adamantly against me shipping these before his group gave it the thumbs up. So we were at odds. He told me the helmet was not ready and that I did not have the authority to put it in the field without his okay. His argument was that we need to do more testing down the road, but I thought do we need a 100 percent solution or a good enough solution that is three times better than what they have now?

I told him that I was fielding it anyway and it was in my authority to do so. The chief then escalated our disagreement up the chain of command for final resolution. I got lots of pushback, but while he was escalating the debate, I put the helmets into production because as prototypes there was no limit to how many we made. We made thousands of them and shipped them to the field before anyone was able to counter my decision. And because of this decision, these helmets were in place when 9/11 hit.

A couple of years later I was at a SEAL reunion, and I met a guy whose life was saved by that new helmet. If it wasn't for that helmet, he would not have been at the party. I never told him I was the one who got it fielded. I was satisfied just hearing his story.

Walt did get some "back channel effect" as he calls it from his pushing forward with the helmet project. The head of the testing division did escalate the conflict up the chain of command, which Walt felt he had a perfect right to do, but when the final decision came down, Walt got the thumbs up. Of course, by then, it was a little late to recall thousands of helmets in the field. By the time the final decision came down, they had been shipping helmets for three to four months.

Walt cautions against pulling rank or going to the authority toolkit too often.

If you always go to your authority lever all the time you become ineffective. You have to know when to work within the system and when you have to test it. If you always work within the system you might not be taking enough risks, but if you work too often outside the system you become labeled a "wildcard." You have to keep the tool in the toolbox until you absolutely need it, then you can put it away again.

> *I was passionate enough about the helmet situation to take the risk that I would be challenged, and the decision could have gone against me. But I felt I was within my decision-making authority and took the chance. I knew I was taking some risk. They could have removed my authority, or taken me out of my position, if they found my decision unjustified or improper. It is easier not to make a decision. Let the bureaucracy play out, don't take any position until things are on your side, but if you have passion and are committed to doing the right thing, then you act.*

The Congressional Visit

In the previous example, Walt demonstrated the ability to take advantage of an opening. When there was a fight over who had the decision-making authority over fielding the helmets, he saw his opening and made his move. As he said by the time the haggling was over it was four months later and thousands of helmets had been shipped. I liked Walt as an Innovation Judo master because of his ability to spot and/or leverage openings to pursue innovation and always using right-mindedness. His use of Innovation Judo is never self-serving as the next example will show you.

> *For some reason my command was moved from San Diego to Hawaii. We had a facility on Ford Island and we were asked to take up residence in very old, vintage WWII hangars. My people not only had to be uprooted from their families in San Diego, we had no real mission in Hawaii, and our barracks were hardly livable. So there we were in these buildings with busted-out windows, rusted pipes, and peeling paint. It was unsightly and uncomfortable. But it was the quality of life I had to focus on. It affected morale and because we had no real mission to sink our teeth into, this made things worse. I needed money to fix the place up and I had asked for funds, but they were not put into the budget. But then I had a chance to host a congressional delegation visiting the base. When they came to visit, I could have taken them to one of the more physically presentable parts of our command, but instead I took then on a tour of the worst places in the*

command and said this is where my people work, where they take their breaks. I made sure to take them up the back stairwell, and not through our beautiful front office. One of the delegates asked me why we didn't fix up the place, and I said, "I can't go outside my command to ask for more money."

A couple of months later I was out on a sub off Korea doing some warfare exercises. The sub was the Kamehameha. We were underwater when we got a communications telling us to surface so someone could talk to Walt Pullar. It was my boss back in San Diego, and he was agitated. "What did you say to that staffer from the congressional delegation? I want to know everything you said and write it down! Did you ask for money?" And of course, I said no. He continued to interrogate me and then hung up.

It turned out that there was a commanders' conference for SOCOM, and an admiral was briefing a four-star about how wonderful everything was in our command (SEAL Team 1). So the four-star says, "If everything is so great why is there a two million dollar congressional insert in this group's budget? Tell me why SEAL Team 1 needs two million?" The presenting admiral, who was the boss of my boss had no idea about this, so he flamed on my boss who flamed on me during the sub call. I never asked for money outside of the command so I never broke any rules. But my special tour of the delegation got $2 million that year and $1 million the next year for fixing up our digs, and this is stuff that commands don't like to spend money on. We used that money to fix up our quarters, but we used some of the money to get better boats as well. Remember, I had put all these requests in my boss's formal budget, and they were turned down. Fortunately, I saw a new opportunity to address the problems without breaking any rules.

As you can see from the previous two stories, Walt is not a rule breaker, nor is he a rule bender, but he is not afraid to challenge the bounds of authority. There are many occasions when the lines between one person's authority and another's look clear, but at the edges there are shades of gray. I like to call these seams in the organization because they provide opportunities for the innovator who is right-minded to exploit those seams and openings when pursuing innovation. Seams exist in every organization no matter how bureaucratic or rule bound it is. In fact, really wacky environments often have countermanding rules. These situations can either be seen as impediments or opportunities for the innovator.

Parachuting into Peril

Walt told me another story about his exploits as a SEAL that I found particularly compelling. Again, it involved the exploitation of an opening, but he and his team were also able to save a life surely lost had it not been for Walt's willingness to act while others debated his authority to act.

Walt and his team were still in Hawaii at the time, and while he had been able to fix up the barracks, he was still looking for some kind of mission that would keep his guys sharp and motivated. There had been so much focus on the move from San Diego that he was worried his folks would get rusty, and practicing missions is not the same thing as completing real ones. Additionally, his command was in a strange position from a reporting perspective. They were located on a base in Hawaii but did not report to anyone on the base because the rest of his command and his boss were back in San Diego. Thus, no one on the base was authorized to give them orders.

> One Easter, I get a phone call from the PACOM (Pacific Command) duty officer. He said, "You guys parachute, don't you?" And I answered in the affirmative as parachuting is part of the SEAL training (sea, air, land). Everyone else on the base reported through PACOM except my group because we reported to the Special Ops command in San Diego, and my boss actually reported to a four-star in the Army.
>
> The PACOM (Pacific Command) duty officer told me he had an emergency situation. An American citizen and his girlfriend were

sailing his yacht in the middle of the Pacific stopping off at different islands along his route. He had been fishing and accidently got a fish hook stuck in his foot. Unfortunately, he had been wading in a lagoon that the natives used as a cesspool and got a bad infection while back out at sea. The infection got worse and turned into gangrene. This is when the Coast Guard in Hawaii got a distress call from the boat that the owner was in serious trouble. Normally, it is the Coast Guard's job to conduct rescues of citizens at sea, but in this case none of their helicopters had the range necessary to get to the boat. The Coast Guard told Walt that they had planes that could get that far out in the Pacific, but no one who knew how to parachute. For SEALs to do a mission they need orders from their command, and I worked for a four-star Army general. Thus, the Coast Guard had no ability to issue orders to the SEALs, and the SEALs did not have permission from their command to do this kind of rescue, which would require them parachuting into the sea, boarding the boat, administering medical help, and then sailing the boat to the nearest land that had hospital facilities or where they could land a plane and then fly the yachtsman to a hospital.

Walt knew he would have to get permission from at least one if not two levels up the chain of command to go on this mission. And time was of the essence. Gangrene moves fast and the Coast Guard predicted that this yachtsman would only last a day or two before the gangrene went systemic and killed him.

First, I called my immediate boss. He wasn't in at first, but when I did hear back from him the next morning he told me, "Stand by. I will see if I can get permission." I knew that we had no time to waste, so I told the Coast Guard officer to task me to do a rescue at sea. (Normally a rescue at sea means a boat is going down and they have to get people off.) I knew that the Navy has a law that you are required to assist in an emergency rescue at sea if that is how the request is worded.

In the meantime, I did a command recall since it was Easter and I needed to get my team back to the base. We built a rubber duck boat, put it on a pallet, and picked six guys from the team: two who could free fall, two who were medical corpsmen, and two who could sail the boat. Our plan was to hop a Coast Guard plane, jump into the sea where we could board the vessel, stabilize the guy, and get him to a place where he could either get hospital treatment or be picked up by a plane and flown to the nearest medical facilities. Even though I was still waiting to hear from my boss, we began to execute the plan. We worked all night putting our equipment together so that we could catch the first Ford Island ferry in the morning to the main base. We had the equipment and the team on the ferry, got them to the airplane, and sent them off. It would take them twelve hours from Hawaii before they made it to the boat. I told them to do whatever it takes to save the man's life. I went back to my office and my boss called and said, "I almost have your permission to proceed." I told him the team had already left and I was executing this as a rescue at sea and therefore I really don't need any permission. He said we should still get permission, but I knew it was now too late to call them back.

Walt's team made it to the boat and headed it toward Christmas Island while the two corpsmen started to deal with the gangrene. They gave the man two rounds of medication that didn't work, so they had to call on some of their other exceptional first aid skills to finally stop the gangrene from spreading. And this was all done while navigating through two significant Pacific storms.

This incident got briefed all the way to Colin Powell, and then it hit the press that the SEALs were doing the mission. My boss told me to get to Hawaii. When I got off the plane, there were microphones, cameras, and the press everywhere because it had been in the paper. We saved his life and we saved his leg. But up until the success of the mission became public, everyone was telling me that I couldn't do it. As an ironic note to this story, the guy's girlfriend insisted that the SEALs reimburse her for a toothbrush one of them borrowed during the mission.

Judo Application Summary

- **Discipline**
  - *Preparation*
  - *Self-control*
- **Openings**
  - *Human hot button*
  - *Organizational hot buttons—values*
  - *Pilot/Prototypes*
  - *Seams*
- **Leverage**
  - *Know the rules*
- **Speed**
  - *Dash into opening*
  - *Embed quickly*
  - *Ask forgiveness not permission*

Note that Walt Pullar's use of Innovation Judo principles is somewhat different in terms of both orientation and intent than those applied in the other landscape profiles you have read. Jungles are complex and wacky and are most evident in large bureaucratic, hierarchical organizations. They move at their own pace, and they typically don't deal with surprise and unbalancing as well as the other landscapes do. You probably don't want to pull any big surprises at the Department of Motor Vehicles or you probably won't get your license renewed. In the military, breaking or even bending the rules can be job limiting as well as career limiting. Walt is measured and judicious in his use of Innovation Judo principles, which are appropriate for innovating in Jungle landscapes. And remember that Walt always applies these skills with right-mindedness and for the greater good. When he challenges authority or sees an opportunity, an opening if you will, to influence a congressional delegation or fly out to the Pacific on a rescue mission, he is not doing these things for self-aggrandizement. It is always for others and for morally right reasons. As he said, "You have to choose your battles." Fighting for a better living environment for his command was worth fighting for and taking some chances as was saving a person at sea or protecting a special operator from a bullet to the head. And Walt always disagrees respectfully unlike General Billy Mitchell whom we talked about earlier in the book. Now let's analyze the specific Innovation Judo principles that Walt employed.

DISCIPLINE

Walt's use of *discipline* is not that of writing a business plan or making sure he presents opportunities rather than ideas, it's about understanding the rules and lines of authority as well if not better than the rule makers, and then using this knowledge to justify action. It is quite usual in strong hierarchical organizations for the management level below to push a decision up to the next level to avoid accountability or to reduce the risk of second-guessing. We refer to this as "upward delegation." And, of course, there are times when this is appropriate. But there are times when you have to do the right thing while protecting yourself from unnecessary interference or protracted decision making.

"Rescue at sea" is an explicit phrase in the Navy that carries both legal implications and personal obligations. It is a much different phrase than saying, "Apply first aid to an injured yachtsman," or "Sail ship to nearest medical facilities." This helped justify the mission and protect his team from damaging blowback. If you are in a Jungle environment and you want to innovate, you better learn the rules and the rules that can countermand other rules. Learning these rules and specifics of authority is not necessarily fun work for the innovator, but it can pay huge dividends in helping you overcome both roadblocks and blockheads on the pathway to innovation. Here is another example of Walt's knowledge of the rules.

> After we did the renovations to our buildings, we started to take over several other buildings on the island that were not being used. A couple of years later, the Navy decided they wanted to fix up Ford Island and make it more of a showcase, but they realized that they had a bunch of SEALs now taking up the real estate. The Navy said we were going to have to move out, and I said, "No. The law says that you have to move me to comparable space and if nothing is available you have to fund the building of a comparable space." So we carved out fifty-five acres including two piers on Pearl Harbor as compensation for moving. They gave us money to move and $15 million to build a new headquarters. But the rest of the space had to be comparable as well so we got an additional $55 million to build out the rest. This enclave is now jokingly referred to as "the world that Walt built." We took a bad thing, getting thrown out of our facilities, and turned it into a great thing. We were a tenant command on the Navy base and had already established tenant command at their invite; thus, they were then obligated to pay for our move and comparable facilities. We said, "We're happy to move but you will have to pay, or we are happy to stay!"

OPENINGS

Walt's stories also show the importance of openings for the innovator. If you can't make your own opening, you can certainly take advantage of those that come your way if you find your pathway obstructed. The helmets story demonstrates the importance of knowing where your authority leaves off and another's begins. Even though his authority was challenged, he believed the decision to field the not-yet-perfect helmets was in his purview, and he had the courage to make the decision and act because he knew that every day they sought perfection was a day another special operator could get killed.

These openings or seams between authority and the tendency toward upward delegation create more opportunities for moving an innovation along. Upward escalation of an authority issue or seeking a higher level manager to make the final decision takes time and allows the innovator to act while the debate is going on. Embedding much of the innovation quickly makes it harder to undo later. You can't easily recall 3,000 helmets that are saving lives or bring back a SEAL team that is halfway over the Pacific under the legal obligation to carry out a rescue at sea.

The visit of the congressional delegation also created another opening for Walt in trying to improve his command's working conditions. I know a number of commanders who would have gone out of their way to make sure that this delegation saw the best of the environment not the worst. But Walt saw his opening and moved.

LEVERAGE

Walt not only knew the rules; he also leveraged them to his advantage. By offsetting rules, he acted for the greater good despite the odds. But he also used referent power as leverage when he purposefully brought the congressional delegation through the SEALs' ill-kept facilities on Ford Island in Hawaii. He never asked for money, which would have been illegal, but he did utilize the people who could influence funding by giving them the "back door" tour.

SPEED

Seeing or creating an opening is no good unless you can exploit that opening by moving into and through it quickly. So speed is of the essence. Walt didn't sit on his hands waiting for his boss to okay his rescue at sea. He got his team ready and they headed out.

He didn't wait for a higher level decision regarding the helmets. He quickly contracted to have them made and started shipping. In many of our Innovation Judo examples, you have seen the importance of speed. Openings can appear quickly, but they can close just as quickly. The good thing about Jungles is that members of this landscape often have a tough time making a quick decision due to both complexity and wackiness. These vacuums in decision making actually work to the innovator's advantage if he or she is quick to see or create them and then moves relatively quickly to take advantage of them.

7 Principles Quick Guide Self-Test

Reread the preceding profile and look for the use of other Judo principles that I have not referred to in the summary. Place a check mark beside each tactic which you can identify.

Discipline
☐ Preparation
☐ Passion
☐ Bring opportunities
☐ Patience
☐ Self-control

Leverage
☐ Corporate values
☐ Customer
☐ Competitor
☐ Referent power
☐ Strategy
☐ Informal network
☐ Dote on quotes

Redirection
☐ Feigning
☐ Pulling

Circling
☐ Walk around opponents
☐ Walk around ideas
☐ Circle the wagons
☐ Brand enhancement
☐ Numbers
☐ Pilots/Prototypes
☐ Seams

Openings
☐ Hot buttons
☐ Cost cutting/Containment
☐ Efficiency/Effectiveness

Speed
☐ Idea to opportunity
☐ Fail fast
☐ Quick to reshape/Pull plug
☐ Dash into openings
☐ Forgiveness, not permission
☐ Embed quickly

Unbalancing
☐ Surprise
☐ Underpromise/Overdeliver
☐ Foot sweep criticism
☐ Shock therapy
☐ Power shifting

Part IV *Counterbalancing*

In many respects, Innovation Judo is a necessary evil. Ideally, this skill set and the seven principles that underlie it should not be necessary because organizations should be as naturally innovative as the human race, and the roadblocks and blockheads would be few and far between. And some organizations, despite their size and complexity, have figured out how to systemically enable innovation, thus lessening the need for this secret leadership skill. Innovation Judo becomes less important and less effective as organizational complexity and organizational wackiness decrease or are structurally counterbalanced. Over the long term, however, most established or growing organizations still have a propensity to increase these two factors. Thus one or more of the seven secret skills will have some role to play in keeping ideas alive in the organization.

Since most established organizations have a great deal of difficulty in deconstructing themselves, a counterbalancing strategy can help them mitigate against some of the innovation roadblocks and blockheads that live within. Part IV of this book is aimed not just at innovators, but also at senior leaders whose job it is to create both the architecture and culture necessary for serial innovation. It is not enough to say, "We need innovation." Senior leaders must also value it and then create the organizational architecture for it.

In Part IV, you will learn how to utilize Dragon Dens, Dragon Serum, Dragon Cultures, and Dragon Borrowing as counterbalancing mechanisms that will help promote, nourish, protect, and defend ideas so they have a chance of staying alive long enough to create value. While many counterbalancing mechanisms involve the establishment of formalized structures and processes, you will still need some Innovation Judo masters to span the boundaries between logic and illogic. There will never be "no politics," and organizations will always have a penchant for creating complexity where simplicity would suffice. Counterbalancing strategies always involve the right combination of people and processes.

Near the end of the book, you will be introduced to Lt. Cmdr. Chris Kluckhuhn and the United States Coast Guard (USCG) Innovation Council. The USCG, as with most military and governmental organizations, is replete with Jungle landscapes, but the USCG has figured out how to both structure for and recruit for innovation. The USCG is one of a handful of organizations that has been successful at embedding and sustaining innovation over the long run, despite the odds. And finally in Part IV, readers will be challenged to become a sensei (Japanese for "revered teacher") of other Innovation Judo experts until organizations can create more permanent counterbalancing mechanisms.

CHAPTER 11

In Search of the Dragon
Counterbalancing Strategies

In Search of the Dragon

- Large and agile

- Organized and flexible

- Controlled and empowered

- Operationally excellent and innovative

- Effective and efficient

- Budget constrained and opportunity focused

- Corporate and innovative

Whenever I speak to people in large organizations about how they can become more innovative, I always tell them that it is important to understand and embrace the concept of a paradox—two things that do not fit together comfortably or logically. In the figure above, you will see a list of paradoxes that are appropriate for large organizations wishing to increase their IQ (innovation quotient). I say there is no on/off switch for large companies that allows them to go from innovation killers to innovation enablers, and it doesn't make sense for them to do so even if they could. You cannot run an organization that is large without some form of hierarchy, controls, or budget constraints. But when these good management practices suffocate innovation, then some counterbalancing is necessary, so organizations must be comfortable with the fact that some days they will be examples of innovation and others they will be quite stupid. It can't be helped. The secret, however, is to try to marry these paradoxes so that both can exist. For example, later, I will talk about how to have a Land of Oz living inside a Jungle. The Jungle is still there, but it has been structurally counterbalanced by building a Land of Oz within it. Innovation Judo is a counterbalancing mechanism as well, but if this is your only mechanism then your chances of embedding and sustaining innovation on a wide scale over the long term will be limited.

WHAT'S WITH THE DRAGON?

A couple of years ago, I was asked by Tsinghua University in Beijing to speak to a group of company directors about innovation and in-company entrepreneurship. I was told that most of these directors were members of the communist party, did not speak English, and had little or no understanding of how to build a more entrepreneurial orientation within a company that took orders from the government's Central Planning authority. I had to find some metaphor or analogy that would help carry my points so one of my Chinese friends suggested the dragon; the Eastern one, not the Western one. In the West we still have images of fire-breathing man-eaters, but in the East, dragons are revered because they are both large and powerful, but simultaneously are quick and agile. And this was a great metaphor for me to convey that in-company innovation and entrepreneurial thinking was in many respects a form of "dragon building"—making large, bureaucratic, perhaps even dinosaur–like companies into dragons.

You will also find a lot of images of dragons in the martial arts. Perhaps the most famous karate movie starred Bruce Lee and was appropriately titled *Enter the Dragon*. You will see dragon images on martial arts uniforms, in clubhouses, and even as tattoos on some martial arts practitioners. For the martial artist the dragon also symbolizes the rare combination of power and agility.

The challenge then for most organizations wishing to embed and sustain innovation requires some form of dragon building so as to marry the best in size, scope, structure, and processes that come with large companies to the agility and power that is inherent in the dragon. There are typically four ways in which organizations can institutionalize this marriage, and I will refer to them as

- Dragon dens
- Dragon serum
- Dragon cultures
- Dragon borrowing

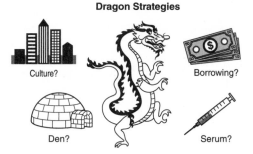

Dragon Strategies

Culture?

Borrowing?

Den?

Serum?

Dragon Dens

A number of organizations including Intel, P&G, Kimberly-Clark, and the Coast Guard have utilized this strategy to help counterbalance both roadblocks and blockheads in a sustained way. This approach involves the building of a structure within the structure to help support, nurture, and implement innovative ideas. In this chapter you will read about Lieutenant Commander Chris Kluckhuhn and the U.S. Coast Guard Innovation Council. The Innovation Council is a perfect example of a dragon den combined with dragon serum. The Innovation Council is a small den within the Coast Guard. It is a formal structure within the structure—it has a reporting relationship directly to the commandant's office, it is populated by some pretty good Innovation Judo masters like Chris, it has a small seed capital fund, and it has a specified process as to how to move ideas along the road to implementation. The council members are told that 70 percent of their job is to innovate, and senior leaders are willing to intervene on the innovator's behalf if a boss tries to change or challenge this ratio. They also hold a yearly Innovation Expo, which allows the innovators a chance to showcase their ideas and interact with not only the brass but members of the defense industry and other military branches who might take advantage of these ideas.

The Coast Guard Innovation Council is a good example of how a dragon den should be set up and run. It has the following elements that have helped sustain its impact over the years.

- Top-level commitment and support
- Resourcing, although purposefully limited
- Formalized structures and processes to move an idea along
- Recruiting of "chip on the shoulder" members
- High visibility
- Innovation prizes and awards
- Top cover from those who try to interfere
- Innovation as the member's primary job
- Council members stay long enough to see their ideas take flight

Since I consider the Innovative Council a model, I will discuss it at the end of this chapter so that you can see how it sustains innovation within the organization.

You will find most of the characteristics mentioned previously in successful dragon dens whether they are in the public or private sector, with one exception. In the private sector, companies often utilize the allure of rapid promotion for those in the dragon den if they are willing to take a risk and step out of their normal jobs and innovate, knowing that there is always some degree of failure involved. In the Coast Guard's model, it is not looking for the wannabe admiral but for the kind of person who enjoys innovating for innovation's sake and is willing to step out of an admiral track to do this particular job. Military people especially value recognition from the brass and their peers like the "Innovator of the Year" award. In Chris Kluckhuhn's case, he stayed with the Coast Guard just because he was having so much fun. He got a great head start on his private business as well because of his innovation, while the Coast Guard, and other branches of the military, got great value as well. A win-win.

In many respects dragon dens are often an attempt to build a Land of Oz landscape within one of the other less innovation-friendly landscapes in order to create an effective and sustainable counterbalance. Much of Chris's work was in the Jungles of the military and the federal government, but his base camp was in the Land of Oz in the Coast Guard's Innovation Council.

The Coast Guard's model was well thought-out in that it considered what people needed to not only get great ideas on the table but also how to cut a path through the Jungle so that these ideas can be implemented. The Innovation Council seeks out midgrade officers who have a little chip on their shoulders—they are not afraid of their bosses and have some savvy when it comes to Innovation Judo.

Many organizations focus too much time and energy on the ideation process and not nearly enough time on the process and politics of getting these ideas into action. I am currently working with two groups who have just started to create their versions of a dragon den. They have spent all their time thinking about how to reward people for giving them ideas and how to vet them when they come in, but they have not spent nearly enough time on how to turn these ideas into reality. Dragon dens need both entrances and exits for the ideas that are created. For example, P&G and Kimberly-Clark have their versions of the dragon den as does Intel, but they know that someone has to adopt the ideas that are created and help nurture them to maturity if they are ever going to deliver potential value. So not only have these companies built the entrances into the den, they have also built the exits that lead to entities who have clear responsibility and accountability for seeing ideas through to fruition. If you don't think of a dragon den as part of the company's internal ecosystem, then sustainability is almost impossible, because the den is not woven into the fabric of the organization.

Skunkworks can also have some of the attributes of a dragon den. ONR is a big player in innovation especially in science and technology. They have set up a purpose-built skunkworks to help get ideas into rapid prototyping and full-scale implementation. The Navy has many attributes of a Jungle landscape, but ONR has created their own brands of skunkworks as counterbalance to the inertia and bureaucracy that often stands in the way of a good idea. In addition, the head of the skunkworks is Jim Blesse, a former Navy master chief. Master chiefs not only teach the new captain of a ship how to lead; they also get the newbies to scrub the decks. Not a bad choice to have these people make sure an idea is not stalled on the path to creativity.

The choice of building a dragon den depends on the company's intent for having such a structure. If it is just to have a place in the corner to incubate ideas for others to implement, that's great as long as you have the cooperation of those other people who will be implementing the idea. Often potential adopters are not brought in early enough in the innovation process to make them co-creators, thus making the adoption process much more difficult. Well-thought-out dragon dens have a clear process of identifying and involving key stakeholders throughout the innovation process. If you don't help create the idea, it is hard to have passion for it.

Dragon Serum

Another strategy companies use to institutionalize innovation is to inject many of their key managers with a dose of "dragon serum" mixed with entrepreneurial education. In my last book, *Lead Like an Entrepreneur: Keeping the Entrepreneurial Spirit Alive Within the Corporation* (McGraw-Hill 2006), I profiled a number of organizations that tried to train their key leaders to think and act more like entrepreneurs in the pursuit of innovative new businesses. I worked closely with Siemens Corporation for a number of years on just such a dragon serum program. Siemens put several thousands of their high-potential middle managers through an eight-month program where participants had to present a full-blown business plan to the executive committee in order to graduate. One of these new business ideas led to a $250,000 revenue generator within two years of its inception. The entire investment in the educational program was less than $2 million. Against conventional wisdom, Siemens focused on the middle of the organization because this is where some of the best new ideas come from. Middle managers have been around for a while, they know what works and what doesn't, and under the right circumstances they can come up with really impactful ideas. Notice that all my profiles of Innovative Judo masters are people I consider middle managers, like Jim Repp. The downside is that middle managers can also be the most resistant to change and innovation if they are not at least co-creators of the ideas. But once they buy in, they can make things happen because they are typically the implementers. It is too bad that many U.S. companies often cut the middle when it comes time for downsizing. This is because they have never really seen or leveraged the great font of innovation that can come from this group when properly induced.

Dragon Cultures

Building dragon cultures is the most challenging of the counterbalancing strategies because you are not trying to build a Land of Oz within another landscape, you are trying to transform the entire landscape into a Land of Oz. If you already have this kind of landscape, you probably shouldn't have picked up this book because you are most likely in a company like 3M, Disney, Google, Apple, P&G, or Zappos. These kinds of innovation cultures do exist, and innovation is part of their corporate strategy. The founders or investors in these organizations realize the importance of sustaining innovation and have built their organizations accordingly.

A SYSTEMIC APPROACH

I have made the point that innovation is not a destination but a tool. When we ask the "intent" question, we need to specify what we want the tool of innovation to do. Let's assume for a second that we want a more innovative culture. Then we have to ask, "To do what?" When I talk to CEOs who say they want a more innovative culture, they usually mean that they want greater growth, fueled by harnessing the ideas and energy of their employees. This growth allows cash generation, reinvestment, and a dynamism that helps the organization develop and dominate its competitors. When the Navy brass say they want a more innovative culture, the intent is to generate and harvest good ideas to make the Navy run better, faster, and cheaper within a fiscally constrained environment. "Readiness at less cost" has now become their mantra.

But just getting good ideas does not mean that you have an innovative culture. It is much more complex than that and requires a systemic longer term view of innovation. The 7S model of organizations[3] describes why some organizations were able to bring about large-scale change while others tried and failed. Emanating from its comparative studies, it came up with a descriptive model of what I call the "anatomy of the organization" using a now famous model called the 7S framework. The model was originally intended to help executives understand the systemic nature of organizational change. I have found it to be a very useful tool, with a couple of key modifications that I have added, to help executives develop cultures of innovation. I now refer to it as the 9S model because I have added two S categories.

Figure 11.1 shows the 9S model I adapted from the McKinsey 7S model because it left out a couple of important elements: assets and strategic communication (a compelling story). Some of my participants have suggested I use *Stuff* instead of *Assets* to stay within the S framework, but I prefer to use the term *A$$ets*. I use dollar signs to signify that we are talking about assets in terms of resources both material and human. Every organization has a financial footprint that underlies its activities. McKinsey did not mention this in its original model, which was clearly an oversight. For example, an organization that has champagne taste on a beer budget has a problem. It either has to scale back its strategy to fit its budget or seek more funds in order to fulfill its strategy. There is one other option, of course, and that is to use innovation to get champagne on a beer budget. Much of my work with the Navy today is aimed at helping it maintain defensive readiness with a much lower budget, and innovation is a key tool for accomplishing this seemingly paradoxical goal.

---

[3] Robert Waterman, Thomas J. Peters, and Julien R. Phillips, "Structure Is Not Organization," *Business Horizons,* 1980.

Organizational Alignment

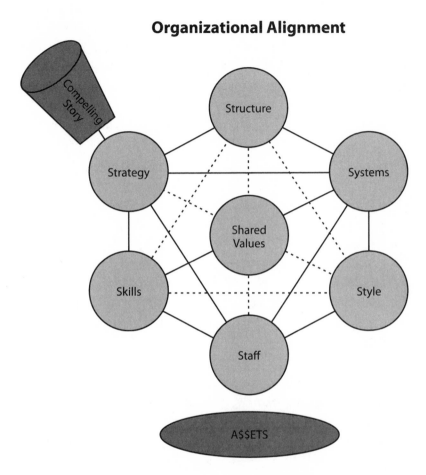

The strategic communications part I refer to as a compelling story. If I, as the CEO, and my executive team know where we are taking the company and no one else inside or outside the company does, then we have failed at strategic communications. And if we can't come up with a compelling story, then we probably can't communicate it to others with any sense of clarity or passion. I have always made the case for the "rocket pitch" when it comes to communicating a compelling value proposition for a new idea, and the same is true for the organization's strategy. If you can't tell others about your idea in a few short sentences then you probably don't understand it yourself. When it comes to innovation, the compelling story is about intent. My biggest challenge as an innovation consultant is to help senior leadership clarify and communicate their "intent" for innovation. Without understanding the intent, or as McKinsey would refer to it, strategy for innovation, then it is very hard to organize for it.

Let's see how this model can help create a culture of innovation. It is very important to note that "shared values" or culture is at the center, but a culture of innovation cannot be built without aligning the other S's to either support it or create it. If I were to spend enough time in your organization, I could probably describe it to others with some degree of accuracy by understanding each of these S's and how they work together. Think of these as part of the organization's anatomy. And just like people, we cannot be a whole person in the anatomical sense if any of our parts are disaggregated. And just like people, when something goes wrong in one part of the anatomy it can affect all the others.

About two years ago I was forced to wear an arm sling for a number of months due to three failed biceps tendon operations on my right arm. This was not the doctor's fault but the impatient patient's fault. This injury has now affected my left arm because I am overusing it, it affects my ability to sleep at night, and I have back problems resulting from favoring my left side. These systemic effects are not unexpected. For all of you who have had similar injuries, you know that something wrong in one part of your body often has systemic effects on other parts. And so it is with organizations. Next are some brief explanations of each of these S's. For those of you wishing to build a more innovative culture, you may want to think of the 9S model as a checklist so that you make sure you are doing all you can to embed and sustain innovation as it is often easily snuffed out if not institutionally embedded.

- **Strategy:** The ways in which competitive advantage will be achieved. It is the company's direction whether it is written or not.

- **Structure:** The way in which tasks and people are divided. The basic groupings of activities and reporting relationships. The primary basis for specialization and integration. Structure is most readily observed by looking at an organizational chart to see how the organization is organized.

- **Systems:** Formal systems and procedures including management control systems, performance measurement and reward systems, budgeting systems, information systems, planning systems, and capital budgeting systems. Systems are typically documented and have performance metrics.

- **Shared values (culture):** The guiding concepts, fundamental ideas, and principles around which the company is built and tries to operate. They focus attention and give purpose and meaning to the organization. Values, if they are real and shared, are the most observable aspects of culture.

- **Staff:** The people and their backgrounds and competencies. How an organization staffs including its approaches to recruitment, selection, and socialization; how managers are developed; how young recruits are trained, socialized, and integrated; and career management. It also means where we place our people. If we say we are the leaders in technology in our industry, we would expect to find a fair number of engineers working for the company and eventually winding up in higher management positions.

- **Skills:** The basic competencies that reside in the organization. Can be distinctive competencies of people, management practices, technology, etc. If the company is a technology-driven one, we would expect it to recruit from the best engineering schools. If the company is financially driven, we would expect it to have more than a few Wharton graduates.

- **Style:** The leadership style of top management and the overall operating style of the organization. If leadership is autocratic and hierarchical then it sets a tone for how leaders should act through the ranks. If democratic and participative, that sets a different tone. We often say that leadership is set at the top, and research studies demonstrate that what top leaders evidence as their style tends to get emulated in many other parts of the organization.

- **A$$ets:** This refers to the resources, both people and material, that we have at our disposal to support our strategy. A$$ets could also be other people's money. P&G has had some great success in the innovation arena by getting other folks, for example, suppliers, to co-invest in a new product's development, thus allowing both risk sharing and reward sharing.

- **Story:** This is how clearly, articulately, and compellingly we are able to tell other people where we are going as an organization, and this is not simply about the numbers. It is guidance for people working with us and for us. The story needs to be short, simple, and memorable so that it can be easily communicated.

The leader's job is to align all these S's in a harmonic way in order to achieve the implementation of strategy. If an organization truly wants a more innovative culture then the head of the organization (or subcomponent) must manage and align the S's so that innovation is not only a value in theory it is supported by all the other S's.

The 9S model has two key takeaways for managers. It demonstrates the importance of aligning these elements so that the company's strategy can actually be implemented. If the parts are not supportive of one another then you get a lot of activity but very little in the way of real change. It is also a good diagnostic tool to help executives think though how to change their organizations so that the change actually becomes embedded.

Here is a perfect example. Siemens embarked on a new strategy of having "one face to the customer." Before this new strategy, it was not uncommon for multiple divisions to call on the same customer. But these salespeople did not talk to each other or co-ordinate their efforts. So customers began to complain. And some suggested that, since Siemens had a number of complementary divisions, they were missing opportunities to present a solution sale to some of its bigger global clients. If you are in the business of power plant building and building controls technology why not have both these divisions make a pitch to a customer? Seems like a no-brainer.

ONE FACE TO THE CUSTOMER

Siemens's answer to this challenge was to develop a solutions sell-ing strategy and back it up with a new structure that involved cre-ating a new role of global account manager responsible for selling joint solutions based on Siemens's broad divisional capabilities. But, at least for the four years I worked with them, it never panned out because they did not modify the other S's in order to support the necessary changes in strategy and structure. For example, they left untouched the sales incentives system, which only rewarded salespeople for selling products from their own divisions. Thus there was no incentive for a salesperson to help sell another divi-sion's products or services. Cross-selling was made more difficult because divisional salespeople were not trained to sell the other division's products. Also, Siemens's divisionalized structure had not developed a good culture for salespeople to work together amicably.

You can see how the 9S model can help a company bring about a sustainable change. If you want a culture of innovation, then you have to think systemically about what in the organization needs to be aligned, to implement and sustain innovation. The Coast Guard or 3M model provide examples of creating the architecture within the organization so that innovation is not a one shot deal and has a chance of being truly embedded in the organization's culture. When I am asked to consult with organizations about innovation, one of the first questions I ask is, "How are you currently going about innovation?" This tells me pretty quickly whether they are thinking systemically or not. Creating a culture of innovation takes a while because of the need to develop the organizational elements (9S's) necessary to embed and sustain it. Clearly this cannot happen without top-level commitment.

The original 7S model presumes that the starting point would be strategy and then you would logically build or modify the other S's to support the strategy. But practitioners soon realized that you can actually start to bring about a desired change from any one of the S's as long as you continue the alignment process. If I change reward systems to reward innovators and they come up with some innovative business ideas, these ideas could potentially lead the company in a new direction, thus changing the current strategy. Apple didn't think it would be in the music business, but the advent of digitized music sent it, through iTunes, on a whole new trajectory including buying music rights from a host of artists and production companies.

I could also try to start with culture change, but this is a long, drawn-out process where the old culture could reasonably survive the tenure of those who change it. I am a fan of innovation-induced cultural change. If you reward innovators, recruit folks into key positions who have some of that entrepreneurial spirit, and develop processes for routinely coming up with great ideas, you may affect culture change more effectively and efficiently than if you started with culture change as your objective.

Simply telling your employees you want them to use their talents to come up with great ideas is not even a baby step toward the evolution of a culture of innovation. 3M, P&G, Apple, and others have developed a systemic approach to developing cultures of innovation. However, innovation is a delicate balance as we saw with NcNerny's tenure at 3M. All he had to do was apply Lean Six Sigma (processes fall under systems) to researchers to kill innovation.

Dragon Borrowing

Dragon borrowing is a more recent approach that is starting to accrue large numbers of advocates. Dragon borrowing refers to open innovation or crowdsourcing as some people call it. *The Innovator's Playbook* (Deloitte, 2009) gives an excellent overview of this approach or you can easily Google the phrase for more information. In fact, this movement has spawned a number of new organizations whose job is to innovate for and/or with their clients. IDEO in Palo Alto is an example of a company whose sole purpose is innovation. Thousands of companies come to them each year for help with "ideating" new ideas for their respective businesses. IDEO utilizes its specialization in the process of innovation to help companies like P&G (squishy toothbrushes) or Apple (first computer mouse) to create and design new products for them.

But other companies have also emerged to help other companies "borrow their brilliance" (see David K. Murray's book *Borrowing Brilliance*). YourEncore, for example, is a spin-off from P&G that utilizes retirees from companies like P&G and others to help clients solve particularly challenging problems with new insights. Yet2.com helps its clients realize a return on their IP investments. It excels at locating unrealized IP (intellectual property, like patents, licenses, etc.) value potential, especially in situations where IP and technology offer substantial market opportunities for products, services, or cooperative relationships with third parties. Yet2.com also finds IP and technology around the globe, enabling clients to enhance their own resources quickly and efficiently and to address gaps in their IP portfolios. Note that many of these firms are relatively smaller than the typical organization that hires them. Their smaller size and agility allows them to do things faster and less bureaucratically.

The Internet has allowed companies and individuals alike to reach out around the world for new ideas to enhance their IQ (innovation quotient). P&G now insists that 80 percent of their new product ideas come from people who do not work for them. Their motto is now "Proudly not invented here," and is a 180-degree turn from their philosophy ten years ago. This approach is clearly one way to utilize a Land of Oz that may not necessarily exist in your own company's landscape. The CIA and NASA have both taken advantage of open innovation by giving some of their partially developed software away free to others with the request that if they can improve on it to send back the improved versions. Both organizations got millions of dollars' worth of free software development from this kind of open innovation. In some respects dragon borrowing allows you to not only get new ideas that you would never have come up with on your own, it may be both more effective and efficient in the ideation process if you do not have a particularly internally friendly environment for innovation. But you can't outsource implementation, so you are still on the hook for building a pathway through the Jungle, the Maze, or the Asylum.

Putting It All Together

These various approaches are not independent. In fact, you can utilize multiple approaches simultaneously to provide counterbalance. In the last profile in the book, I want to introduce you to Lieutenant Commander Chris Kluckhuhn and the Coast Guard Innovation Council. I have saved this one for last to show that no matter how difficult your innovation landscape there is still hope for engendering, embedding, and sustaining innovation. Much of Chris's work was in a Jungle landscape, but the Coast Guard picked him well because of his inherent Innovation Judo skills and provided a Land of Oz base camp and top cover to make sure that the Jungle did not consume him.

The Coast Guard represents a hybrid approach to innovation that has allowed it to embed and sustain innovation over the long term. As with all Jungle base camps, the Innovation Council has the possibility of being overrun if it doesn't keep its defenses up and guard its perimeter. As new leaders come and go in the military, or other organizations that have embedded innovation, they may or may not continue to support innovation, or they may not support a past approach. As you saw at the beginning of this section, 3M's innovation culture was almost killed by the new president's slavish application of Lean Six Sigma.

But the Coast Guard's story is a good one that showcases how Innovation Judo masters can still be of immense help in navigating the borders between the Land of Oz and other landscapes within the same organization. Here is his and their story. I have put it last so you can see how you cannot separate innovation architecture from the innovator if you seek long-term value creation through innovation. Even though this is a military example, it represents the ability to triumph over complexity and wackiness in any organization, public or private.

Counterbalancing in Action: Lieutenant Commander Chris Kluckhuhn and the Coast Guard Innovation Council

One of the most defining moments in Chris Kluckhuhn's life was 9/11. Some people say that innovators are born not made, but on that day Chris developed an instant passion for innovation that led him on a path that eventually won him the award for the Coast Guard's innovator of the year. Upon hearing of the attacks on the Twin Towers in New York City (NYC), Chris and a fellow officer flew a Coast Guard helicopter to NYC to offer any assistance they could provide. They were desperately hoping to pull people off the tops of the Twin Towers. Unfortunately, they were grounded in New York and had to observe the collapse of the second tower and experienced that awful feeling of helplessness as they watched victims plunging to their deaths. Poor situational awareness and lack of adequate technology to assist in search efforts hindered their attempts to support the efforts of local and national agencies on the scene. Chris knew there had to be a better way.

The initial energy and passion was 9/11. I was sitting in a helicopter on deck at the U.S. Coast Guard Air Station in Cape Cod. We were not scheduled to fly or do anything that day but check a few things on the chopper like rotor motion, etc. That's when we got word about the first

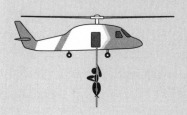

9/11 attack. I didn't have gloves, I didn't have anything to go do a mission, the operations officer in the other aircraft that was taking off was going to go out and do training. They didn't have a full tank of gas and we did. We said

we're ready and launched immediately to NYC. The max power on the H-60 helicopter is 106 percent continuous power. You can pull 120 percent power temporarily for up to 10 seconds. This kind of power is only used when fast takeoffs are desired. But this was an emergency so we were pulling 120 percent, counting to ten, dropping it for one second to 105 percent, then pulling up to 120 percent again to get there as fast as we could. We did this all the way from Cape Cod to NYC. We were pushing the limits. We got over Montauk, tuned up the NYPD's frequency and heard that the south tower collapsed. We flew a little bit farther, and we were ordered to land, just fifteen minutes away from the city. We sat on the ground for a while, loaded some equipment, and then watched as the second tower collapsed.

We finally got clearance to take off, but it was too late to save anyone who was on top of the tower. We flew over and around the city, dropping off some people, but stood by for two days to do medical evacuations that never materialized.

Even today Chris is haunted by the thought of the people jumping to their deaths and the lives they might have saved had he and his copilot been permitted to fly directly to the towers. They had the time to make it to the second tower before it collapsed.

We were there. We beat the hell out of ourselves for landing in the first place, for not taking off quicker. We didn't need that gear that we waited for. We should have just gone right away. The next day, we're in Gabreski Airport in Southampton. A lot of the victims' families were in the area and we were seeing them on the streets. The newspaper showed people diving headfirst out of the buildings— the people diving out of the buildings is what resonated the most. The NYPD said the updrafts were too high to let us attempt the rooftop rescues, but even to this day I wonder. Still, I would like to have tried.

9/11 was life-changing for me. I know that absolutely without that tragedy, I wouldn't have had enough passion or enough commitment to take the risks that are necessary to be an innovator.

Fortunately for both Chris and the Coast Guard, Chris's profound frustration became a passion for better situational awareness, something they didn't have during 9/11. Perhaps the updrafts were not as strong as people thought, but there was no real way of knowing. Chris's newfound passion and some past history of risk taking made him the kind of officer that the Coast Guard was looking for to work as a field member in their Innovation Council.

On a Mission

My parents divorced when I was five. I went to live with my stepfather who was a senior chief aviation survival man in Elizabeth City, North Carolina. That's one of our biggest air stations. I grew up there around the Coast Guard. My stepfather was in the Coast Guard. I moved back to Maryland with my dad for high school, and he was right next to the Naval Academy. Top Gun came out when I was ten, and I said, "I want to be a Naval fighter pilot. I want to go to Annapolis." I visited Annapolis. My stepfather and mom had me visit the Coast Guard Academy, and I spent a week there and said, "I want to go fly for the Coast Guard. I want to do that."

I graduated May 22, 1996. My first assignment was as a leadership instructor at the academy teaching cadets leadership. I went to the Coast Guard cutter Bear out of Portsmouth, Virginia. I was the first lieutenant on board there, deck watch officer, and boarding officer. Two years after joining, I got to go to the Naval flight school. Until recently, every Coast Guard Academy graduate had to go to a ship for two years, and then you compete to go to flight school. I had my heart set on flying top gun fighters, but after I got introduced to helicopters and saw the Coast Guard's reliance on them in emergency situations, I thought there would be more action flying helicopters than flying jets.

And aside from his 9/11 rescue attempt, he has seen plenty of action.

The Coast Guard looks for Innovation Council members who aren't afraid to take some risks, and Chris fit the bill perfectly. As a wrestler at the Coast Guard Academy, he broke his neck. Despite the recurrent pain, he kept quiet about it and just barely passed the flight school physical.

Given my condition, I knew there would be some physical risk, and after flying for five years my neck problems got bad enough that I was medically grounded. The weight, the vibration, the heavy night goggles, it all took a toll. I had discectomy surgery hoping to fly again, but it wasn't in the cards.

Chris also showed a willingness to bend or break some rules if it meant doing the right thing.

There was a snowstorm off of New England. There was a ship 150 miles offshore. Typically if we go more than 100 miles offshore, we have the fixed-wing aircraft cover it, but because of the snow it couldn't take off. So we flew out without anybody. To go that distance, you have to roll out on HF radio to talk. We tried to establish an HF connection and couldn't get anybody. So we chose to continue going and relaying our position from ships on VHF. We got out and said, "We know exactly where they're at. Once we get on scene, we'll drop the pump and we'll head back." We were kind of breaking the rules by not having direct communications with the Coast Guard, but the vessel was taking on water and we did what we had to do.

My most dangerous mission was picking up a guy off of Martha's Vineyard with 300-foot overcast, forty to fifty knot winds, and icing. We picked up a half an inch of ice just flying between Cape Cod and there. So we weren't going to go unless he was going to die. He was at the hospital. He'd had a heart attack, and they needed us to evacuate him and get him up to Boston. They said, "He's going to die if you don't." So we said, "Okay. We'll do it." We picked up all this ice getting over there. We said, "We're not going to Boston. We're just going to bring him back to the Cape and transport him via ambulance." We barely managed to get him back to the Cape, and the ambulance couldn't drive him up to Boston because the conditions were so bad. They took him up to

Hyannis, and he ended up being my wife's patient. She said, "Yeah, he would have died if you hadn't have gone to get him."

Chris and the OPC

In Part IV, I talked about dragon dens as counterbalancing strategies for innovation-challenged landscapes, and the Coast Guard's Innovation Council is a great example of such a strategy. The Coast Guard has always had innovation as a core value, but it is not always easy to operationalize it. It is still part of the military and thus hierarchical, and it has many rules, guidelines, and policies that help it run as well as get in the way of innovation. With it now a part of DHS (Department of Homeland Security), which has its own bureaucracy via the federal government, it is very important that the Coast Guard establish and maintain its own innovative values.

Some foresighted leaders knew that it was not enough just to wish for innovation; they had to be the architects of some protective structure so that new ideas could not only be generated but developed and implemented. As you read on, decide if you also need to develop some safe havens in your organization for innovation as well, and also note the application of the 9S model. To build a Land of Oz, you need a strategy and a supportive structure. You also have to have systems that can help you engender and evaluate good ideas, and then help you implement these ideas. Fortunately, the Coast Guard was able to build the whole package, which included the use of Innovation Judo masters to help navigate the Jungle outside the den.

Guard Innovation Philosophy and Structure

Historically, the Coast Guard has been open to innovation as a core value. The first formal structuring of an organization solely dedicated to innovation within the Coast Guard began with Captain

Johnson's recommendations and the creation of the Commandant's Innovation Council in November 2000. The Coast Guard's
innovation philosophy and organization was outlined formally in
2003 in *The Coast Guard Innovation Process* pamphlet.[4] This document detailed the council's *intent* and guided the efforts of those
involved in driving innovation and communicated the Coast
Guard's innovation process. These precepts include the following:

Innovation Philosophy: The Coast Guard recognized the
potential of the individual to solve key organizational challenges through the ingenious application of existing resources
focused and applied toward the many and diverse challenges
facing the organization. The Innovation Staff was created to
support the work of the Commandant's Innovation Council (Council), which served as the champion of these innovators, by discovering promising innovations, evaluating them
for organizational use, and facilitating their enterprise-wide
implementation. While the Council was a catalyst for change
in the way the Coast Guard conducted operational and support business, the Innovation Staff supported the Council in its
endeavors. As the framework and support for innovation and
performance excellence, the staff:

- Promoted an innovative culture that entertains all ideas to
  resolve organizational challenges,
- Infused innovation and risk-based decision making as a
  cultural tenet,
- Promoted enabling technology to enjoy significant productivity and efficiency gains,
- Championed innovative solutions to program managers
  for enterprise-wide implementation, and

---

[4] Excerpted from *The Coast Guard Innovation Process,* distributed by the Office of
Quality and Management Effectiveness, 2003.

- Cultivated and sustained relationships with the two Coast Guard Field Innovation Councils (created later) and major support commands as principle incubators of innovation.

The Commandant's Innovation Council would champion the innovation initiative with support from the LANTAREA (Atlantic Area) and PACAREA (Pacific Area) Field Innovation Councils, and the Headquarters Innovation Team.

Commandant's Intent: The Council was created as a cross-programmatic catalyst for productivity improvements through innovative reengineering of business processes in support of the Coast Guard's strategic plan. The Office of Quality and Management Effectiveness chief assumed the task of chairing the Commandant's Innovation Council. The Council's job was to prioritize and champion competing Coast Guard innovation projects and liaison with Area Innovation Councils to ensure enterprise-wide initiative alignment.

Area Innovation Councils: The LANTAREA and PACAREA Councils prioritized and championed innovation projects promoted from their areas of responsibility. Each liaisoned with the Commandant's Innovation Council, their counterpart Field Innovation Council, and cognizant program offices to ensure enterprise-wide initiative alignment. The Field Innovation Councils also served as communication and collaboration conduits to assist units in sharing their innovative productivity and process improvements.

Innovation Staff: Though small, the Innovation and Initiatives Team was staffed to administer the Commandant's Innovation Council processes. Staff responsibilities also included promotion of innovative solutions, technologies, devices, and practices of all Coast Guard members by working with the Commandant's Innovation Council and other mechanisms to promote enterprise-wide implementation to achieve organizational excellence.

Innovation Execution: The Commandant's Innovation Council in alignment with the strategic and business plans facilitated this endeavor through:

- **Innovation Funding:** The Commandant's Innovation Council funds are comprised of an annually reoccurring budget managed by the Council. It was designated to fund innovative solutions to Coast Guard challenges. The fund also underwrites the annual Innovation Exposition. The fund was not designed to support long-term funding of innovative ideas, only the initial start-up. Long-term funding becomes the responsibility of the headquarters program managers and must compete with other internal Coast Guard priorities.

- **Innovation Exposition:** Initiated in 2000, the Coast Guard Innovation Exposition has become an annually held event. Its purpose was to bring together the Coast Guard and industry to establish open dialogue among the technology users, innovators, academia, research and development centers, and Coast Guard support elements to promote innovation. The exposition focused on major Coast Guard challenges such as transitioning to the new Department of Homeland Security. The agendas encompass a full range of issues pertaining to homeland security.

- **Innovation Award:** The Captain Niels P. Thomsen Innovation Award Program was created to celebrate the best ideas that had been implemented. Managed by the Commandant's Innovation Council and the Innovation and Initiatives Team, the award recognized an individual or teams for creative solutions that resulted in a successfully implemented solution. All Coast Guard employees are eligible to participate in the program, and instructions were crafted to provide specific guidance and nomination requirements. Individual and/or team awards are specified for the following areas: Science or Technology, Operations or Readiness, and Support, Administration, or Training categories.

If you are looking for a compelling story you can see that they have taken considerable time and effort to not only create an innovative culture but to communicate it as well.

Top Cover and Support

Admiral Thad Allen, twenty-third commandant of the U.S. Coast Guard, was a staunch supporter of the Coast Guard's innovation efforts. In his thirty-eight years of service, Admiral Allen had held operational command both at sea and ashore, conducting missions to support the maritime safety, security, and environmental stewardship interests of the nation. As a flag officer, he served as the principal federal official for response and recovery operations for hurricanes Katrina and Rita, while also serving as the Coast Guard chief of staff. Under Admiral Allen's tutelage the Coast Guard underwent significant modernization efforts to better organize, train, equip, and deploy its assets in response to twenty-first-century challenges like terrorism. While serving as the Coast Guard chief of staff, he was an avid supporter of the Innovation Council. From his perspective, soliciting and listening to ideas and taking calculated risks on innovative ideas were critical to enhancing and improving the Coast Guard's capabilities.

Since the inception of the innovation initiative in 2000, over $10.5 million has been invested in Coast Guard innovation through the Commandant's Innovation Council, generating an estimated $300 million in savings. However, concern had developed over the potential for funding to continue in an era of dwindling resources and competing priorities. From a high of $4 million in

2003, the budget has been reduced to $1 million in each of the last three years, of which, $500,000 was budgeted for the Innovation Exposition, and the other $500,000 for the annual innovation awards. The process for funding innovation within the Coast Guard is very informal. In discussing the budget process:

Funding of innovative initiatives that showed demonstrable improvements in efficiency and effectiveness come from surpluses generated by cost savings. For example, voice over IP capitalizes on an existing Ethernet backbone and can produce immediate savings through the elimination of traditional phone company expenses. Only innovation that resulted in a new requirement required additional funding, and Chris found himself operating more and more in this domain.

The Innovation Exposition

From its start in the early 2000s, the annual Innovation Exposition quickly became a focus for highlighting innovation in the Coast Guard. Participants include Coast Guard innovators and senior leadership, academia, and the private sector. The Coast Guard uses the Innovation Exposition to educate and communicate its innovation efforts to the Coast Guard and both public and private sector vendors. Innovation Expositions typically receive just over 50 percent of the Coast Guard's total innovation budget. However, as chief of staff, Admiral Allen conjoined the semiannual Coast Guard Flag and SES Conference with the Innovation Exposition to ensure all senior leaders had the opportunity to see the ideas firsthand.

Admiral Allen stated in an interview, "There is stuff that has walked off the floor of the Expo and been institutionalized six months later because a flag officer (admiral) sees it. The Expo brings senior leaders face to face with the deck plate innovators who, in a five minute conversation, can make a value proposition." He went on to discuss an example involving the vice commandant during a recent Innovation Exposition. The operating design of EPIRBS (Emergency Position Indicating Radio Beacons) changed with the advent of the 406 version. As a result, legacy Coast Guard aircraft lost some direction-finding capabilities. In other words, patrol aircraft could not hone in on the 406 distress signal and had to rely on positions provided by shore-based units, fly to the location, and perform a visual search in the area. Program elements had been unable to fast-track the implementation of the necessary equipment. Because of an extemporaneous Innovation Exposition floor conversation between a vice admiral and an aviation maintenance warrant officer attending the event, the project was jumpstarted, the equipment was acquired, and the capability regained. The impact that the chance meeting and the subsequent equipment installation had on mission efficiency can't be overstated—it has saved lives and resources.

Another example highlights the benefits of networking that the Innovation Exposition provides. About five years ago, the master chief petty officer of the Coast Guard (MCPO-CG) began sponsoring the Enlisted Innovators initiative. Command master chiefs at the various districts identified the best and brightest enlisted Coast Guard innovators doing a great job in their units and sponsored their attendance to the Innovation Exposition. In reward for their hard work, they enjoy breakfast with the commandant, MCPO-CG, and other senior leaders. During their attendance, they are exposed to what the Coast Guard is doing in the world of innovation, and it gives them a chance to see the various ideas and projects being displayed at the various booths.

Finally, the Innovation Exposition also offers the opportunity for many Coast Guard enlistees to demonstrate their innovative ideas at a national venue. One such example involved the innovative product Petty Officer First Class (MK1) Arturo Munoz of the USCGC *Seneca* (WMEC-906) brought to the Exposition in 2008. Aboard ship, engineering logs are principally maintained by hand. Over the course of a four-hour watch, crewmembers annotate readings of various valves and gauges on a paper log. At the end of their watch, they hand their logs in, where they are typically "filed" away in a drawer. Little analysis is conducted on the readings, and if any was attempted, entries were difficult to read due to oil, coffee, or sloppy handwriting. MK1 Munoz created an Excel spreadsheet to capture required readings and upload it to a personal digital assistant (PDA). Placing bar codes at each reading site and adding a bar code reader to the PDA allowed crewmembers to key in their readings during a watch. At the end of a watch, their readings were downloaded to a master spreadsheet where the data could be analyzed and trends spotted. MK1 Munoz's innovation created a better process and the ability to analyze the data allowed the reallocation of assets for a better purpose.

MK1 Munoz was grateful for the opportunity to attend the conference, see other ideas on display, and share his own. He commented that he felt there is often resistance to new ideas from veteran "Coasties," and he didn't really know how or where to communicate his ideas within the organization until the advent of the Innovation Council and the Innovation Exposition. This was one of two common themes resonating throughout the Exposition, at individual booths, lunch conversations, and even discussed by some general session speakers. "We have lots of great ideas that never get beyond a single unit." Thanks to the Exposition, now they can.

Innovation Scholarships

In the past the Coast Guard collaborated with the National Graduate School to provide personnel the opportunity to pursue a master of science degree in quality systems management while on full-time active duty. From 2003 until 2005, a scholarship program funded by the Innovation Council, combined with reduced tuition from the National Graduate School and the Coast Guard tuition assistance program, allowed personnel the opportunity to achieve an advanced degree at minimal personal cost. As a requirement of the scholarship program, participating students worked on a Coast Guard–focused process improvement project that had to demonstrate a positive return on the scholarship investment. Each project team applied quality management concept tools under academic supervision. Though the scholarship program ended, the advanced degree program remains a huge success: from 2002 to early 2008, 450 students graduated, 107 process improvement teams were formed, and over $300 million in process improvements, cost avoidances, cost savings, and productivity gains were delivered by these teams.

Innovating—Formally and Informally

The Coast Guard has a formal process for managing innovation projects. Projects can be submitted by anyone within the Coast Guard by accessing the Coast Guard Innovation database. After a simple data entry process that includes a request for funds, the applicable Innovation Council reviews the idea and a recommendation is made to the Headquarters Innovation Council. If approved, funding is provided by the Commandant's Innovation Council.

Additionally, the Coast Guard staffs its districts with two OPC (organizational performance consultants) billets (positions). These performance and process experts help commands/units/individuals pursue quality and innovation. These billets included both civilian personnel and active duty Coast Guard personnel who rotate from an operational tour into an OPC billet for four years then return to an operational billet. Most of the initial OPCs had advanced degrees and all received training in quality consultation and facilitation. OPCs are "internal consultants with expertise in organizational assessments and development. They help commands and staffs implement Coast Guard management programs."[5] OPCs also

---

[5] *U.S. Coast Guard Leadership Development Center, Performance Improvement Guide*, 5th ed. (Boston: U.S. Government Printing Office, 2008), p. 163.

served on Field Innovation Councils and may act as reviewers for projects submitted to the Coast Guard Innovation database.

As the Coast Guard chief of staff and innovation program champion, Admiral Allen and the chief of quality management, Captain Abbott, understood the need to "buffer" OPCs from the various district agendas in order to push the Coast Guard innovation agenda forward. As a result, OPCs maintained a dotted-line relationship with headquarters. However, the billets resided on each district's PAL (personnel allowance list); OPC's were assigned to the district staff with the district exercising administrative control over the OPCs (including preparing their performance reports). District staff rarely dealt directly with the headquarters innovation staff on innovation or quality issues. The OPC had to manage the needs of the headquarters while simultaneously managing local expectations. It became the communication buffer for the quality program.

STRATEGIC AND SYSTEMIC

I have laid out the Coast Guard approach to innovation in some detail because it is such a good example of strategically well thought-out approach that recognizes the systemic nature of the organization. Notice how it has operated in all the 9S's so that innovation is embedded and thus sustainable. The Coast Guard has a strategy, a structure, and a process for getting ideas on the table and into the system. In addition it uses the OPCs who have the skills and personalities to drive innovation initiatives. The leadership tone for valuing innovation is set at the top.

The Innovation Council represents a good example of infusing just enough Land of Oz into the landscape so that ideas have a chance of surviving. I also like this story because of the Coast Guard's ability to follow the steps in the 7I model I presented to you earlier in the book: intent, infrastructure, investigation, ideation, identification, infection, and implementation/integration. The

Coast Guard's innovation database and local area councils allow them to infect others with the best ideas. But once outside the Land of Oz, things get more hairy for the innovator. That's why the Coast Guard picked Chris Kluckhuhn as one of its innovators. Chris was very skilled in traversing the Jungle where a little Innovation Judo can make the difference between success and failure.

From 9/11 to Katrina

The lack of situational awareness on 9/11 became Chris's passion as an innovator. He would do whatever it took to help the Coast Guard and other governmental organizations develop a greater capability in this area. One of his first jobs as a helicopter pilot was to fly ship spotting missions. Now more than ever, it is important for the country to have increased vigilance and accurate information about vessels that move in and around U.S. coastal areas and waterways especially in light of the immense danger posed by international terrorists.

But in 2001, just after 9/11, Chris knew right away that our ability to track ships in real time with up-to-date information was woefully inadequate. Pilots might be lucky to have ten accurate spottings during an entire day's mission, if they were lucky. Sightings were visual, and while the pilots had lists of what ships might be out there from yesterday's sightings and ships records, they would often have to fly at XXX feet or less to be able to see the hull's markings, and even then they did not know which ship it was.

We in Coast Guard aviation were required to do vessel sightings. We were supposed to record where vessels were out in the ocean so that boarding officers and others would know who was out there and who they wanted to board. When we did those sightings, we were supposed to check several lists to see if the ships we sighted were on any of the lists. In practical terms that was impossible because we'd be on to the next vessel before we could check the list to see whether the last ship was on it or not. By the time we landed and manually entered our visual sightings into our system so that others could use the information, it was generally four to eight hours old. So we were basically doing a useless mission, because the information wasn't getting to anybody in a timely manner. And when we went out the next day we could print out a tabular spreadsheet of the ships that were supposed to be out there and we could look up information on them but we really didn't know exactly where they were. The information wasn't in the form of a map where you could see it, so we were going out blind each time and just hoping to spot some of the ships for possible boarding actions. It reminded me of 9/11 where we were woefully short of situational awareness data, and I knew there had to be a better way.

Outsmarting/Outmaneuvering

Even in landscapes that have built a dragon den, you can still run into roadblocks and blockheads that aren't with the program. All it takes is for one boss who either doesn't understand or doesn't buy into the innovator's role and innovation can be stymied. Fortunately, Chris has some inherent Innovation Judo skills that have allowed him to either outsmart or overcome these obstacles. As I mentioned, Chris's job as an OPC consultant designated that 70 percent of his time was to be allocated to innovation. And since working on innovation is hard to measure until the innovation shows value creation, it is understandable that a boss would have to have some faith that the innovator is indeed innovating and that something good will happen as a result of these efforts. Add to this a boss who likes to micromanage and thinks that 70 percent of time spent on something like innovation is a waste of time, and then you have a blockhead and a roadblock. On one of his tours Chris had such a boss, and this is when his Innovation Judo skills came in handy.

The fun part of my job as an OPC consultant was working at the local level. I got into a new billet and shortly after I arrived, the captain who was my direct supervisor transferred out, so I had very little interaction with him before he left. There was a three- or four-month gap where I had no local boss. It was great. I was learning my new job and figuring out what the job was really about, what areas of innovation to focus on. But then I got a new boss, a commander who didn't like the OPC model because he could not equate traditional quality with innovation. We butted heads quite a bit when he first got there. He didn't understand what I was doing. He wanted to see me and know that I was actually doing work and accomplishing things. Innovation can't be micromanaged so I just started copying him on emails from 4:00 in the morning until 11:00 or 12:00 at night until he cried mercy. I did this because I tried to make him feel comfortable that I was actually doing work and knew that all these emails would require his time to read them, which would make keeping tabs on me all the time not a good use of his time.

I also protected him politically. His first question was, "What does this innovation stuff have to do with quality?" I said, "It's all quality, sir." He said, "It's good stuff, but I don't understand how it's quality." I said, "Sir, you've got the best of both worlds right now. Anything I do wrong, you have plausible deniability. Any of the good things I do you get to take credit for." He smiled and laughed, and said, "I like the way you say that."

So once he was comfortable I was doing good work and working hard, he left me alone. He transferred out and then a new captain transferred in who understood what I was doing and was supportive. Fortunately the way my job was structured with 70 percent of my time allocated to innovation fenced me off and in many ways helped protect me from a boss who wanted to allocate 100 percent of my time to his tasking and zero for innovation. I could always go over his head if I had to but in my case just unbalancing my boss and then redirecting his concerns to either plausible deniability of taking credit solved the problem and let me get on with my work.

Chris spent four years as an OPC working on his passion for better situational awareness always having in the back of his mind the haunting memories of 9/11 when he and his copilot were grounded because authorities had very little real data about the situation in and around the towers and whether it was safe enough for helicopters to attempt rooftop rescues. So how could first responders fly into a disaster area like that of Hurricane Katrina and know whether live wires were in the water or a helicopter landing pad on top of a hospital was no longer there due to the roof collapsing, or how could you save someone from the ravaging waters from the air if you only had an address? You can only read street addresses from the ground, which aren't much good for a chopper pilot flying into a flooded area. You need GPS coordinates derived from this address and a moving map that is being populated with real-time data as reported from rescue workers, satellite data, Google maps, and other bits of information that give first responders real-time situational awareness.

Thanks to Chris's innovative thinking, some Coast Guard seed funding, emerging technology from industry and government, and his ability to pull people and resources together, we now have these capabilities. Chris is now a Coast Guard reservist, but he had a thriving entrepreneurial business based on what he had learned and developed as an Innovation Council member. In the recent Gulf Oil spill, Chris was hired to help bring his situational awareness knowledge and technology to help track and manage the movement of oil and ships in the area.

Despite the Coast Guard's support for innovation, its innovators still face roadblocks and blockheads as indicated in the boss example I described earlier. But my favorite Innovation Judo stories from Chris were about overcoming two particularly difficult bureaucratic obstacles with relatively simple but very clever solutions.

Jousting with the Jungle

You know you might be meeting roadblocks when you deal with any group that has the words *Board* or *Process* attached to its name. In Chris's case one group was called the Aviation Control Configuration Board (ACCB) and the other was the Local Control Configuration Board (CCB). I am not suggesting that these boards are unimportant; in fact they are essential in command and control environments, but in some cases they put process before problem solving, and Chris had to use his cleverness and some Innovation Judo skills to neutralize these two entities.

One of Chris's greatest attributes as a Coast Guard innovator was his ability to spot and capitalize on emerging technologies that could truly enhance situational awareness. For example, he met a colleague at one of the Coast Guard's yearly Innovation Expositions who was demonstrating how the use of a PDA could lead to faster, cheaper, safer, and more effective ship boardings. Before the advent of the PDA, ship boarding was labor intensive and lacked real-time data to help determine who to board and what to look for. In the old approach, the Coast Guard would physically board a ship, interview people on board, check the cargo, and log all these data by hand. With the advent of the PDA things changed dramatically, and with the application of this tool and the appropriate software, everything is logged in real time: fingerprints, identities, pictures of passports, etc. These data can now be processed in seconds and minutes, not hours, and can be distributed instantly.

Chris saw immediately how that this kind of technology might be modified and adapted for use in his ship-sighting missions and potentially provide even greater capabilities for situational awareness in all kinds of venues. He migrated this approach to Panasonic Toughbook laptop computers so that much more data could be stored and processed. Now pilots would know what ships were in the area from previous reports, track their routes, and merge known data about cargo, port of embarkation, destination, unscheduled movements, and ship history, making their sighting mission much more effective. And, of course, his experience in pulling all these data together through a technological advancement led him to his insights regarding moving maps and situational awareness capabilities necessary for disasters and emergency situations.

But before you can hardwire a computer or an intelligent system to an aircraft, the system must be assessed and approved by a board, and that could easily take a year to deliberate the safety and efficacy of any hardwired avionic.

> We wanted to automate the GPS, putting in the position and time as much as possible. That was 2002 and the PDA couldn't handle that type of work, so we ended up migrating to Toughbook tablet computers. We built a graphical user interface, basically a web page that extracted all the data out of the Coast Guard's web-based information system called MISLE (Maritime Information and Law Enforcement) and downloaded information to the Panasonic Toughbook. We integrated it with a moving map system called Falcon View. We had it down to the point where a sighting used to take ten minutes to record on a piece of paper. Once you land it, you had to go back and enter it, and it took ten minutes to enter the information into the web-based system. We got it down to ten seconds to actually record the information into the tablet, and when you landed, you plug the tablet in, you hit "Export" and you are done.

> The solution that we built was pretty incredible. We said, "Hey, let us know who you already know about and we'll display that to our moving map." So we linked this system that ended up being called MISLE Lite with Falcon View. Before we went for a flight, we plugged a computer into the network. We'd hit "Plot common operating picture," and it would plot out a static picture of all the vessels that the Coast Guard had, an unclassified picture of all the vessels, as we would go fly. Within a two- to three-hour period those vessels aren't going to move very far. The system allowed us to hit a button and project a ship's path based on its course and speed if we wanted to. It was

color-coded so that we could see which vessels had lookouts on them or didn't and what type of fisheries they were doing. We could click on it and pull up information like when was the last time it was sighted, when was the last time it was boarded. These are called right of approach questions. But getting these capabilities accepted and then implemented presented their own set of challenges.

For Chris to shepherd his idea through the bureaucracy, he had to navigate around two gatekeeping boards, the ACCB and the CCB.

We had two major bureaucracies to deal with. One was the IT computer bureaucracy, the other one was the aviation control configuration process. Trying to navigate both of those simultaneously was a challenge. It basically takes a year to get an approval to make a permanent modification to the aircraft. But there are certain loopholes you can use to avoid this committee. For aviation, it was the portable electronic device policy. So you had to do some simple tests and a couple of hours' worth or testing to verify that any electronic equipment you want to use inside the aircraft didn't cause any interference with the aircraft. I could do that at my level and sign off on it, send it in, and get it approved. According to that policy, you couldn't connect anything to the aircraft. You couldn't get the aircraft GPS, you couldn't get aircraft power, so I bought lots of batteries.

We had a GPS that we put in the window, and it was a total stand-alone device that we put in a bag and people carried it on their laps or whatever. But headquarters, which was trying to get control of what we were doing and stop what we were doing, I don't know if they were trying to stop it, but they were definitely trying to get control of it, they kept demanding that we go through the Aircraft Control Configuration Board process. It's a long process that generally takes about six months to a year to get approval.

I believed and so did my boss at the time that if we went the board route, it was going to kill what we were doing. So we kept throwing out the portable electronic device policy and refusing to go through the Control Configuration Board. We just kept firing back telling them that we were in compliance with the portable electronic device policy. We also made the device Wi-Fi between the front and rear of the aircraft so the folks up front could coordinate with the people in back without using any hardwired communication devices. It was a slick solution. I never mentioned that it was Wi-Fi. I did all of the testing, but I just used the acronyms. Panasonic called it an MDWD or Mobile Data Wireless Device. I just called it an MDWD. It got approved and went on the Coast Guard Aviation website as approved equipment. It was wireless, and we had over 100 hours of operational testing. Once the Control Configuration Board found out about a year later that it was just wireless Wi-Fi, then they turned that part of it off. But by then the solution had proven its value and saved lives in the process. I also had a 1,000 page NASA study that demonstrated that Wi-Fi inside an aircraft causes less interference than the screen itself.

Chris got around the ACCB hurdle but then had to figure out how to deal with the local CCB board. The problem was that the moving map solution required the use of a nonstandard laptop that was rugged enough to withstand rough weather flying conditions and that could be put in and taken out of the aircraft at will without fear of breakage. The answer at the time was the Panasonic Toughbook, which is similar to what our servicemen and -women are using today in Afghanistan and Iraq. Today, these types of laptops are standard issue for troops, but at this time, this type of computer was not approved for purchase by the Coast Guard. It was considered "nonstandard" and therefore needed to be approved by the local CCB, which would have taken a long time.

They didn't understand our world of work. There's a local CCB process that allows you to buy nonstandard stuff for applications like ours. I used the innovation money. I got that sent to me, but I knew I had to go through the Cell CCB process, and I knew the people who would be voting on it would be hard to convince why we needed it in our world of work. Quite frankly at the time I didn't have the energy to *fight that bureaucratic battle, so I went straight to the procurement guys, the junior petty officers. I brought them the non-rugged device that we procured under the $2,500 procurement cap. So we just used the credit card. It was on us. Basically I didn't think the bureaucracy— with all the things going on—would ever notice that we bought that. That happens all the time. It was a small enough purchase that it was below the radar. This one was going to be a $50,000 purchase. I had to get procurement specialists involved.*

I took the Toughbook and showed them the benefit that it provided to us. I showed how it would have saved Coast Guardsmans' lives in Niagara. We had lost a helicopter that flew into terrain out in Humboldt Bay at Shelter Cove. The 6541 crew flew into a cove and then turned into what they thought was a safe course. But they forgot that they were in a cove and flew right into a cliff. So I showed the board how this new situational awareness system would have prevented that accident. They said, "You know we have to follow the policy book," but then they figured out if we were getting these funds from something called the innovation fund it could be considered separate from regular Coast Guard policy and thus allow for purchasing them without having to make a policy decision. So they bought in to what we were trying to do. They had sixty days to make the procurement, and they completed all the paperwork in one week.

Innovating in Jungle environments is particularly tricky and time consuming. Often Jungle environments will either run out or wear out the innovator, but Chris survived and thrived in this type of environment. You have already gotten some insight into his success via his profile, but at the end of the interview, I asked him if he had any other advice for innovators who find themselves operating in difficult innovation landscapes. Here are some of his thoughts.

1. *Stay under the radar long enough so that your idea can have a couple of operational successes to demonstrate the power of what you're trying to do, and then all those walls, all that resistance, turns around and starts supporting it.*

2. *Look for and create opportunities to communicate your ideas to the right audience. The 2002 Innovation Exposition basically taught me the benefit of having the Coast Guard Expositions. This is one of the few venues where you have all these admirals together in one place, and junior-level Coasties have access to them.*

3. *Understand the difference between* kairos *and* chronos *time. Chronos is that every second is the same as every other second or minute, and kairos is the belief that some time is more valuable than other time and knowing when time's important. When I flew to the site of Hurricane Katrina to help with the disaster efforts, I found out that an admiral was going there as well, so I offered to fly him down in my plane. This gave me numerous hours of interaction with him to help socialize and demonstrate my system to him, thus winning another advocate. Again, I made this contact at the Exposition, and this is when I found out he was headed to the Hurricane Katrina site.*

4. *Don't pick open fights. Listening carefully to the negative inputs you get about your idea and try to meet that criticism with things that either solve their needs or mute their opinions.*

5. *Get enough resources to keep your ideas alive. The other big key in all of this is what I've learned in government, which is the power of resources. It's not just government, it's anywhere, but it's important to have enough resources to survive. I've been very good at getting resources in the first place. I used the innovation grant to get the first Toughbooks and all the other equipment. Also, don't be afraid to use other people's money. Not only did I get some modest resources from the Coast Guard to help move my idea forward, I also got some resources from industry, other governmental agencies, and the Air Force. But I had to demonstrate some proof of concept before they were willing to help. So you need enough to develop some working models and prototypes.*

CONDENSE COMPLEXITY

Complex organizations are just that—hard to get your arms around in terms of structures, processes, and relationships. And most complex organizations have a tendency to add to their complexity as Greiner showed us in his work on evolution and revolutions that I talked about earlier. Even good intentions can create their own unintended complexities. For example, Lean Six Sigma is a great toolkit, but many organizations have built a bureaucracy around the administration of Lean Six Sigma, which is ironic since it is supposed to help make the organization "lean" so that it is more effective and efficient.

The best thing senior management can do is to make the road to innovation clear. If managers haven't built it or, worse, yet haven't communicated it, they need to do so. This suggestion may seem like a no-brainer but in complex organizations it is not unusual for people to be unaware of vital information. I have tested people on their own company's vision, strategy, corporate values, financial health, and the path to innovation. You would be amazed at how many people fail the test. They can tell you a lot about their little part of the organization, but often display ignorance of the company at large. This is not unexpected in complex organizations.

I was doing some executive education for managers in a large, complex multinational corporation. I was not only an instructor of the course, but I was the main program designer and faculty director. I designed the course so that there would be a mix of presenters, both outside academics and internal executives. The program was about innovation and corporate entrepreneurship, so I invited the company's director of innovation to speak to our group. He laid out the company's process for getting ideas heard. Only two participants out of the thirty-eight in the class, all of whom were middle managers, knew that there was a director of innovation, and it was news to them that there was any process.

It is very hard to dismantle complexity, but it can be done as GE shows. GE used external consultants and internal teams to ferret out worthless work and therefore worthless processes. One team found triplicate copies of a document that was created sent to numerous others who added to the document so that it could wind up in a file cabinet that no one ever looked at. CEOs need to spend as much time reducing unnecessary complexity within their organizations as they do focusing on stock price. This is especially true when it comes to innovation. If people don't know where to go or who to talk to when they have a good idea, that is a problem that can be easily handled by proper communication. But if the processes are difficult, unclear, and unnecessarily bureaucratic, why would anyone want to spend the time trying to get an idea heard? There are several specific things that leaders can do regarding reducing complexity:

1. Spell out and communicate the company's innovation road map and put it in an e-brochure that is sent out to everyone.

2. Create a web portal spelling out the process and give names, email addresses, and phone numbers of people who play a role in the process.

3. Post examples of successful innovation and put in links to the innovators so that others can talk to them about how they managed the process.

4. Create that diagonal slice of the organization and task it to ferret out unnecessary complexities and redundancies and

create a goal of simplifying the organization rather than complicating it.

5. Think three times before adding any processes or controls without taking others out.

6. Think through the possible unintended consequences or possibilities of creating bureaucracies within processes that are meant to create efficiencies and effectiveness.

7. Create a SUC (simplify unnecessary complexity) award and incentive for people who recognize the ability to simplify work.

8. Don't read the latest gurus' business books (except mine) or go to their seminars and immediately come back and try to implement what they said.

9. If you don't have a road map, pick out the five best innovators in the company, ask them to describe how they got it done, codify the similarities, and publish the stories with the road map.

Whack Wackiness

Complexity is mostly a structural problem, and some form of destructuring is necessary. This is not an easy task, but it is amazing what budget cuts in the right areas can produce. Wackiness on the other hand is primarily behavioral. This is not to say that the behavior is not in part motivated by structure. If there are only a few slots in the pyramid that I might be promoted into, I might engage in some backstabbing or other moves that would give me an edge. Our behavior can only be partially explained by structure, the rest lies with us and our personal value system. Most of us hate politics, but sometimes others force us into it. For example, the guy who emails you a diatribe about what you have failed to do and then emails everyone and his brother in the company has to be neutralized, which may require some sort of political maneuvering, but it is not something that you should resort to first.

In highly wacky companies, however, playing politics may be the only way to survive. But a heavy emphasis on politics or outsmarting wacky rules and processes takes a lot of energy that should be used to innovate. Senior leaders, to a great extent, dictate the degree of wackiness in their organizations. Leadership at the top sets the organization's tone.

I once worked in a consulting capacity for a CEO who liked to pit each one of his vice presidents against each other. He would personally tell each of the VPs that they were the one he saw as his replacement, but they should not tell anyone else in the company until the time was right. You can imagine the kind of wacky behavior and subsequent culture that this behavior yielded. The VPs became extremely competitive with one another and not in a nice way. The sad part is that before the arrival of this CEO, many of the VPs were very friendly and team-oriented. But they weren't after this guy came on board. There was backstabbing, rumor mongering, and open hostility among this team. The CEO's view was that this competition would be good for the organization as it would make every VP strive to be the best that he or she could be. Instead it promoted just the opposite. It brought out the worst. This nasty competition was not lost on employees and soon enormous silos formed as each VP tried to blame the others for any problems in the company's performance. The manufacturing VP was the reason for the quality problems, the engineering VP overdesigned the product, or the marketing VP promised unrealistic delivery dates. When the CEO left, the board brought in someone from the outside, which was probably best for everyone.

So what can you do to whack wackiness?

1. Do not make company values discretionary. Fire even the most talented employees if they don't live the values. This of course assumes that the values are essential for the organization's success.

2. Visit your most disgruntled customers and listen to them very carefully. Internal wackiness, like in Asylum organizations, almost always has an impact on customers. It is very hard to hide wackiness from the outside. How you are treated indicates the way management treats its employees. I recently asked two flight attendants what they thought about their airline's merger with another one. They both said that it hadn't changed their lives but made senior management rich while their benefits were being cut. The airline says it stresses customer service, but it is much more interested in making a few people very, very rich. Nothing wrong with wealth, but it should not come at the sacrifice of the people who help create it.

3. Provide top cover for innovators. Seek out innovators and give them some protection from the politics. Call yourself a champion or mentor and make some innovations your pet projects. It gives credibility to the innovator and lets others know that you are watching closely.

4. Look for rules or processes that get in the way. Remember IBM had to use project metrics not financial metrics to keep its new innovations alive. It was brainlessly forcing innovative new business ventures to show a return on capital within the first year or be shut down. That might work for mature businesses, but not newbies. This rule was killing innovation. Hold contests and give prizes to those who can uncover the worst example of wackiness in the organization.

Often senior leaders are not aware of these roadblocks or blockheads unless they create a communications channel or network that purposefully surfaces them.

5. Promote innovators. Who you promote says a lot about a company. If you promote sycophants then that is who you get. If you promote innovators who aren't afraid to try and fail and who aren't afraid of you, then you have found innovation gold that sends a message around the organization that you are serious about doing new things or doing things differently.

6. Manage and celebrate failure. The worst thing you can do as a senior leader is to ask for risk taking and then shoot the first mistake maker. Of course you don't want to just roll the dice either. Use a staging approach for innovation—pay a little, learn a lot. Fail early and small so that you can manage the risks. And don't be afraid to pull the plug or change direction quickly to try something different if some aspect of the idea does not work.

7. Make the company values clear, live them yourself, and make others live them. Asylums are most likely to happen in vacuums where values are either ambiguous or the ones in place are not enforced. Make innovation a value, live it, and encourage others to live it. But be prudent. Not every organization needs or wants innovation everywhere. The tool must be consonant with the strategy.

CHAPTER 12

···

Become a Sensei

In Chapter 5, I talked about leverage as one of the key principles of Innovation Judo and I presented the story of KCI's VP of R&D, Kien Nguyen. On his first day of work, his boss at J&J gave him a piece of paper with six names on it and ordered Kien to meet and befriend six key people. Kien was told that each week he would have to meet with the boss to give him the results of all of these meetings. The six names, of course, were the informal leaders of the organization who could either make or break him.

Kien was extremely fortunate to have a boss who mentored him to success. Most of us are not that lucky. Some of us are lucky enough to get good coaching from our boss, but it is very rare to have a sensei who gives you the keys to the informal organization on day one. In this chapter, I am suggesting that Innovation Judo masters also become senseis and pass their secrets along to trusted others. In organizations that have less than friendly innovation landscapes, I encourage management to actually look for and subtly support these kinds of people. John Kilcullen, the Dummies books founder, calls these people "rebels within."

For those of you old enough to remember the TV series *Kung Fu* starring David Carradine, you might recall that he learned all of his lessons as a Kung Fu master from a blind Shaolin priest (played by actor Keye Luke), who himself was the master of masters. The blind priest was the epitome of a sensei.

In this chapter, I suggest that there is a role for Innovation Judo masters that is akin to being a sensei. And just like the priest in *Kung Fu*, the sensei requires that the principles remain subtle and only passed on to the most trusted of students. As I have mentioned throughout the book, it is pretty hard for companies to admit that they need Innovation Judo skills because it is an admission of being somewhat screwed up when it comes to innovation. They may not even be conscious that they need this at all.

The Japanese word *sensei* literally means "one who has gone before" and has quite a different meaning from the Western word *coach*, which is quite different. I know many professional business coaches, and 75 to 80 percent have never been an executive yet they coach executives. They are not senseis because they do not have any executive experience. Mentors are more like senseis in the Eastern sense because they are usually higher level managers and executives who coach and advise lower level managers within the same organization.

I referred to all of my black-belt Judo instructors not by their given names but by addressing them as *sensei*. This term is used as a title of honor that connotes respect, affection, reverence, and deference. Most black belts would tell you that they are always learning the art of Judo and will never truly master it, even though they might be a tenth- or twelfth-degree expert. But the black belt means you have mastered enough that you can now be a teacher of others, because you have demonstrated your ability to "go before."

So in this chapter, I suggest eleven ways an Innovation Judo master can help others practice their art for the good of the organization. In addition, I suggest to senior managers how they can spot these Innovation Judo masters and subtly support them in their endeavors. Perhaps they should support them overtly as well, but let's start with small steps.

SHOWING OTHERS THE WAY

Apart from admitting that you need Innovation Judo masters, you can be a sensei to those who show promise. You can share the seven principles with them, and you can also show them the pathway to innovation that you have either made or discovered. You can give them the secret map. In my last book *Lead Like an Entrepreneur,* I came across a fascinating, mostly unnoticed, study in the *Journal of Business Venturing* that demonstrates how a few innovation-oriented leadership behaviors can make a real difference. The authors describe how a large southeastern U.S. utility organization, upon becoming privatized, attempted to infuse more creative thinking and leadership behaviors into its managers. As we all know, government utilities are poster children for inefficient bureaucracies. Their typical motto is "If we need more money, we'll raise the rates."

With privatization, of course, this attitude is severely challenged. In this study, managers were given a course in how to foster and nurture a more creative climate for their direct reports, in which their subordinates would be challenged to think of new and different ways of doing things. They were taught to push their subordinates to gain new skills and knowledge and to try to circumvent bureaucratic red tape. Figure 11.3 shows the eleven entrepreneurial leadership behaviors, defined by the company, that the managers were asked to practice to create a more innovative and entrepreneurial culture within their own departments.

Corporate Entrepreneurship Behaviors

Efficiently gets proposed actions through bureaucratic red tape and into practice	Devotes time to helping others find ways to improve our products and services
Displays an enthusiasm for acquiring skills	Goes to bat for the good ideas of others
Quickly changes course of action when results aren't being achieved	Boldly moves ahead with a promising new approach when others might be more cautious
Encourages others to take the initiative for their own ideas	Vividly describes how things could be in the future and what is needed to get us there
Inspires others to think about their work in new and stimulating ways	Gets people to rally together to meet a challenge
	Creates an environment where people get excited about making improvements

However, the most fascinating aspects of the study were its results. The authors followed up with the managers to see if they were practicing these behaviors, using a 360-degree management survey that included those eleven specific behaviors along with numerous other generic leadership survey items. They found the managers who consistently practiced these behaviors had significantly higher results in terms of employee satisfaction, customer satisfaction, and financial district margin contributions than do their peers who did not practice these behaviors.

Let's take a look at each of these behaviors individually to see what messages we can glean about coaching others in the art of Innovation Judo.

1. *Efficiently gets proposed actions through bureaucratic red tape and into practice.* This small statement has a tremendous degree of significance for the innovator and the sensei. Earlier I told you about Kien Nguyen's boss at J&J who taught him how to do this by proactively meeting with the informal network of movers and shakers within the company as one of his first assignments as a new employee. His boss gave him the actual names of the decision makers. Helping people find the shortest way through the bureaucracy is no small gift. It could have taken many months if not longer for Kien to identify these people on his own. Instead, his boss gave him the list, but then held him accountable for meeting with these people and making the most of these meetings.

   I had no such mentors when I first started at NPS. It took me more than a year to find out who the really helpful people were versus the ones who always said no or stalled so they would not have to make a decision at all. If you as a sensei can help people navigate around the organization, particularly the informal network that you use to bypass roadblocks and blockheads, you will be doing them a great service.

2. *Displays an enthusiasm for acquiring skills.* As a leader this means you display an enthusiasm for *your* people acquiring new skills. Innovation often comes from insight when people learn new things. Innovation often comes from being exposed to things outside of your own experience, therefore, going to educational events or programs can spark great new ideas. In Wales, for example, the Greenfield Valley historic site had to be closed numerous times to repair damage caused by vandalism. Obviously, one preventive measure would be to install cameras or hire guards, all of which incur expenses. Instead, people put their heads together and decided to borrow from nature. Since there were

numerous bees in the area, the proprietors placed beehives in strategic places around the property where vandals typically scaled the fences. They made sure the beehives were visible and away from where the public walked the property. Only someone trying to scale a fence would have an unfortunate encounter with these flying defenders, and thus vandalism was greatly reduced.

If you asked a security consultant what to do about vandalism you would get a very different answer than you would from someone asked to utilize one of nature's natural defense mechanisms. Someone had to connect the dots from one idea to another, and that often happens with knowledge. When seeking innovation, leaders should probably not send one of their engineers to another course in circuit board design, but to a course in art, or music, or something very different than what they already know.

3. *Quickly changes course when results aren't being achieved.* Innovation requires flexibility, adaptability, and fast learning. When things aren't working, you need to turn quickly and try something else or take a different path to the same thing. This is what Einstein was referring to in his famous quote in which he defined insanity as "doing the same thing over and over again and expecting different results." My friend at ADP whom I talked about earlier in the book was right when he said he learned to have the door hit his face in a different spot each time it was slammed on him when he presented his various innovations. He was saying that it is important to take a different angle of attack if you run into the word *no*. Persistence is fine when you know your idea is an opportunity, but sometimes you realize that what you really need to do is change your idea so that it becomes an opportunity.

IDEO, the famous design organization in Palo Alto, instills its mantra into its employees and clients alike: Fail early and fail fast so that you can learn about your idea, reduce risks in the process, and quickly change course accordingly. Small failures and learning from these failures is much more valuable to the innovator than sticking with one idea until the end. Innovation Judo rewards the combatants who can react quickly and adapt to the different challenges put forward by their opponents.

4. *Encourages others to take the initiative for their own ideas.* Of course this sounds like a good behavior for a sensei who wants to encourage greater innovation within the organization. But there is more to it than just saying, "Great, go look into it." Under the principle of *leverage*, I talked a great deal about ideas versus opportunities. In Appendix B I've included an Opportunity Template. I encourage you to use this short but very powerful document to help people flesh out their ideas to see if they have opportunity characteristics. When people come to you with an idea about how to make things work better, cheaper, faster, of differently, applaud them. Then give them this two-page document, schedule a meeting in the next five days, and ask them to fill in as much as they know about their idea. Meet with them to figure out whether this is just an idea or a real opportunity, or whether you need more research to determine this. Of course if they never come back for that meeting then they probably did not have an opportunity, just an idea. If two pages seems too long, you can follow Steve Paljieg's advice at Kimberly-Clark and ask them to summarize their idea and proposed benefits in no more than one page. I prefer the Opportunity Template because it also coaches people on the difference between just an idea and an actual

opportunity, but a one-paragraph or one-page summary is still a great starting point. Your follow-up says you care about innovation and you are willing to work with them to pursue it.

5. *Inspires others to think about their work in new and stimulating ways.* This behavior is one of the most important as it sends a message that you expect others to see how they can do things better, faster, cheaper, and more innovatively. This behavior in not practiced by email, it must be done in real time both individually and in a group setting. Innovation doesn't occur by having timed meetings, it happens by people looking around them and being inspired to come up with new ideas that can improve performance outcomes. One of my captain friends in the Navy is excellent at this. Everybody who works for him from his direct staff to the people on the deck plate know that when they meet him, they are likely to be asked, "So, what do you think we can do better, or more effectively?" And they also know that they better have an answer. In the Navy we call this a "drumbeat"—a consistency and frequency of message that continually signals that this is important and I will stay on top of this as your leader.

6. *Devotes time to helping others find ways to improve our products and services.* This behavior sounds materially like several of the other behaviors, but it is actually different since it focuses on what our organization produces to create value for customers. Products and services are what companies offer, and the value of these products and services to customers eventually determines organizational survival. I can innovate around the margins, like deciding to go paperless in our office, or utilize innovative technology to be more efficient, but none of this innovation is as important as

innovating for the people who pay us or will pay us if we offer something new or different.

This particular behavior focuses on innovation from the customer perspective. The leader not only keeps a drumbeat going about how we can do things better and more innovatively inside the organization, but also more importantly how we can translate innovation to the outside (our customers). All of the internal innovation we can produce probably doesn't help us as much as one external innovation that shows our customers/constituents that we are not only keeping up with them, we are thinking ahead of them.

IDEO goes to extreme users for its inspiration. It is especially good at innovating because it examines the fringe customers who may be way ahead of the mainstream in utilization of a company's goods or services. Many of these extreme users adapt a company's product in ways that the company never anticipated. Kimberly-Clark goes to moms who have created products for their children, because they have found a need that no company has filled so they try to do it themselves. The sippy cup is one such example.

The sippy cup uses the surface tension of liquid to prevent spillage, even if the cup is turned upside down. Sucking retains a vacuum that maintains the surface tension. To practice this behavior effectively, the sensei must make sure that people realize how their work can have an effect on the customer and thus focus on innovation that can create value for them.

7. *Goes to bat for the good ideas of others.* This behavior means that you will demonstrate your support for someone else's idea regardless of whether it comes from your particular unit or elsewhere if you truly believe it has merit. Innovation has risks and always brings some detractors who do

not like change. This behavior requires some guts. I once witnessed a manager's subordinate make a presentation on a new product development idea to some higher-ups in the organization. These folks were pretty conservative and quickly shot it down without giving the idea much of a hearing. The manager sat there silently and was clearly unwilling to back his employee despite his own belief in the idea. You can imagine the employee's feelings when his boss did not back him given all the work he had spent on developing the concept. It was clear his boss never brought a bat to the meeting or intended to use one. Why would anyone want to innovate for this guy?

In silos and competitive organizations where NIH (not invented here) is the first reaction to some other department's innovative idea, going to bat can be more challenging, but it is the right-minded thing to do. A good idea is a good idea not matter who comes up with it. Senseis who practice this behavior are often the first to support someone else's good idea even if the group did not propose it.

8. *Boldly moves ahead with a promising new approach when others might be more cautious.* When I first saw this behavior, I harkened back to Billy Mitchell's experience and thought about how bold you can really be. Billy was too bold and lacked organizational savvy, which he needed to get others to back innovation. If you don't have the courage to face the inevitable roadblocks and blockheads on the path to creativity, then you should not turn down the path. Using the word *courage* in that last sentence does not mean an inherent personality trait that endures across time and circumstances no matter what. Instead, *courage* refers to standing by your convictions for a *promising* new idea. You will not have the courage to face the roadblocks and blockheads for just any

idea, this courage comes from seeing that you have a real opportunity, which is what I mean by a *promising idea.* Your willingness to take a risk should go up as you move from idea to opportunity. If an idea has opportunity characteristics that gives the innovator confidence in his or her idea, and that in turn allows for courage to face all the obstacles put in front of you. I would not bet my job on an idea, but I might on an opportunity.

9. *Vividly describes how things could be in the future and what is needed to get us there.* Unless you are engaged in basic research, some challenge is necessary to spark innovation. The innovative leader's job is to describe and position the challenge giving the parameters, assumptions, and constraints. Now all of these things can and should be challenged, but without some guidelines, innovative energy cannot focus. I always laugh when people say, "Let's think outside the box." If everyone is outside the box, who is still in it doing the work? Innovation needs guidelines so that the challenge produces opportunities that others can work with. How do babies drink from cups without spilling the contents? How can you type on a computer without having a keypad? How can the Navy do its job with 20 percent fewer ships? How can the IDEO team bring the shopping cart into the modern world? As a leader, you need to formulate a clear vision to challenge innovators to come up with real workable solutions.

John Kilcullen's message to his team spawned Dummies. He challenged them to build a world where smart people did not have to feel dumb and where complex things could be explained simply. My interpretation of this behavior is that it is much less about what is and more about what if?

10. *Gets people to rally together to meet a challenge.* Here again we see the word *challenge*, but the key is "rally together." No innovation gets off the ground with only one advocate. You need more than one, but you do not need an army. As Steve Paljieg from Kimberly-Clark reminds us, "You just need to build your team one at a time." Not only is Steve a great pitchman; he is also very attuned to finding like-minded people who he believes will develop passion for his idea. Rallying can only happen if you show passion for your idea, when it has opportunity characteristics, and when you can demonstrate that it has value for someone else. People believed in John Kilcullen's idea not only because he believed in it but key customers did as well.

11. *Creates an environment where people get excited about making improvements.* This last one is really a summary and culmination of much of the other ones. If you practice behaviors one through ten, then you are likely to create a culture where innovation is an integral part of the organization, or at least the unit that you control.

REFERENCES

1. Arie de Geuss, *The Living Company*, HBS Press, 2002.

2. D. Eggers & K.S. Singh, *The Innovator's Playbook: Nurturing Bold Ideas in Government.* http//www.Deloitte.com// InnovatorsPlaybook.

3. D.K. Murray, *Borrowing Brilliance.* Gotham Books, 2009.

4. D.M. Smick, *The World Is Curved: Hidden Dangers in the Global Economy.* Penguin Group, 2008.

5. Herbert T. Spiro, *Finance for the Nonfinancial Manager*, 4th ed. (Hoboken, NJ: Wiley & Sons, 1996).

6. http://www.mindtools.com/pages/article/newCDV_ 45.htm

7. http://www.36hourbooks.com/0071749551.php?c=book

8. IBM Global CEO Study-US, http://www.IBM/Services/Us/ En/C-Suite/CEOStudy/2012.

9. J. Pinto, *ABB Corporate Culture—Winners Shaped by History.* Automation.com 2009, p. 170.

10. J. Timmons, *The Timmons Model of the Entrepreneurial Process. Innovation Ventures*, 2008, pp. 326-328.

11. K. Lewin, *Field Theory in Social Science. Harper*, 1951, p. 170.

12. Les Livingstone, *Finance Made Easy* (Les Livingstone, 2009).

13. L. Greiner, *Evolution and Revolutions as Organizations Grow. HBR Magazine*, 1998, p 51.

14. Lita Epstein, *Reading Financial Reports for Dummies* (Hoboken, NJ: Wiley & Sons, 2009).

15. M. Goldsmith & M. Reiter, *What Got You Here, Won't Get You There.* Hyperion, 2007.

16. Neal Thornberry, *Lead Like an Entrepreneur: Keeping the Entrepreneurial Spirit Alive Within the Corporation.* McGraw-Hill, 2006.

17. N.J. Webb & C. Thoen, *The Innovation Playbook: A Revolu tion in Business Excellence.* Wiley, 2011.

18. N.J. Webb & C. Thoen, *The Innovation Playbook.* Wiley & Sons, 2011.

19. R.H. Waterman, T. Peters, & J. Phillips, *Structure Is Not Organization. Business Horizons*, June 1980, p. 273.

20. T.L. Friedman, *The World Is Flat: A Brief History of the Twenty-First Century.* Farrar, Strauss, & Giroux, 2005.

....

Innovation Landscape Survey (ILS)

A Dangerous Intersection

High

Maze   Jungle

Complexity

Land of Oz   Asylum

Low   Wackiness   High

The purpose of the questionnaire is to help you assess the innovation landscape in which you operate. More than likely you already know based on my description of the four landscapes created by the intersection of Complexity and Wackiness. But if you would like to hone your understanding and/or validate it with others, please feel free to use this questionnaire. Next to some of the questions you will notice an (R) at the end. This R means that you need to reverse-score the question.

For example, if someone strongly agrees with a statement that indicates low wackiness, then a 5 (Strongly Agree) is reverse-scored to a 1. If you rate a 5 for "Very rarely do people take credit for the ideas of others," then you need to give a 1 when you add the scores because this question indicates low wackiness on this question. I have done it like this as good survey development forces people to read each question carefully. If, for example, I made all of the questions under wackiness negatively stated, e.g., "We are a pretty siloed organization," some people would feel that, since this is the pattern, they can just rate all the questions one way without really reading them. I have tried to help the rater avoid this "patterning" so he can glean as much information from the ratings as possible on each question as opposed to just looking at the summed score.

A little more work on your part to be sure, but it makes for a more valid survey in the end. Make sure you pick a frame of reference when you or others take the ILQ. You could rate just the part of the organization in which you work or the organization as a whole. It's your choice.

Senior executives would most likely want to have people rate the organization as a whole. They could then break down the ratings by department, level, or unit to get a better feel as to where the innovation landscapes are most favorable. For example, it would be bad news to find out that your R&D folks were living in either an Asylum or Jungle if their task is to create new products, or if your advertising and marketing people were there as well, given their respective missions.

Please rate the following question on a 1 to 5 scale by placing a circle around your choice: 1 designating "strongly disagree" to 5, "strongly agree." At the end of the questionnaire, you will see the scoring key, and then you can plot about where your innovation landscape falls on the Landscape Map.

WACKINESS

1. *Risk-taking is encouraged, but you better not make a mistake.*

1	2	3	4	5
Strongly Disagree	*Disagree*	*Neutral*	*Agree*	*Strongly Agree*

2. *We are a pretty siloed organization.*

1	2	3	4	5
Strongly Disagree	*Disagree*	*Neutral*	*Agree*	*Strongly Agree*

3. *It is fairly common for people to CC their boss or others on emails to gain leverage over another employee or group.*

1	2	3	4	5
Strongly Disagree	*Disagree*	*Neutral*	*Agree*	*Strongly Agree*

4. *Very rarely do people try to take credit for the ideas of others. (R)*

1	2	3	4	5
Strongly Disagree	*Disagree*	*Neutral*	*Agree*	*Strongly Agree*

5. *The best way to sell a new idea around here is to make a logical case for it as opposed to taking a political approach. (R)*

1	2	3	4	5
Strongly Disagree	*Disagree*	*Neutral*	*Agree*	*Strongly Agree*

6. **Our organization does not encourage us to challenge the status quo even though we may have a better idea of doing things.**

1	2	3	4	5
Strongly Disagree	*Disagree*	*Neutral*	*Agree*	*Strongly Agree*

7. *Creative ideas are encouraged and listened to. (R)*

1	2	3	4	5
Strongly Disagree	*Disagree*	*Neutral*	*Agree*	*Strongly Agree*

8. *Innovation is a core value, and we live it in reality. (R)*

1	2	3	4	5
Strongly Disagree	*Disagree*	*Neutral*	*Agree*	*Strongly Agree*

9. **Our organization consistently comes up with successful new products/services. (R)**

1	2	3	4	5
Strongly Disagree	*Disagree*	*Neutral*	*Agree*	*Strongly Agree*

10. *Company innovators are well-known within the organization and are held in high esteem. (R)*

1	2	3	4	5
Strongly Disagree	Disagree	Neutral	Agree	Strongly Agree

11. *Our customers do not view us as particularly innovative.*

1	2	3	4	5
Strongly Disagree	Disagree	Neutral	Agree	Strongly Agree

12. *We are encouraged to spend company time on interesting ideas that we come up with. (R)*

1	2	3	4	5
Strongly Disagree	Disagree	Neutral	Agree	Strongly Agree

13. *People get promoted here for what they do, not because of who they know. (R)*

1	2	3	4	5
Strongly Disagree	Disagree	Neutral	Agree	Strongly Agree

14. *Backstabbers and rumormongers are not tolerated here. (R)*

1	2	3	4	5
Strongly Disagree	Disagree	Neutral	Agree	Strongly Agree

15. *Status symbols like office size, parking places. etc. are highly valued in our culture.*

1	2	3	4	5
Strongly Disagree	Disagree	Neutral	Agree	Strongly Agree

16. *Executive secretaries are very protective of their boss's time and often block easy access.*

1	2	3	4	5
Strongly Disagree	Disagree	Neutral	Agree	Strongly Agree

17. *Promotions here are mostly made on a political basis.*

1	2	3	4	5
Strongly Disagree	Disagree	Neutral	Agree	Strongly Agree

18. *Information is power in our organization, and people often use it to gain an advantage.*

1	2	3	4	5
Strongly Disagree	Disagree	Neutral	Agree	Strongly Agree

19. *Our executives openly disagree with each other in front of employees.*

1	2	3	4	5
Strongly Disagree	Disagree	Neutral	Agree	Strongly Agree

20. *We lose good people because of the political nature of our culture.*

1	2	3	4	5
Strongly Disagree	Disagree	Neutral	Agree	Strongly Agree

21. *Getting results is the only thing that really counts in our organization.*

1	2	3	4	5
Strongly Disagree	Disagree	Neutral	Agree	Strongly Agree

22. *Those employees who "kiss up" to their bosses are the ones who get ahead.*

1	2	3	4	5
Strongly Disagree	Disagree	Neutral	Agree	Strongly Agree

23. *There is a genuine spirit of cooperation within the organization. (R)*

1	2	3	4	5
Strongly Disagree	Disagree	Neutral	Agree	Strongly Agree

24. *We don't live up to our stated values.*

1	2	3	4	5
Strongly Disagree	Disagree	Neutral	Agree	Strongly Agree

25. *Even the person with the best results will get fired if they are not a team player. (R)*

1	2	3	4	5
Strongly Disagree	Disagree	Neutral	Agree	Strongly Agree

Mean Score _____ Add all of your ratings for Wackiness together, then divide by 25 to get your average or mean score on this dimension. Remember to reverse-score the items with an (R) next to them. Thus a 5 would be re-scored as a 1, a 4 would be re-scored as a 2, and a 3 should remain the same.

COMPLEXITY

1. *There is a clear pathway to innovation in this company. (R)*

1	2	3	4	5
Strongly Disagree	Disagree	Neutral	Agree	Strongly Agree

2. *We use a lot of acronyms that outsiders would have difficulty understanding.*

1	2	3	4	5
Strongly Disagree	Disagree	Neutral	Agree	Strongly Agree

3. *If you have an innovative idea, you can easily find someone who can help you push it forward. (R)*

1	2	3	4	5
Strongly Disagree	Disagree	Neutral	Agree	Strongly Agree

4. *People would be more innovative here if we did not have to go through so many layers of bureaucracy to get a decision to move ahead.*

1	2	3	4	5
Strongly Disagree	Disagree	Neutral	Agree	Strongly Agree

5. *Our organization is difficult for new employees to figure out.*

1	2	3	4	5
Strongly Disagree	Disagree	Neutral	Agree	Strongly Agree

6. *Our organizational structure is clear, and we know who to go to for what. (R)*

1	2	3	4	5
Strongly Disagree	Disagree	Neutral	Agree	Strongly Agree

7. *We have a clear pathway to innovation. (R)*

1	2	3	4	5
Strongly Disagree	Disagree	Neutral	Agree	Strongly Agree

8. *Innovation is one of our core values, and we strive to live it. (R)*

1	2	3	4	5
Strongly Disagree	Disagree	Neutral	Agree	Strongly Agree

9. *Lines of authority and responsibility are not well defined here.*

1	2	3	4	5
Strongly Disagree	Disagree	Neutral	Agree	Strongly Agree

10. *We often debate who has the authority to make decisions.*

1	2	3	4	5
Strongly Disagree	Disagree	Neutral	Agree	Strongly Agree

11. *We are pretty clear about our own roles and responsibilities, but not that sure about what others do in the organization.*

1	2	3	4	5
Strongly Disagree	Disagree	Neutral	Agree	Strongly Agree

12. *It takes a while to learn who the true decision-makers are.*

1	2	3	4	5
Strongly Disagree	Disagree	Neutral	Agree	Strongly Agree

13. *The informal organization in our company often works better than the formal one.*

1	2	3	4	5
Strongly Disagree	Disagree	Neutral	Agree	Strongly Agree

14. *It would be difficult to explain to others how our company works in simple layman's terms.*

1	2	3	4	5
Strongly Disagree	Disagree	Neutral	Agree	Strongly Agree

15. *We use many task forces/committees and temporary project groups to do our work.*

1	2	3	4	5
Strongly Disagree	Disagree	Neutral	Agree	Strongly Agree

16. *When we decide to do things differently, it takes a long time to implement.*

1	2	3	4	5
Strongly Disagree	Disagree	Neutral	Agree	Strongly Agree

17. *We don't have to deal with a lot of rules and regulations in our organization. (R)*

1	2	3	4	5
Strongly Disagree	Disagree	Neutral	Agree	Strongly Agree

18. *We have very few layers of bureaucracy. (R)*

1	2	3	4	5
Strongly Disagree	*Disagree*	*Neutral*	*Agree*	*Strongly Agree*

19. *Getting a timely decision is normal in our organization. (R)*

1	2	3	4	5
Strongly Disagree	*Disagree*	*Neutral*	*Agree*	*Strongly Agree*

20. **Employees need extensive orientation training to understand how the organization works.**

1	2	3	4	5
Strongly Disagree	*Disagree*	*Neutral*	*Agree*	*Strongly Agree*

21. *We are an organization that can react quickly to solve customer problems. (R)*

1	2	3	4	5
Strongly Disagree	*Disagree*	*Neutral*	*Agree*	*Strongly Agree*

22. **Getting the right information from the right people is a real challenge for us.**

1	2	3	4	5
Strongly Disagree	*Disagree*	*Neutral*	*Agree*	*Strongly Agree*

23. *Many parts of our organization are geographically dispersed.*

1	2	3	4	5
Strongly Disagree	*Disagree*	*Neutral*	*Agree*	*Strongly Agree*

24. *Outsiders find our organization hard to navigate.*

1	2	3	4	5
Strongly Disagree	Disagree	Neutral	Agree	Strongly Agree

25. *If you have an innovative idea, it is easy to find others who have a similar interest. (R)*

1	2	3	4	5
Strongly Disagree	Disagree	Neutral	Agree	Strongly Agree

Mean Score _____ *Add all of your ratings for Complexity together, then divide by 25 to get your average or mean score on this dimension. Remember to reverse-score the items with an (R) next to them. Thus a 5 would be re-scored as a 1, a 4 would be re-scored as a 2, and a 3 should remain the same.*

Then follow the directions below.

Plotting Your Scores

On the following graph, find the intersection between your mean (average) score on Wackiness against your mean score on Complexity, and place an X on the graph where these two mean scores intersect. As I said, you probably already have a good intuitive idea, but the survey may help you pinpoint your position indicating how much innovation judo you may have to employ to innovate against the odds.

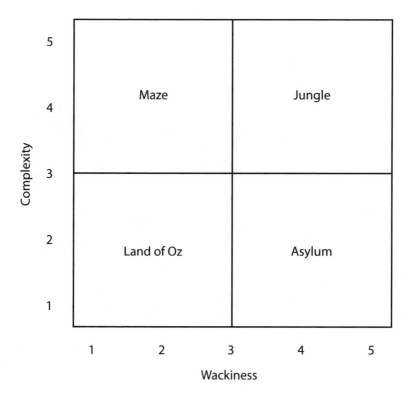

A Dangerous Intersection

High

Complexity

Maze   Jungle

Land of Oz   Asylum

Low   Wackiness   High

APPENDIX B

Opportunity Template[6]

Please fill in as much of this document as you can before coming to the program. Please make a copy and send it either electronically or by fax to _____.

We realize that you may not have enough information to fill in all these categories but please put in as much as you can. The purpose of the course is to help you move your idea closer to reality. Thus, this template may also help you to think about what you need to do in a more systematic way.

Statement of the Opportunity: Write a brief one paragraph description of the opportunity you wish to pursue. Tell us what is innovative about your idea and how it differs from your normal day-to-day objectives and goals. Also, please describe how your idea will give the company a competitive advantage that will be durable (hard for others to imitate) and sustainable (have staying power).

---

[6] Copyright: IMSTRAT LLC, 2012.

Customer Value Proposition: Briefly describe who your customer (internal or external) is and what unique value they will receive from your idea if it is implemented. Remember that value is defined as V = Benefits/Costs.

Economic Value Proposition: What do you think the value to your firm will be if your idea comes to fruition and what will the risk profile (high, medium, or low) look like? Keep in mind that as risk increases, a company would expect higher returns to cover the risk.

Research: Other than your personal opinion, what data do you have to support your notion that this idea is worth pursuing? Have you talked with potential customers? If so, how many? Have you done any market surveys, competitor analysis, or other external data collection? If your idea is internally focused, with whom have you spoken inside the company about your idea and what were their reactions/suggestions?

Resources: Please describe the resources you think you will need. These resources could be financial, human, time, etc. Remember, customers who are really interested in your idea can be a source of resources as well.

Cash Flow and Pay Back: Many opportunities require financial resources to implement. What would the investment cycles look like? What sort of cash flow projections do you foresee? And when would you expect to return this investment (with interest for the cost of capital)?

The Team: Whose help will you need in pursuing this opportunity? List the key stakeholders. These stakeholders could be internal or external.

Risk Mitigation: Briefly outline the key risks that you will have to manage in making sure that your idea does not fail. What plans do you have or will have to develop for mitigating these risks?

APPENDIX C

....

Seven Principles Planning Tool

You are now more than familiar with the 7 Principles and their associated tactics. It is now time for you to do a little strategic thinking about which of these principles and tactics you will utilize in your particular situation.

A. *Write a one-sentence statement that spells out the INTENT of your Innovation and why it is right-minded. If you cannot do this, then you are not yet clear about your own idea.*

B. *Identify the roadblocks/blockheads you are currently facing or anticipate you will face. List them in priority of difficulty to overcome.*

Roadblocks/Blockheads

1

2

3

4

5

C. *Go through the 7 Principles Quick Guide and place the principles you believe would be most effective next to the roadblocks and blockheads listed previously. To do this you will need to ask yourself questions like*

- *Do I need leverage? Against whom or what? If so, what tactic(s) would be best to employ?*
- *Can I identify or create a seam that allows me to move quickly through contradictory rule sets?*
- *Am I sure that I am communicating an opportunity, not just an idea?*
- *If I face an illogical attack on my innovation, can I circle a small group of supporters to help fend off the attack?*
- *Could I utilize a customer or vendor to help validate my idea and thus gain leverage to pursue it?*

Discipline

Preparation
Passion
Bring opportunities
Patience
Self-control

Leverage

Corporate values
Customer
Competitor
Referent power
Strategy
Informal network
Dote on quotes

Redirection

Feigning
Pulling

Circling

Walk around opponents
Walk around ideas
Circle the wagons
Brand enhancement
Numbers
Pilots/Prototypes
Seams

Openings

Hot buttons
Cost cutting/Containment
Efficiency/Effectiveness

Speed

Idea to opportunity
Fail fast
Quick to reshape/Pull plug
Dash into openings
Forgiveness, not permission
Embed quickly

Unbalancing

Surprise
Underpromise/Overdeliver
Foot sweep criticism
Shock therapy
Power shifting

APPENDIX D

Most importantly, don't talk about this strategy, just do it!!

ABOUT THE AUTHOR

Neal E. Thornberry, Ph.D.

Dr. Neal Thornberry is the founder and CEO of IMSTRAT LLC, a consulting firm that specializes in helping private and public sector organizations develop innovation strategies that create economic value by increasing an organization's effectiveness and efficiency. A respected thought leader in innovation, Thornberry is a highly sought-after international speaker and consultant.

With offices in Florida and California, Thornberry and his associates work with organizations around the world, including Ford Motor Company, Daimler AG, Chrysler, IBM, KCI, SmithKline-Glaxo, SAP, Nationwide Insurance, Home Depot, France Telecom, Sodexho, Arcelor Steel, Alfa Laval, GE, Fresenius Medical, Cisco Systems, and Motts.

As an innovation subject matter expert, Thornberry is often a keynote speaker for NGO's as well as public sector organizations, including the Navy (NWDC, CNIC, Bumed, and NAE), the United States Coast Guard, the Human Capital Institute, the U.S. Government, ATB Financial (Alberta Treasury Branches), PDI (Professional Developers of Iowa), IRI (retail industry group), the Republic of Thailand, St. Elizabeth's Hospital of Boston, Kimberly-Clark, and Homeland Security.

Thornberry also works as Faculty Director for Innovation Initiatives in the Center for Executive Education at the Naval Postgraduate School in Monterey, California, where he heads up the "Leading Innovation" program for Navy Admirals, Marines, and Senior Executive Services.

Index